Fishing Lure Collectibles

VOLUME TWO
THE MODERN ERA

An Identification and Value Guide
to the Most Collectible
Fishing Lures Made Since 1940

Dudley Murphy and Deanie Murphy

COLLECTOR BOOKS
A Division of Schroeder Publishing Co., Inc.

ABOUT THE AUTHORS

As a child growing up in a family of fishermen, it was only natural for Dudley Murphy to develop a healthy interest in fishing. His father, Dudley C. Murphy, Sr., manufactured one of the early vibrating lures of the 1950s. His grandfather, Dudley A. Murphy, was a conductor on the L&N Railroad who whittled fine examples of folk art which often included fishing lures. But it was his grandfather, Frank D. Royce, who presented him with a gift of old Heddon, Jamison, and Clark lures that encouraged Dudley to become a lifelong collector at age 13. As one of the original three founders of the National Fishing Lure Collector's Club, Dudley is an active collector with a variety of interests, including fishing.

Having received his MFA degree in 1971 from the University of Oklahoma, Dudley teaches graphic design and directs the Visual Communication Program at Drury University in Springfield, Missouri. In addition to teaching, Dudley designs, photographs, and edits the *NFLCC Magazine* and plays guitar with the popular bluegrass music group, Radio Flyer.

Springfield, Missouri artist Deanie Murphy was born in Tulsa, Oklahoma, and was married to Dudley in 1968. They are the parents of two adult children, Quinn and Jennifer. Deanie is also a musician, having played semi-professionally in a bluegrass band with Dudley for 10 years; she also does the typesetting and production for the *NFLCC Magazine*.

Deanie juggled family responsibilities, work, music, and art until 1995 when a summer of painting in Italy with her daughter convinced her to sell her graphic design business, Adworks, and set aside all other creative pursuits in order to focus on her passion for painting. With a degree in art from Oklahoma State University and post graduate studies at Drury University, Deanie has taught art in the Oklahoma and Missouri public schools. Her paintings have been exhibited throughout Missouri, Oklahoma, and Michigan.

Dudley, Deanie, and their two dogs, Tipton and Cosmo, enjoy life together in the beautiful Missouri Ozarks.

Book design and photography by Dudley Murphy

Front cover, clockwise from top: Kingfish Wobbler #6535 (p. 88); Jitterbug, wood (p. 124); Jamison Bottle Bass Popper (p. 193); Bon-Net Lure (p. 189); Live Action Frog (p. 19); "Spin-Wiggle Minnow" (p. 267).

Back cover, clockwise from top: "Musky" Electrolure (p. 204); Dozey Boy (p. 117); Rat Bait (p. 265); Pretz-L-Lure (p. 123).

COLLECTOR BOOKS
P.O. Box 3009
Paducah, KY 42002-3009

Copyright © 2003 Dudley Murphy and Deanie Murphy

This book focuses on lures made since 1940 but on occasion includes pre-1940 lures which were carried over into the 1940s or influenced the development of post-1940 lures. Since many of the lures included in this book were popular for a long period of time, introductory years are occasionally approximated or indicated by a range of dates.

The current values in this book should be used only as a guide. They are not intended to set prices, which vary from one section of the country to another. Auction prices as well as dealer prices vary greatly and are affected by condition as well as demand. Neither the authors nor the publisher assumes responsibility for any losses that might be incurred as a result of consulting this guide.

CONTENTS

The current values in this book should be used only as a guide. They are not intended to set prices, which vary from one section of the country to another. Auction prices as well as dealer prices vary greatly and are affected by physical condition as well as demand. Neither the authors nor the publisher assumes responsibility for any losses that might be incurred as a result of consulting this guide.

This book concerns itself primarily with the most collectible antique fishing lures made since 1940. Therefore if certain lures do not appear in this guide, it may be because of their age, similarity to other versions pictured or possibly an oversight by the authors which may be corrected in subsequent revisions. It should not be assumed that lures excluded from this printing have no collector value. While the focus of this book is on the most collectible lures made since 1940, certain earlier lures are included as necessary to complete the overall picture of a company's production.

Some lures cannot be accurately valued since they do not exist in sufficient quantities to create a history of transactions which might establish a value scale. It should be remembered that values are arbitrary, and true current market values can only be determined when someone is willing to pay the seller's price, or when the seller accepts the buyer's offer. Listed values, therefore, are based on what a lure in average condition should bring in an average market.

In the past few years, sensationalized auction prices have tended to create the impression that all "old lures" are valuable, and while certain lures are indeed valuable, the vast majority of antique fishing lures are quite affordable and available in adequate quantities to allow collectors to comfortably enjoy the hobby. High auction prices have caused sellers to bring lures "out of the woodwork" in hopes of matching the publicized prices, but when rare lures begin to become available in large quantities, their value tends to decrease dramatically. Record setting lures simply do not exist in quantities of 50 or 60, but rather in quantities of usually a dozen or less. There must be a quantity sufficient to establish a desire, but few enough to prove rarity.

While lures will appear to some extent chronologically within the following chapters, the authors believe that the organization of lures by similarity of design provides a superior working reference. It is hoped that quick comparisons of similar features of a lure throughout its many variations will allow a more thorough understanding and enjoyment of the hobby.

Please refer to **Fishing Lure Collectibles Volume 1** by Dudley Murphy and Rick Edmisten to view early lures in production prior to 1940.

ACKNOWLEDGMENTS

The authors wish to thank their family for being understanding and encouraging despite piles of lures, photographs, seemingly unending manuscripts, countless coast-to-coast phone calls, and all of the other trying circumstances which throughout history have stood discouragingly in opposition to countless writers. Without understanding families and help from many fine friends, this project would have remained an unachieved dream.

While the precedent of husband and wife authors is a bit unique in the fishing lure collecting field, it is not without numerous examples in books on various other collectibles. Husband/wife collecting teams are quite common within the lure collecting fraternity.

As with *Fishing Lure Collectibles Volume I* (lures made before 1940), this volume has turned out to be unusual among books of its type in that it is a collaborative effort — a "we thing," not a "me thing" — the representation of a large number of knowledgeable opinions providing credibility to the information contained herein. We thank our collector friends from all over the United States and Canada for their unselfish and helpful contributions.

For the use of their extensive lure collections and for their writing contributions (listed in chapter order), the authors thank **Harold Smith** – Hermitage, TN; **Bruce Dyer** – Lindsay, Ontario; **Dennis Boulai**s – Danielson, CT; **David Stalnaker** – Magnolia, AR; **Drew Reese** – Reeds Spring, MO; **Dan Zemke** – Robbinsdale, MN; **Terry Wong** – Phoenix, AZ; and **Gary Smith** – Woodstock, GA.

For their inspiration and continual encouragement, we thank **Bill Calhoun** – Springfield, MO, and **Rick Edmisten** – Studio City, CA.

For the use of lures from their excellent collections, we thank **John Anderson** – Park Ridge, IL; **Bob Baird** – Salt Lake City, Utah; **Butch Bartz** – Bellaire, MI; **George Chrisman** – Allen, TX; **Garry Clements** – Rogers, AR; **Jim Cook** – Tulsa, OK; **Bob Curington** – Tulsa, OK; **Bob Dell** – Siloam Springs, AR; **Rich Dickman** – West Harrison, IN; **Peter Duguay** – Cumberland Beach, Ontario; **Lanier Feemster** – Springfield, MO; **Johnny Garland** – Johnson City, TN; **Harvey Garrison** – Ft. Lauderdale, FL; **Ron Gast** – Kissimmee, FL; **Bill Grossman** – Lower Hudson Valley, NY; **Bob Halver** – Grand Rapids, MN; **Ron Hanley** – Commerce, GA; **Bob Hart** – Long Island, NY; **Adam Hartmann** – Jacksonville, FL; **Rufus Harris** – Springfield, MO; **Ron Hoseney** – Rapid City, MI; **Vince Ingle** – Maryville, TN; **Casey Jones** – Stockton, MO; **David Martin** – Sparks, NV; **Dennis McNulty** – Chesapeake, VA; **Bill Mitzel** – Bismarck, ND; **Ron Mize** – Lufkin, TX; **Donnie Moore** – Strafford, MO; **Michael Muth** – Grand Island, NE; **Bob Nickel** – Thornfield, MO; **Emil Polansky** – Corpus Christi, TX; **George Richey** – Honor, MI; **Dan Ross** – Cincinnati, OH; **Charles and Annette Sanders** – Columbia, MO; **Dean Smith** – Ridgefield, CT; **Riley Smith** – Battle Creek, MI; **Tony Smith** – Holland, MI; **Jack Swedberg** – Webster, WI; **Ken Webb** – Shreveport, LA; **James A. White** – Effingham, KS; **Steve White** – Chesterfield, MO; **Richard Whitehead** – Colmesneil, TX; **Jerry Wible** – Springfield, MO; **Matt Wickham** – Louisville, KY; and **Charlie Wilson** – Lincoln, NE.

The authors are especially appreciative to **Bill Schroeder** for commissioning this book back in 1995, to **Billy Schroeder** for allowing us to design the book, and to **Lisa Stroup** for her undying patience and encouragement.

For their excellent assistance in printing photographs of lures for this book, the authors thank **Mark Shipley** and **Miriam Huffman** in the Processing Service Department at Lawrence Photo and Video, – Springfield, MO.

The Passion

When my father returned from World War II, he was not alone in longing for the peaceful cool waters he had fished back home prior to the mighty conflict... countless returning servicemen shared the same desire. The longing to return to wives, children, girlfriends, and families was often too much to bear and other dreams came calling. For Dad, Kentucky's rushing Cumberland River burned vividly in his memory during those long years with the Air Corps in Burma and later in Panama, giving him great encouragement during trying times.

We lived in Lexington, Kentucky and when I was old enough to fish, Dad told me about fishing the Cumberland and showed me an old Pflueger Tandem Spinner which he claimed always filled his stringer with fat smallmouth bass ... he said it was the flash along with the red, white, and speckled guinea feathers that attracted them. It was to be my first lesson on the particulars of fishing lure design, but by no means my last.

During the late 1940s and early 1950s Dad made and marketed a vibrating lure which was way ahead of its time: Murph's Irish Shad. Made of Kentucky red cedar with a molded lead weight carefully inserted for proper balance, Dad's lures were finished with lacquer and sent with eager fishermen to the lakes to do their magic. The Irish Shad was an outstanding fish catcher on impounded lakes like Kentucky's Herrington Lake and Tennessee's Dale Hollow. I recall fishing the Irish Shad among frantic schools of white bass churning the surface as they fed on shad. When the fish jumped, I cast optimistically and seldom retrieved the lure without a good strike. Demand for Dad's lures overtook his ability to continue making them by hand, and he joined forces with two other men interested in manufacturing the lure out of molded tenite plastic. Dad contributed the design and research, a man named Bacon contributed his machinist skills, and George Gordon provided materials for the molds from his scrap metal yard. The acronym for the new lure became MuBaGo's Irish Shad. Throughout the process I continued to learn, not only how Dad's lures were made but how other companies made their lures.

Fishing the "jumps" was only part of the fishing picture, and Dad accepted the challenge of each fishing season enthusiastically. I recall my father purchasing a large number of Creek Chub lures from an old hardware store in a small town near Lexington. Darters were carefully scooped out at the belly to give a sideways lurch to the lure when it was twitched, and Injured Minnows were cut down to make stubby Dalton Specials. Darters also might become River Pups, and the tail sections of Pikies sometimes became small Plunkers. I was lucky enough to rescue a Pikie and an Injured Minnow, both mint in the box, not very valuable lures but priceless memories. Thus, I became a lure collector.

One memorable summer evening on Herrington Lake, I attached a Paw Paw Wottafrog to my line and cast toward the shore without warning. The loud splash of the large bait brought first surprise and then good natured ribbing from Dad

and a fishing buddy, Waller Miller, who happened to be fishing from a nearby boat. The lure was immediately retired to a special place in my tackle box reserved for lures I admired but never fished with. Collecting lures came naturally to me as yet another dimension of my schooling on lure construction.

My tackle box grew with lures — the Grumpy I caught my biggest bass on while Dad and I fished the bushy willows overhanging the bottle green Kentucky River, the no-eye frog finish Bomber that was just too beautiful to fish with, the glittering little Pippin Wobblers we often trolled behind Bombers on 24" of leader, and others — many others.

When I was about thirteen years old, my maternal grandfather gave me some really old lures dating from about 1900. He could see I had become a collector, and his contribution pushed me irretrievably over the edge into a fascinating world of fishing lures which I would often contemplatively enjoy.

I still have Dad's tackle box, and I occasionally peruse its nostalgic contents. The musty smell of time, reel oil, and 6-12 mosquito repellent still lingers in the old Kennedy box, and that faint scent always transports me to a cold morning walking down the steep flight of worn limestone steps at Ashley's Camp on Herrington Lake. Closing my eyes, I am motoring downlake in the bow of a gray wooden boat propelled by a green 1950 Johnson 5 HP motor. The man in the stern, with a cigarette in one hand and the tiller in the other, is wearing an old felt hat with a few flies stuck in the band. He is leaning slightly forward against the breeze, huddled in a worn wool shirt to ward off the chill until the morning sun can take over. We will catch fish today, I think — lots of them, my Dad and I.

Dudley Murphy
January 2002

The Hobby

Along with two collecting buddies, John Goodwin and Jerry Routh, I was privileged to found the National Fishing Lure Collectors Club (NFLCC) in 1975. In the ensuing years our club has grown from the original three of us to about 5,500 members who actively pursue a unique form of pleasure by collecting antique fishing lures. Through the group efforts of our members, the lure collecting hobby has gained exposure, definition, and refinement. Histories of lure design and manufacturing have been tediously extracted from the past by persevering members, resulting in numerous helpful articles published in the two club publications, *The NFLCC Gazette* and *The NFLCC Magazine*. A number of helpful books and national magazine articles have been written by NFLCC members as well.

The History

Looking back, we see that the exactness of lure history is clouded by time and the lack of foresight or need to document the introduction of the old lures. What we perceive now is the good design and thoughtful insight that characterize the most notable and collectible antique lures. These are the qualities that give the lure collecting hobby its appeal but yet often cause the hobby to become overwhelmingly complicated and difficult to learn and understand. In addition, antique lures have increased in value in the marketplace, creating a need for a clear understanding of the hobby before making a major purchase.

While most lures are still readily affordable, there are a good number that exceed the limits of casual affordability. This book will attempt to identify, date, and provide an approximate value of the most collectible antique lures made since 1940. It must be remembered that lure prices can vary as widely as pork bellies in the commodity market. The state of the national economy and the variables of eye appeal such as color, version, condition, and desirability based on factors such as rarity and vintage all tend to prevent values from crystallizing into a predictable pattern. Values rise and fall, and collectors learn to expect the fluctuations and adapt in a manner that allows them to continue collecting.

The directions that lure collectors choose in developing their collections can be awe inspiring. While some collect by company, others collect by vintage, design, material, and color. Thus the chapters in this book have been organized to include the "big six" companies, miscellaneous companies (many of which had production rivaling the larger companies), folk art lures, spinning lures, and finally the creative works of contemporary lure designers.

Every effort has been made to be as thorough as possible in assembling this collection of information, but just as there is said to be "many a slip twixt the cup and the lip," some oversights may have occurred. New information will be included, as it becomes available, in future printings.

It is hoped that the old adage "a picture is worth a thousand words" is indeed true, for it is primarily with pictures that we present the subtleties which make lures desirable in hopes that they can be better recognized and understood.

Desirability

Three major factors orchestrate the desirability of a lure:

1. Vintage – Early versions are usually the most desirable.

2. Rarity – While this factor is very important, it is still too early in the development of the lure collecting hobby to completely pinpoint rarity and its effects on collecting. Some extremely rare lures are surprisingly affordable in contrast with their more numerous counterparts, and what is rare today may turn up in abundance somewhere tomorrow. A fisherman who may have had one or two rods and reels might also have owned dozens of lures.

3. Condition – It is often said that condition is everything, and indeed it seems to play a major part in a lure's desirability. It is important however to note that many older lures often appear in poorer condition than those from a more recent time but because of their age and rarity are sometimes given special consideration when graded.

Ten Suggestions For An Enjoyable Collecting Experience

1. **Join the National Fishing Lure Collector's Club.**
   NFLCC, 197 Scottsdale Circle, Reeds Spring, MO 65737, telephone: 417-338-4427
2. **Seek other collectors to trade with.**
3. **Begin slowly and affordably.** It is much easier to survive a bad deal with an inexpensive lure than with an expensive one.
4. **Advertise for lures.**
5. **Learn to trust the right people, after you've learned to trust yourself.**
6. **Caveat emptor.** "Let the buyer beware."
7. **Carpe diem.** "Seize the day (opportunity)." Buy it! Some lures become available so infrequently that it might be considered unwise to let a few dollars prevent you from owning a desired lure. Great lures often only pass by once, so be ready!

8. Choose a reasonable direction and develop your collection patiently. In time you should have chances at most of the lures you seek.

9. Keep an open mind to new lure collecting directions. It stimulates one's interest to have a variety of directions to pursue.

10. Enjoy the hobby for its contemplative merits. When one begins to look at the hobby as an investment, the element of competition can destroy the pure enjoyment of collecting.

The NFLCC Standard Lure Grading System – Originated by R. L. Streater.

Scale		Description/Condition
10	New-in-box (**NIB**)	*Unused with original box.*
9	Mint (**M**)	*Unused without box.*
8	Excellent (**E**)	*Very little or no age cracks; very minor defects.*
7	Very Good (**VG**)	*Little age cracks; some minor defects.*
5-6	Good (**G**)	*Some age cracks; starting to chip, small defects.*
3-4	Average (**AVG**)	*Some paint loss and/or chipping.*
2	Fair (**F**)	*Major paint loss and/or defects. Much chipping.*
1	Poor (**P**)	*Parts missing, poor color and/or major chipping.*
0	Repaint (**R**)	*Original paint covered over in part or all.*

Conditions may be clarified by the use of (+) or (-) ratings with the regular description, or by using the numerical scale and adding or subtracting .5 to the rating number.

The values indicated in this book are based on a lure in average condition and color. For particular lures average condition means some paint loss and defects may be common while other lures may usually appear in excellent condition.

Knowledge

One cannot overemphasize the need for the serious collector to read everything available about lures if a thorough knowledge is to be gained. The following books should prove helpful additions in the reader's library of research materials: *Fishing Lure Collectibles Volume One* - The Most Collectible Antique Fishing Lures Made Prior To 1940, Dudley Murphy and Rick Edmisten (2001), P.O. Box 686, North Hollywood, CA 91603; *Streater's Reference Catalog of Old Fishing Lures*, R. L. Streater, Rick Edmisten and Dudley Murphy (1999), Collector Books, 5801 Kentucky Dam Road, Paducah, KY, 42003; *Creek Chub Bait Company,* Harold Smith (2002), 2277 Stewarts Ferry Pike, Hermitage, TN 37076; *South Bend Fishing Lures* - Terry Wong (2000), 1657 W. Acoma Drive, Phoenix, AZ 85023; *19th Century Fishing Lures* - Arlan Carter (2000), Box 107, Fall Creek, WI 54742; *Old Fishing Lures and Tackle,* Carl F. Luckey (1991) Books Americana, Inc., P.O. Box 2326, Florence, AL 35630; *Fishing Tackle Antiques and Collectibles*, Karl White, P.O. Box 9, Luther, Oklahoma 73054. *Early Fishing Plugs of the USA* - Kimball, Art and Scott (1989), Aardvark Publications, Inc., P.O. Box 252, Boulder Junction, WI 54512; *Heddon Historical Footprints* - Clyde A. Harbin (1995), 1105 Marlin Road, Memphis, TN 38116; *The Peppers of Rome, N.Y.,* Jack Gallagher with Larry Mayer, 30 Reedy Ct., Manning, S.C. 29102; *Made in Michigan Fishing Lures,* George Richey (1995), Rt. 1, Box 280, Honor, MI 49640; *Fishing Tackle Made in Missouri,* Dean A. Murphy (1993), DAMMO Publishing Company, 7076 North Shore Drive, Hartsburg, MO 65039; *The Heddon Legacy,* Bill Roberts and Rob Pavey (2002), Collector Books, P.O. Box 3009, Paducah, KY, 42002-3009; *The Best of British Baits,* Chris Sanford (1997), P.O. Box 256, Esher, Surrey, KT10 9WA, U.K.

In an undertaking of the magnitude of this book, it is inevitable that some items will be overlooked and omitted. If readers have items, corrections or information they feel need to be included in future printings, please call the authors at (417) 881-1907.

The authors sincerely hope that as collectors peruse this volume that new understanding and respect for the fishing lures made since 1940 will result and that the fires of interest will be kindled, leading the reader to the peace and enjoyment of this most noble and contemplative pursuit, the collecting of antique fishing lures.

Creek Chub Bait Co.
Garrett, Indiana

In 1916 three fishermen friends from the small town of Garrett, Indiana, came together to form the Creek Chub Bait Company. Henry Dills was the creative genius with two industry changing patents; a lip that made a bait wiggle through the water, and spraying paint through netting to create a scale finish. Carl Heinzerling and George Schulthess brought business skills to the enterprise. High quality lures that caught fish vaulted Creek Chub to success.

By 1940 Creek Chub baits were well established. Wigglers, Darters, Pikies, Injured Minnows, Dingbats, and Wigglefish were standard equipment for fishermen. World War II brought shortages that created some stresses for Creek Chub, but by 1950 the company was thriving once again. The timely introduction of plastic lures, the development of lures for the growing legions of spin fishermen, large baits for the saltwater fishermen, and plastic models of old standards kept the company strong in an increasingly competitive environment in the years that followed.

For over 50 years Creek Chub created innovative lures of great quality. The labor intensive production methods of Creek Chub were the key to their success but signaled the eventual end of an era. Creek Chub continued in business under its original owners longer than any other classic bait company, but competition and labor costs resulted in the sale of Creek Chub to the Lazy Ike Corporation in September of 1978. Creek Chub lures are still produced in limited numbers by Pradco Inc.

Dr. Harold Smith
Hermitage, Tennessee
Collector's Guide to Creek Chub Bait Co. and Collectibles

Wiggler #100
Date: c. 1906 – 1964
Length: 3½"
Notes: This is the final version of Creek Chub's first lure. The late model #100 Wigglers had a reinforced lip and a screw replacing the "line tie" on the head. The reinforced lip was introduced in 1935.
Value: $40.00 – 50.00

Baby Wiggler #200
Date: 1917 – 1954
Length: 2¾"
Notes: The #200 is the small version of the CCBCO #100 Wiggler.
Value: $20.00 – 30.00

Husky Musky #600
Date: 1919 – 1954
Length: 5"
Notes: The late model #600 had one line tie, a "two screw" reinforced lip, and "thru-wire" hook rigging.
Value: $40.00 – 50.00

Deluxe Wagtail Cub #800
Date: 1921 – 1953
Length: 2¾"
Notes: The early #800s featured a flat metal tail which was replaced with a fluted version in later years.
Value: $130.00 – 200.00

Crawdad #300; Baby Crawdad #400
Date: 1917 – 1964
Length: 2¾" (top); 2¼" (bottom)
Notes: The bead-eyed Crawdad remained a mainstay in the CCBCO line until 1964 when it was replaced by the plastic Cray-Z-Fish.
Value: $20.00 – 30.00

The Seven Thousand #7000

Date: 1950 – 1954
Length: 2¾"
Note: Shown here in rare Western Auto sable color, the #7000 was in production for only four years.
Value: $30.00 – 75.00

Creek Darter #2000; Jointed Darter #4900; SW Creek Darter #2000

Date: 1924 – 1978; 1938 – 1964; 1924 – 1978
Length: 3¾" (top); 3¾" (middle); 3¾" (bottom)
Value: $10.00 – 50.00; $10.00 – 15.00; $30.00 – 45.00

CB Darter #8000; Midget Darter #8000

Date: 1947 – 1978; 1938 – 1978
Length: 3" (top); 3" (bottom)
Notes: The #8000 CB has a concave belly.
Value: $10.00 – 15.00; $25.00 – 30.00

Surf Darter #7600

Date: 1955 – 1959
Length: 7"
Notes: Like the #7400, #7500, and #7700, the #7600 Surf Darter was produced for only four years due to a shortage of suitable cedar.
Value: $100.00 – 125.00

Salt Spin Darter #7700

Date: 1955 – 1959
Length: 5¾" (5½")
Notes: This is the small version of the #7600 Surf Darter.
Value: $90.00 – 125.00

Pikie #700 (glass eyed, tack-eyed, painted-eyed)
Date: 1920 – 1978
Length: 4½"
Notes: These three examples of the famous Pikie demonstrate the lure's evolution over the years from wood to plastic, and from glass eyes to tack and simple painted eyes.
Value: $30.00 – 70.00

Jointed Pikie #2600
Date: 1926 – 1978
Length: 4½"
Notes: The Deep Diving Lip was added to the Jointed Pikie in 1950. Visible in the photograph are the glass eye detail (top) and painted talk eyes (bottom).
Value: $20.00 – 30.00

Baby Pikie #900; Baby Jointed Pikie #2700
Date: 1921 – 1963 (wood) or 1978 (plastic); 1927 – 1963 (wood) or 1978 (plastic)
Length: 3½" (top); 3½" (bottom)
Value: $35.00 – 60.00

Midget Pikie #2200; Jointed Midget Pikie #4200
Date: 1924 – 1961; 1934 – 1961
Length: 2¾" (top); 2¾" (bottom)
Value: $30.00 – 45.00; $12.00 – 25.00

Husky Pikie #2300
Date: 1925 – 1978
Length: 6"
Notes: The #2300 pictured features painted tack eyes and a reinforced lip attached with two screws.
Value: $20.00 – 45.00

Jointed Pikie #3000
Date: 1931 – 1978
Length: 6"
Note: In 1936 the #3000 was produced with an improved (reinforced) lip and thru-wire construction.
Value: $30.00 – 40.00

Snook Pikie #3400; Jointed Snook Pikie #5500
Date: 1931 – 1978; 1939 – 1964
Length: 4⅞" (top); 4⅞" (bottom)
Value: $60.00 – 80.00; $25.00 – 40.00

Tarpon Pikie #4000
Date: 1933 – 1961
Length: 6½"
Notes: This large tack-eyed bait featured a pair of gigantic 9/0 single hooks.
Value: $200.00 – 275.00

River Scamp #4300
Date: 1934 – 1953
Length: 2½"
Notes: Unlike the rest of the floating/diving Pikies, the River Scamp was lead weighted for underwater use only.
Value: $15.00 – 25.00

Jointed Striper Pikie #6800
Date: 1950 – 1978
Length: 6½"
Notes: The last new production color produced by CCBCO is the #44 Whitefish shown here.
Value: $25.00 – 35.00

Striper Pikie #6900
Date: 1950 – 1978
Length: 6¼"
Notes: With improved lip and thru-wire construction, this is the unjointed or "straight" version of the #6800 Jointed Striper Pikie.
Value: $50.00 – 60.00

Surfster #7200; Husky Surfster #7300; Salt Surfster #7400
Date: 1953 – 1968; 1953 – 1959 (1964); 1953 – 1959 (1964)
Length: 4¼" (top); 6" (middle); 7¼" (bottom)
Value: $50.00 – 60.00; $75.00 – 90.00; $75.00 – 85.00

Giant Straight Pikie #6000
Date: 1960 – 1978
Length: 8"
Notes: The #6000 is the largest of the straight Pikies.
Value: $80.00 – 150.00

Giant Jointed Pikie #800
Date: 1957 – 1978
Length: 14"
Notes: This is the largest of the Pikies. A 17" Pikie was made for display but not for fishing.
Value: $40.00 – 60.00

3-Jointed Pikie #2800-P
Date: 1960 – 1978
Length: 6½"
Notes: The 3-Jointed Pikie was made of plastic with three body sections and two joints.
Value: $20.00 – 30.00

Injured Minnow #1500;
Baby Injured Minnow #1600
Date: 1924 – 1963, 1973 – 1978 (wood); 1964 – 1978 (plastic); 1924 – 1963 (wood), 1964 – 1978 (plastic)
Length: 3¾" (top); 2¾" (bottom)
Value: $20.00 – 35.00

Husky Injured Minnow #3500
Date: 1931 – 1961
Length: 5"
Notes: Out of production from 1947 – 1949, the #3500 returned to the CCBCO line in 1950.
Value: $75.00 – 90.00

Fintail Shiner #2100
Date: 1924 – 1947
Length: 4"
Notes: The original rubber dorsal and pectoral fins on the #2100 tended to harden and break or melt over time. Durable metal fins came into use c. 1938.
Value: $250.00 – 325.00

Wigglefish #2400
Date: 1925 – 1957, 1974 – 1977
Length: 3½"
Notes: The Wigglefish holds the official world record for large-mouth bass — 22 lbs., 4 oz. Caught by George Perry in 1932 from Lake Montgomery, Georgia, the giant bass was cleaned and eaten.
Value: $40.00 – 50.00

Gar Minnow #2900
Date: 1927 – 1953
Length: 5½"
Notes: The Gar Minnow was produced in two standard colors: natural gar and green gar.
Value: $250.00 – 325.00

Castrola #3100
Date: 1927 – 1941
Length: 3⅝"
Notes: The spinner on a wire shaft was a standard feature on the Castrola.
Value: $65.00 – 70.00

Husky Plunker #5800; Plunker #3200; Spinning Plunker #9200; Midget Plunker #5900
Date: 1939 – 1955; 1927 – 1978; 1952 – 1963 (wood), 1978 (plastic); 1939 – 1964, 1973 – 1978
Length: 4¼" (top left); 3" (middle left); 2" (middle right); 2½" (bottom)
Value: $60.00 – 100.00; $35.00 – 60.00; $5.00 – 10.00; $30.00 – 40.00

Snook Plunker #7100
Date: 1952 – 1964
Length: 5"
Notes: First produced with glass eyes as shown, the Snook Plunker featured thru-wire construction.
Value: $50.00 – 90.00

Surf Popper #7500
Date: 1955 – 1959
Length: 7¼"
Notes: Thru-wired with painted eyes, the Surf Popper is the largest in the Plunker family.
Value: $80.00 – 100.00

Pocket Rocket #7000
Date: 1957 – 1962
Length: 4"
Notes: The #7000 designation was also used for the earlier #7000 which was discontinued in 1954.
Value: $200.00 – 300.00

Skipper #4600

Date: 1936 – 1951
Length: 3"
Notes: A weighted tail causes the skipper to float almost vertically in the water.
Value: $15.00 – 25.00

Pop 'N Dunk #6300

Date: 1941 – 1954
Length: 2¾"
Notes: Similar in shape to a Plunker but with a vertical rather than slanted face, the Pop 'N Dunk has an aluminum diving lip.
Value: $30.00 – 45.00

Lucky Mouse #3600

Date: 1931 – 1947
Length: 3"
Notes: Likely due to the WWII metal shortage, the original aluminum ears and diving lip on this neat little mouse were changed to plastic.
Value: $60.00 – 90.00

Beetle #3800; Midget Beetle #6000

Date: 1931 – 1954; 1939 – 1954
Length: 2½" (top); 2" (bottom)
Value: $100.00 – 140.00; $90.00 – 120.00

Jigger #4100; Baby Jigger #4100

Date: 1933 – 1946; 1933 – 1946
Length: 3⅝" (top); 3⅛" (bottom)
Notes: A hole beginning just in front of the scoop lip and exiting out the back caused the Jigger to shoot a stream of water into the air when jerked on retrieve.
Value: $60.00 – 90.00; $60.00 – 75.00

Flip Flap #4400
Date: 1934 – 1941
Length: 3¼"
Notes: The Flip Flap was designed to swim with an "up-and-down movement."
Value: $50.00 – 60.00

Wee Dee #4800
Date: 1936 – 1946
Length: 2½"
Notes: Brimming with eye appeal, the Wee Dee is much sought after and highly prized by collectors.
Value $250.00 – 325.00

Close Pin #5000
Date: 1936 – 1946
Length: 3½"
Notes: Featuring gold plated hooks, the Close Pin was designed for salt water fishing. Only one color was produced.
Value: $400.00 – 600.00

Husky Dingbat #5300; Dingbat #5100; Baby Dingbat #5200
Date: 1939 – 1946; 1937 – 1957 or 1958; 1939 – 1958
Length: 2½" (top); 2" (middle left); 1⅝" (bottom)
Value: $150.00 – 200.00; $40.00 – 50.00; $40.00 – 50.00

Surface Dingbat #5400
Date: 1939 – 1955
Length: 1¾"
Notes: This is the surface version of the Dingbat and features a curving grooved lip.
Value: $45.00 – 55.00

Dinger #5600; Midget Dinger #6100
Date: 1939 – 1954; 1939 – 1949
Length: 4" (top); 3½" (bottom)
Value: $35.00 – 60.00; $40.00 – 50.00

Husky Dinger #5700
Date: 1939 – 1946
Length: 5½"
Notes: The Husky Dinger is the largest of Creek Chub's "Hair Baits."
Value: $200.00 – 350.00

Plunking Dinger #6200
Date: 1939 – 1953
Length: 4"
Notes: Combining characteristics of a Plunker, Injured Minnow, and Dinger, the Plunking Dinger floats on its side in the water.
Value: $40.00 – 60.00

Tiny Tim #6400
Date: 1941 – 1954; 1970 – 1978
Length: 1¾"
Notes: The very collectible Tiny Tim was offered from 1950 – 1954 with a deep diving lip.
Value: $15.00 – 45.00

Big Bomber #6700; Dive Bomber (Kreeker) #6600; Baby Bomber #6500
Date: 1942 – 1946; 1942 – 1954; 1942 – 1946
Length: 3¾" (top); 2⅞" (far right); 2¼" (bottom left)
Notes: This series of CCBCO Bombers are often found in the Dot, Dot, Dot, Dash pattern — Morse Code for "V," for victory.
Value: $125.00 – 300.00; $30.00 – 55.00; $30.00 – 40.00

Spinning Deepster #9600
Date: 1953 – 1955
Length: 2⅛"
Notes: The new #36 Black Sucker color shown was created specifically for the Spinning Deepster.
Value: $20.00 – 25.00

Spinning Pikie #9300 Spinning Injured Minnow #9500; Spinning Darter #9000; Jointed Spinning Pikie #9400; Spinning Plunker #9200
Date: All 1952 – 1963 (wood), 1978 (plastic)
Length: 2¼" (upper left); 2" (upper right); 2¼" (middle left); 2¼" (middle right); 2" (bottom)
Value: $10.00 – 15.00; $10.00 – 20.00; $20.00 – 30.00; $15.00 – 25.00; $5.00 – 15.00

Spoontail #500; Spoontail #9100
Date: 1954 – 1956; 1954 – 1956
Length: 3" (top); 2⅛" (bottom)
Value: $15.00 – 25.00; $20.00 – 30.00

Creek Chub Mouse #6577; Creek Chub Mouse #6380
Date: 1957 – 1962, 1971 – 1978 (wood), 1964 – 1978 (plastic); 1957 – 1962 (wood), 1978 (plastic)
Length: 2½" (top); 2¼" (bottom)
Value: $15.00 – 20.00; $15.00 – 20.00

Mitie Mouse #600-P; Dingbat #5300-P; Cray-Z-Fish #9900-P
Date: 1963 –1978; 1964 – 1978; 1963 – 1978
Length: 1⅝" (top); 2" (bottom left); 1¾" (bottom right)
Value: $15.00 – 25.00; $15.00 – 20.00; $10.00 – 20.00

**Nikie #1000-P; Nikie #9700-P; Nikie #9800-P
(#9700-UL-P)**
Date: 1956 – 1961; 1956 – 1978; 1957 – 1978
Length: 3¼" (top); 2¼" (middle); 1⅝" (bottom)
Value: $10.00 – 15.00; $10.00 – 25.00; $10.00 – 25.00

From left to right:
**Injured Minnow #9500-UL-P; Pikie #9300-UL-P;
Jointed Pikie #9400-UL-P; Plunker #9200-UL-P;
Darter #9000-UL-P**
Date: 1961 – 1978
Length: 1⅝"
Value: $15.00 – 20.00; $20.00 – 30.00; $20.00 – 25.00; $20.00 –
25.00; $20.00 – 30.00

Snark-Eel #1300; Snarkie #1100; Snark #1200
Date: 1957 – 1962; 1957 – 1961; 1957 – 1961
Length: 3" (top); 1½" (middle); 2" (bottom)
Value: $30.00 – 40.00; $30.00 – 40.00; $30.00 – 35.00

Top 'n' Pop #500-P; Viper #8800-P
Date: 1960 – 1968; 1965 – 1978
Length: 3" (top); 3½" (bottom)
Value: $15.00 – 20.00; $5.00 – 15.00

Jig-L-Worm (J-Series)
Date: 1973 – 1978
Length: 5½"
Notes: This lure was designed to be an alternative to the soft plastic worm and had a lead head and floating body segments.
Value: $25.00 – 35.00

Streeker (LS-Series); Streeker (S-Series)
Date: 1973 – 1978; 1971 – 1978
Length: 4½" (top); 3" (bottom)
Value: $15.00 – 20.00; $15.00 – 20.00

Striper Strike #1900-P; Striper Strike #2500-P;
Striper Strike #2400-P
Date: 1960 – 1978; 1961 – 1978; 1961 – 1978
Length: 5½" (top); 3" (middle); 2½" (bottom)
Value: $15.00 – 20.00; $10.00 – 25.00; $15.00 – 20.00

Cheekie C-100
Date: 1975 – 1978
Length: 1⅞" body
Notes: The Cheekie is the last bait introduced by CCBCO.
Value: $25.00 – 40.00

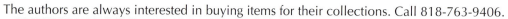

The authors are always interested in buying items for their collections. Call 818-763-9406.

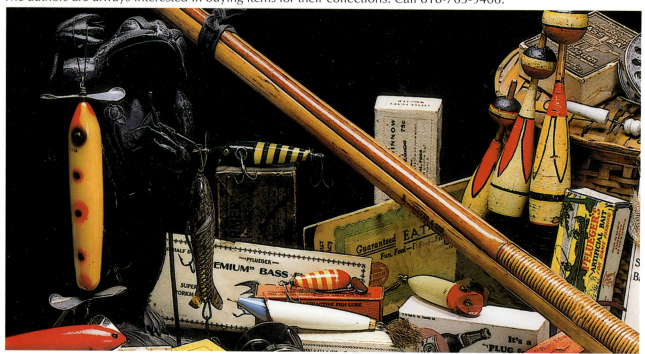

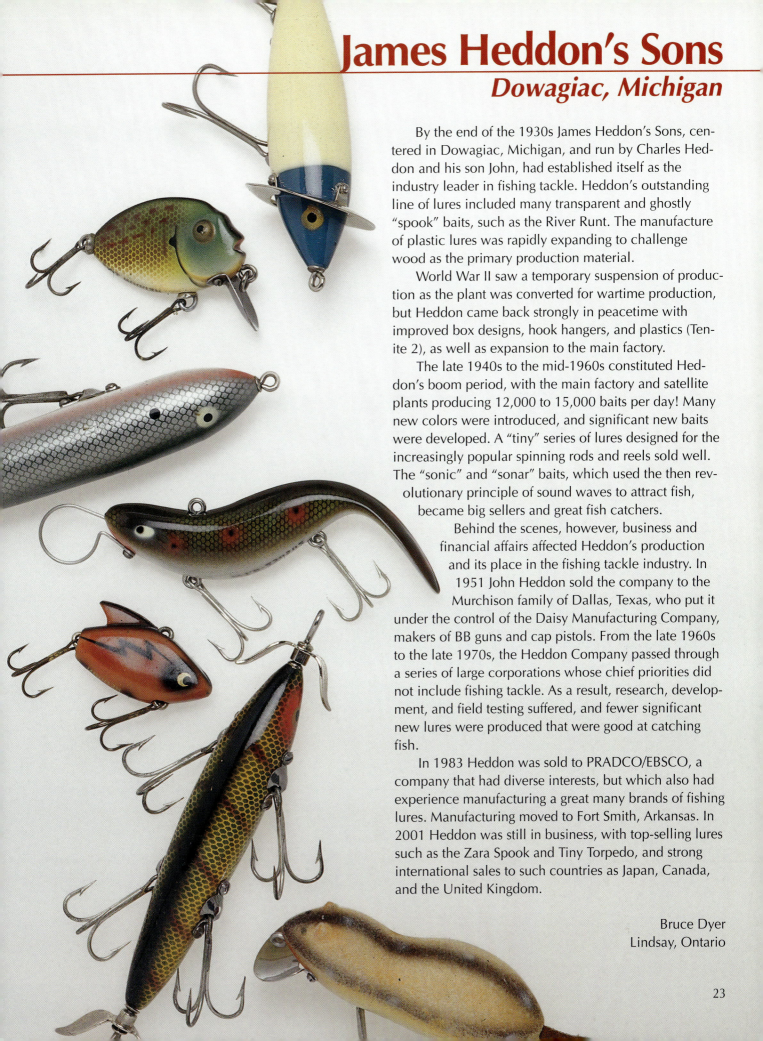

James Heddon's Sons
Dowagiac, Michigan

By the end of the 1930s James Heddon's Sons, centered in Dowagiac, Michigan, and run by Charles Heddon and his son John, had established itself as the industry leader in fishing tackle. Heddon's outstanding line of lures included many transparent and ghostly "spook" baits, such as the River Runt. The manufacture of plastic lures was rapidly expanding to challenge wood as the primary production material.

World War II saw a temporary suspension of production as the plant was converted for wartime production, but Heddon came back strongly in peacetime with improved box designs, hook hangers, and plastics (Tenite 2), as well as expansion to the main factory.

The late 1940s to the mid-1960s constituted Heddon's boom period, with the main factory and satellite plants producing 12,000 to 15,000 baits per day! Many new colors were introduced, and significant new baits were developed. A "tiny" series of lures designed for the increasingly popular spinning rods and reels sold well. The "sonic" and "sonar" baits, which used the then revolutionary principle of sound waves to attract fish, became big sellers and great fish catchers.

Behind the scenes, however, business and financial affairs affected Heddon's production and its place in the fishing tackle industry. In 1951 John Heddon sold the company to the Murchison family of Dallas, Texas, who put it under the control of the Daisy Manufacturing Company, makers of BB guns and cap pistols. From the late 1960s to the late 1970s, the Heddon Company passed through a series of large corporations whose chief priorities did not include fishing tackle. As a result, research, development, and field testing suffered, and fewer significant new lures were produced that were good at catching fish.

In 1983 Heddon was sold to PRADCO/EBSCO, a company that had diverse interests, but which also had experience manufacturing a great many brands of fishing lures. Manufacturing moved to Fort Smith, Arkansas. In 2001 Heddon was still in business, with top-selling lures such as the Zara Spook and Tiny Torpedo, and strong international sales to such countries as Japan, Canada, and the United Kingdom.

Bruce Dyer
Lindsay, Ontario

Super Surface #210
Date: c. 1936
Length: 3⅜"
Notes: Heddon's flocked finish lures are highly sought after by collectors.
Value: $60.00 – 90.00

Super Surface #210
Date: c. 1949
Length: 3⅜"
Notes: This version of the wood #210 represents its final stages of evolution from the early slope nose.
Value: $24.00 – 30.00

Super Surface #210
Date: c. 1977
Length: 3½"
Notes: Heddon's original lure, the Slope Nose, ultimately evolved into the collectible plastic #210.
Value: $15.00 – 20.00

Dowagiac Minnow #150
Date: c. 1904 – mid-1950s
Length: 3⅝"
Notes: This was Heddon's last version of the #150, featuring painted eyes and surface hardware.
Value: $70.00 – 90.00

Baby Dowagiac #20
Date: c. 1952
Length: 2½"
Notes: By 1952, the #20 featured glass eyes and surface hardware.
Value: $24.00 – 30.00

Baby Crab-Spook #9900; Crab-Spook #9900

Date: c. 1936
Length: 2½"; 3"
Notes: The #9900 Crab-Spooks were floating lures designed to dive on retrieve.
Value: $55.00 – 75.00

Go-Deeper Crab #D1900

Date: introduced 1951
Length: 2½"
Notes: Most Go-Deeper Crabs found by collectors show wear from much use and many fish, testimonials of the lures' fish catching ability.
Value: $18.00 – 24.00

Tadpolly Spook (narrow lip) #9000

Date: introduced 1952
Length: 2⅞"
Notes: The narrow-lipped Tadpolly Spook (bottom) is considered to be the first version.
Value: $15.00 – 20.00

Tadpolly Spook Family

Top:
Magnum Tadpolly Spook #9006
Date: introduced 1970
Length: 3⅝"
Value: $5.00 – 15.00

Middle left:
Tadpolly Spook #9000
Date: introduced 1952
Length: 3"
Value: $5.00 – 10.00

Bottom left:
Mini-Tad #590
Date: c. 1992
Length: 1¾"
Value: $5.00 – 10.00

Middle right:
Clatter Tad #9900
Date: c. 1978
Length: 2¼"
Value: $5.00 – 15.00

Bottom right:
Wee Tad
Date: c. 1996
Length: 1½"
Value: $5.00 – 10.00

Lucky 13 Family

Top: **Original Lucky 13 #W2500 (wood),** c. 1967
Left: **Baby Original Lucky 13 #W2400,** c. 1966
Right: **Tiny Lucky 13 Spook #370,** c. 1953
Values: $10.00 – 20.00

Basser #8500
Date: c. 1922 – mid-1950s
Length: 4"
Notes: This is the paint-eyed version of the 1922 Basser.
Value: $18.00 – 24.00

King Basser #8560
Date: c. 1939
Length: 5"
Notes: Produced in 4½", 5", and 6" sizes, the King Basser was designed for salmon and "big water" fishing.
Value: $35.00 – 45.00

"Old Zaragossa" #6500
Date: c. 1920 – mid 1950s
Length: 4¼"
Notes: This is the paint-eyed surface hardware version of the early Zaragossa.
Value: $24.00 – 30.00

Zara Spook #9250
Date: c. 1970s
Length: 4¼"
Notes: The gold eye version of the Zara Spook became highly sought after because of Charlie Campbell's bass tournament success with the "Dog-Walking" lure.
Value: $6.00 – 12.00

Zara Spook Family

Top:
Reinforced Zara Spook #9260
Date: c. 1974
Length: 4¼"

Middle left:
Zara II #9420
Date: c. 1977
Length: 3½"
Values: each type: $6.00 – 10.00

Bottom left:
Zara Puppy
Date: c. 1989
Length: 3"

Middle right:
Baby Zara Spook #365
Date: c. 1956
Length: 2⅝"

Bottom right:
Zara Pooch
Date: c. 1994
Length: 2½"

Prototype Charlie Campbell Zara Spook, Charlie Campbell Zara Spook
Date: c. 1978
Length: 4¼"
Notes: The top lure pictured was one of Heddon's first experimental attempts to produce a Zara Spook that had the same balance and action of the early gold eye versions. Scale patterns are hand drawn.
Value: $90.00 – 120.00; $5.00 – 10.00

Early Japanese Color Zara Spooks
Date: c. 1978
Length: 4¼"
Notes: Designed for the Japanese bass fishing market, these lures were picked up by the authors at the Heddon factory in 1978.
Value: $30.00 – 36.00

Experimental Baby Zaras #365
Date: introduced 1956
Length: 2⅝"
Notes: The authors got these attractive lures from the Heddon factory in 1978.
Value: $18.00 – 24.00

Drop Zara
Date: c. 1980s
Length: 4¼"
Notes: This lure features a dressed dropper hook which would sink behind the bait on retrieve to attract short strikers.
Value: $5.00 – 10.00

Darting Zara #9210

Date: introduced 1951
Length: 3¼"
Notes: Also made in a #9200 3-hook version, the Darting Zara was produced in two-piece hardware. Available with or without tail propeller.
Value: $5.00 –10.00

Chugger Spook Family

Top:
Chugger Spook #9540
Date: introduced 1938
Length: 3"
Value: $9.00 – 15.00

Middle:
Chugger Jr. #9250
Date: c. 1954
Length: 2¼"
Value: $9.00 – 15.00

Bottom:
Tiny Chugger Spook #335
Date: introduced 1962
Length: 2¼"
Value: $5.00 – 8.00

Big Chugg #9550

Date: c. 1970s
Length: 4⅜"
Notes: The Big Chugg is the highly sought after big brother in the Chugger family.
Value: $25.00 – 40.00

Wounded Spook #9140

Date: c. 1970s
Length: 3¼"
Notes: Basically a plastic version of the #140 Flipper (1927), the Wounded Spook was a great fish catcher.
Value: $5.00 – 10.00

Torpedo Family

Magnum Torpedo #362, introduced 1969, 3¼", $30.00 – 40.00
Baby Torpedo #361, introduced 1969, 2½", $5.00 – 10.00
Tiny Torpedo #360, introduced 1952, 1⅞", $5.00 – 10.00
Teeny Torpedo, 1⅜", $2.00 – 5.00
Notes: The surface Torpedo is a colorful and usually affordable collectible with great display potential.

Vamp Spook #9750
Date: introduced 1933
Length: 4" (top); 4⅛" (bottom)
Notes: One of Heddon's great original wood baits. The Vamp remained popular with fishermen after the transition to plastic.
Value: $12.00 – 20.00

Jointed Vamp Spook #9730
Date: introduced 1933
Length: 4¾"
Notes: This is the jointed version of the plastic Vamp Spook.
Value: $15.00 – 25.00

King Fish Vamp-Spook #KF9750
Date: introduced 1934
Length: 4⅛"
Notes: The King Fish Vamp features a nickel plated sleeve around the plastic body to add flash and visibility.
Value: $25.00 – 35.00

Giant Vamp #7550
Date: introduced 1939
Length: 5⅝"
This large Vamp was designed to catch large pike and musky.
Value: $35.00 – 45.00

Jointed Giant Vamp #7350
Date: introduced 1937
Length: 6¾"
Notes: With a more pronounced wiggling action than the #7550 Giant Vamp, this jointed version was popular with fishermen and retains its popularity with collectors.
Value: $35.00 – 45.00

JAMES HEDDON'S SONS

Great Vamp #7540
Date: introduced 1937
Length: 4⅞"
Notes: Using "toilet seat" two-piece hook hardware, the Great Vamp was a big bait for big fish.
Value: $50.00 – 65.00

River Runt #110
Date: c. 1947
Length: 2⅝"
Notes: Originally introduced in 1929 with glass eyes, this is the last version of the wood River Runt and features painted eyes and surface hook hangers.
Value: $24.00 – 36.00

River Runt Spook Sinker #9110
Date: c. 1975
Length: 2½"
Notes: This plastic version of the River Runt was introduced in 1932.
Value: $18.00 – 24.00

Jointed River Runt Spook Sinker #9110
Date: c. 1937 – 1957
Length: 2¾"
Value: $15.00 – 20.00

River Runt Spook Floater #9400
Date: c. 1939 – 1989
Length: 3"
Notes: Heddon's River Runts were among their all-time best sellers as evidenced by the 50-year time period in which they were produced.
Value: $12.00 – 18.00

Jointed River Runt Spook Floater #9430
Date: c. 1935 – 1957
Length: 3⅞"
Value: $20.00 – 25.00

Midget River Runt Spook #9010
Date: c. 1939 – 1982
Length: 2¼"
Value: $20.00 – 25.00

Midget Go-Deeper Runt #D9010;
Go-Deeper Runt #9110
Date: c. 1940
Length: 2¼" (top); 2½" (bottom)
Notes: Early plastic diving River Runts featured scooped lips and two-piece hardware. The scooped lip was not made after WWII.
Value: $20.00 – 25.00

Tiny Go-Deeper River Runt Spook #D-350;
Go-Deeper River Runt #D-9110
Date: c. 1953 – 196, c. 1949 – 1961; 1953 – 1962
Length: 1⅞" (top); 2¾" (bottom)
Notes: Heddon changed from the scooped lip to the step lip after WWII.
Value: $10.00 – 15.00

Jointed River Runt Spook Sinker #9330
Date: c. 1937 – 1957
Length: 3¼"
Value: $20.00 – 25.00

Deep Dive River Runt #DD-9110 (top left)
Deep Diver River Runt #DD-9400 (bottom left)
Midget Deep Dive River Runt #DD-9010 (top right)
Tiny Deep Dive Runt #DD-350 (bottom right)
Date: c. 1962 – 1976
Length: 2½"; 3"; 2¼"; 1⅞"
Value: $12.00 – 20.00 each

Tiny Floating Runt Spook #340
Date: c. 1955 – 1983
Length: 2⅜"
Notes: The #340 was a great pond and river bait.
Value: $5.00 – 10.00

Tiny Runt #350
Date: c. 1952 – 1993
Length: 1⅞"
Value: $10.00 – 15.00

"No Lip" River Runt Spook Floater #S9400SP
Date: c. 1953 – 1955
Length: 3"
Notes: This lipless floater is simply a River Runt without a lip.
Value: $25.00 – 35.00

No Snag River Runt Spook #N9110
Date: c. 1941 – 1943
Notes: At least two versions of wire Weedguards were used on the #N9110.
Value: $30.00 – 40.00

River-Runtie Spook #950
Date: c. 1938 – 1942
Value: $15.00 – 20.00

Midgit Digit #B-110 (wood)
Date: c. 1941 – 1947
Length: 1½"
Notes: This is the smallest of Heddon's wood River Runts.
Value: $20.00 – 30.00

Midgit Digit #9020 (plastic)
Date: c. 1948 – 1976
Length: 1¾"
Notes: The plastic #9020 version replaced the wood #B110 Midgit Digit.
Value: $15.00 – 20.00

Salmon River-Runt #8850
Date: c. 1939
Length: 5"
Notes: The large unsuccessful scooped lip and final shallow lip versions of the salmon River-Runt can be seen here. These lures feature "teddy bear" glass eyes.
Value: $60.00 – 90.00

Salmon River-Runt #8850
Date: c. 1939
Length: 5"
Notes: This lure was originally produced with a large scooped lip which caused the lure to roll unpredictably on retrieve. The lips were cut down as shown to correct the problem.
Value: $60.00 – 90.00

Giant River-Runt #7510
Date: c. 1939 – 1941
Length: 3¼"
Notes: This progression of giant River-Runts shows changes in positioning the tail hook attachment screw.
Value: $60.00 – 90.00

Sea Runt #610
Date: introduced 1937
Length: 2⅝"
Notes: Basically a lipless wood River Runt, the Sea Runt had flattened sides.
Value: $30.00 – 40.00

Laguna Runt L-10
Date: introduced 1939
Length: 2⅝"
Notes: The Laguna Runt is a simplified version of the Sea Runt, having a completely round, body shape.
Value: $30.00 – 40.00

Scissortail #9830
Date: introduced 1953
Length: 3⅛"
Notes: This interesting lure design combined the wiggle of a River Runt with the erratic movement of the two tail sections.
Value: $10.00 – 15.00

SOS #140
Date: c. 1922 – mid 1950s
Length: 2⅞"
Notes: The banana-shaped S.O.S. floated on its side and was produced in three sizes.
Value: $24.00 – 30.00

Flaptail #7000
Date: c. 1940
Length: 4"
Notes: This is the standard Flaptail designed for bait casting.
Value: $15.00 – 20.00

Flaptail Jr. #7110
Date: introduced 1937
Length: 3"
Notes: This glass-eyed, two-piece Flaptail Jr. is the last version of this plug.
Value: $30.00 – 36.00

Flaptail Spook, Jr. #9700
Date: introduced 1951
Length: 3"
Note: Heddon described its plastic "Spook" baits as having a fish-flesh appearance. They also made a smaller Flaptail Spook, 2¾".
Value: $5.00 – 10.00

Giant Flaptail #7050
Date: c. 1937
Length: 6¾"
Notes: Giant Flaptail is the largest of the production models.
Value: $30.00 – 40.00

Husky Flaptail #7040
Date: 1940
Length: 5½"
Notes: The Husky Flaptail bridged the size gap between the 4" Flaptail and the 6¾" Giant Flaptail.
Value: $30.00 – 40.00

Zig-Wag Jr.
Date: c. 1940
Length: 3⅛"
Notes: This is the last version of the Zig-Wag produced and featured painted eyes and one-piece hardware.
Value: $10.00 – 15.00

King Zig-Wag #8350

Date: c. 1940
Length: 5"
Notes: Heddon also made a 6", #8360 King Zig-Wag.
Value: $25.00 – 35.00

Torpedo #130

Date: c. 1949
Length: 4⅛"
Notes: Unlike the early Torpedos which had glass eyes and two-piece hook hardware, the later versions had painted eyes and surface hook hardware.
Value: $15.00 – 20.00

Saltwater Torpedo #30

Date: c. 1949
Length: 4⅛"
Notes: Popular for saltwater fishing, the #30 is shown here in its final configuration with painted eyes and surface hook hangers.
Value: $15.00 – 20.00

Crazy Crawler #2100 (wood);
Tiny Crazy Crawler Spook #2120

Date: introduced 1954
Length: 2¾" (left); 2¼" (right)
Notes: The Crazy Crawler was a "surface crawling" competitor of the Jitterbug.
Value: $15.00 – 20.00

Crazy Crawler #2100 (plastic);
Tiny Crazy Crawler Spook #2120

Date: c. 1952; introduced 1954
Length: 2½" (top); 1¾" (bottom)
Value: $10.00 – 15.00 each

Weedless Widow Jr. #J220
Date: c. 1940
Length: 2¼"
Notes: Also made #220 Weedless Widow, 2½".
Value: $15.00 – 20.00

Meadow Mouse #F4000
Date: c. 1955
Length: 2¾"
Notes: Featuring surface hardware and leather ears, the 1955 Meadow Mouse had tremendous eye appeal.
Value: $15.00 – 20.00

Meadow Mouse Spook #9800
Date: introduced 1956
Length: 2⅞"
Notes: Made of plastic, fatter, and in flocked chipmunk finish, this version of the Meadow Mouse represents the last body shape used for this lure.
Value: $5.00 – 10.00

Experimental Musky Mouse
Date: c. 1983
Length: 3½"
Notes: Given to the author in 1983 by Bob Jones, production manager at Heddon, this lure utilizes a body shape similar to that of a Musky Crazy Crawler.
Value: $100.00 – 150.00

Punkinseed #740; #730 (wood)
Date: c. 1940
Length: 2½"; 2⅛"
Notes: Realistically shaped and painted, the Punkinseeds are highly sought after by collectors.
Value: $40.00 – 50.00

Punkinseed (plastic)

Left: **Punkin-Spin #382, c. 1974,** 1⅝"
Bottom: **Punkinseed Spook #9630, c. 1960s,** 2⅛"
Right: **Tiny Punkinseed #980, c. 1955,** 1⅝"
Notes: Punkinseeds are both highly collectible and attractive.
Value: $20.00 – 30.00 each

River Runtie Spook #950; Punkie Spook #980
Date: introduced 1937; introduced 1951
Length: 1³⁄₁₆" (left); ¹⁵⁄₁₆" (right)
Notes: These lures are flyrod-sized versions of the River Runt and Punkinseed.
Value: $15.00 – 20.00; $30.00 – 40.00

King Spoon #290
Date: c. 1937
Length: 2¾"
Notes: Heddon also made a #280 Queen, 2⅜", and a #190 Ace, 1¾".
Value: $20.00 – 25.00

Ace #190
Date: c. 1927 – 1940
Length: 1¾"
Notes: The center lure is an uncatalogued version of the Ace. At the bottom, the #502 Heddon Spoon is shown for comparison. While the Ace was made of cast brass, the #502 was stamped from thin metal.
Value: $10.00 – 15.00

Dowagiac Spook #9100
Date: c. 1950s
Length: 3⅜"
Notes: Designed to sink on retrieve, the Dowagiac Spooks featured flashing spinners and an attractive fish shape.
Value: $15.00 – 25.00

Tiny Spook #310
Date: introduced 1955
Length: 2¾"
Notes: This lure was Heddon's smallest underwater minnow.
Value: $15.00 – 25.00

Stingaree #9930; Tiny Stingaree #330
Date: c. 1957
Length: 2½"; 1½"
Notes: The Stingaree only survived for one season despite its unique porpoise-like action.
Value: $10.00 – 15.00

Sonic Family

Top: **Firetail Sonic #395, c. 1963,** 2⅝"
Left: **Sonic #385, c. 1956,** 1½"
Right: **Sonic #325, c. 1958,** 1⅛"
Bottom: **Supersonic #9385, c. 1958,** 2"
Value: $15.00 – 20.00 each

Sonar #435, #433
Date: introduced 1959
Top: 2½"; bottom: 2"
Notes: Heddon also made a smaller #431 version.
Value: $5.00 – 8.00

Top Sonic #300
Date: introduced 1967
Length: 1⅞"
Notes: Capitalizing on the Sonic's popularity, Heddon produced Top Sonic, a lure with unique surface vibrating action.
Value: $5.00 – 10.00

Dying Flutter Spook #9205
Date: introduced 1958
Length: 3¾"
Notes: Originally made in plastic, this lure was unsuccessfully tried later in wood.
Value: $5.00 – 10.00

Dying Quiver #9200
Date: introduced 1958
Length: 3¾"
Notes: Originally made in plastic, this lure was a terrific surface fish catcher.
Value: $5.00 – 10.00

Topkick; Hi-Tail #305
Date: c. 1960
Length: 1⅝"
Notes: Heddon was forced to change the name of this little bait from Topkick to Hi-Tail when it was discovered that another company was already using the name "Top Kick."
Value: $40.00 – 50.00; $25.00 – 30.00

Cobra #9930
Date: introduced 1964
Length: 3¾"; 4¾"
Notes: This version of the Cobra featured a fragile foam body which was later replaced with wood.
Value: $5.00 – 10.00

Wood King Cobra #9940

Baby Cobra #9905, 3"
Cobra #9910, 3¾"
King Cobra #9940, 8¼"
Date: introduced 1965
Notes: The Cobra Series was Heddon's entry into the hot Rapala market.
Value: $20.00 – 30.00

Surface Cobra Jr. #9960;
Surface Cobra #9970
Date: introduced 1965
Length: 3⅞"; 4⅝"
Value: $10.00 – 15.00 each

Craw Shrimp #520
Date: c. 1969
Length: 3"
Notes: The highly collectible Craw Shrimp was originally packaged in a wooden slide-top box.
Value: $20.00 – 30.00

Cousin I #7725; Cousin II #7335
Date: c. 1970s; introduced 1974
Length: 4¾" (top); 3½" (bottom)
Notes: These unusual and colorful cousins are growing in popularity with collectors.
Value: $5.00 – 10.00

Prowler Family

Top: **Large Prowler #7050,** 4½"
Middle: **Prowler #7025,** 3½"
Bottom: **Tiny Prowler #7015,** 2⅝"
Date: c. 1970s
Notes: The fish-shaped Prowler had an action similar to a Lazy Ike on retrieve.
Value: $5.00 – 10.00

Hi-Jacker #9355
Date: c. 1980s
Length: 2¾"
Notes: The Hi-Jacker was designed to produce a vibrating action with a fast retrieve.
Value: $5.00 – 10.00

Deep Six

Top: **#345,** 1⅞"
Bottom: **#9345,** 2¼"
Date: introduced 1962
Notes: The deep diving Deep Six featured an unusually long diving lip.
Value: $5.00 – 10.00

Tiger #1020, #1010

Top: **#1020,** 3¼"
Bottom: **#1010,** 2¼"
Date: c. 1960s
Notes: Heddon made four sizes of the Tiger.
Value: $10.00 – 15.00

Deep Dive Tiger, #DD1020
Date: introduced 1968
Length: 4"; 2¼"
Notes: Made in a wide range of colors, the Tiger Series is quite collectible.
Value: $10.00 – 15.00

Crackleback

Top: **#8050, c. 1970s,** 3"
Bottom: **#8000, c. 1970s,** 2¾"
Note: These fish-shaped deep divers were produced in a wide variety of colors, making them highly collectible.
Value: $10.00 – 15.00

Hedd Hunter #9320
Date: introduced 1977
Length: 2⅛"; 2"
Notes: This was one of Heddon's entries into the competitive crankbait market of the 1970s.
Value: $5.00 – 10.00

Preyfish
Date: c. 1988
Length: 3"; 2¼"
Notes: This attractive diving lure has become popular with collectors seeking complete color sets.
Value: $15.00 – 20.00

Timber Rattler #100
Date: c. 1980s
Length: 4½"; 2½"
Notes: Timber Rattlers were made of wood with a beaded rattle chamber inside the body.
Value: $5.00 – 10.00

Big Bud #9410
Date: c. 1970s
Length: 2¾"
Notes: The novel Big Bud was a deep running floating diver.
Value: $10.00 – 15.00

Original wood lures

Vamp #7500 (top left), **introduced 1966**, 4½", $10.00 – 20.00
Basser #8500 (top right), **introduced 1966**, 4½", $10.00 – 20.00
Jointed Vamp #7300 (bottom left), **introduced 1966**, 4¾", $10.00 – 20.00
Zaragossa #6500 (bottom right), **introduced 1966**, 4½", $10.00 – 20.00

Commando #2020
Date: introduced 1968
Length: 4¼"
Notes: The Commando is a weedless plastic lure with a spinning tail.
Value: $5.00 – 10.00

Brush Popper #5440; Brush Popper #5430
Date: introduced 1977
Length: 2"; 1½" (left and right)
Value: $3.00 – 7.00; $5.00 – 10.00

Moss Boss #510; Moss Boss #515
Date: c. 1980s
Length: 2⅜" (left); 2⅞" (right)
Notes: This surface "Skidder" was a great fish catcher in mossy water.
Value: $4.00 – 6.00

Hedd Plug
Date: c. 1980s
Length: 4½" (top); 3½" (bottom)
Notes: The unusual Hedd Plug design can be traced back to the Deluxe Basser of 1936.
Value: $10.00 – 15.00

Saint Spinner #440; Wag Spoon #451
Date: c. 1955 – 1960
Length: ⅞" head (Spinner); 1⅞" body (Spoon)
Value: $10.00 – 15.00; $5.00 – 10.00

Twin Pal #410
Date: introduced 1964
Length: 1½" body
Notes: Heddon also made a smaller #405 model.
Value: $4.00 – 6.00

Spinfin #413
Date: introduced 1956
Length: 2⅝"
Notes: Heddon also produced Spinfins #411 (2¼") and #412 (2½").
Value: $5.00 – 8.00

Toni Spinner #480
Date: c. 1963
Length: 2⅜"
Notes: The Toni was Heddon's answer to the popular Abu Spinner.
Value: $5.00 or less

Multi-Spinner Kit
Date: c. 1950
Notes: Made by Myr Spinnarin, Swedish for Heddon, these spinners featured changeable blades.
Value: $30.00 – 40.00

"Fidgit 3" Spinning Kit
Date: c. 1955
Notes: The Fidgit Kit was developed for the booming market in spinning lures.
Value: $20.00 – 25.00

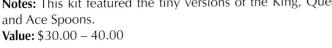

Spoon Kit
Date: c. 1955
Notes: This kit featured the tiny versions of the King, Queen, and Ace Spoons.
Value: $30.00 – 40.00

Hep Kit HK-4
Date: c. 1955
Notes: The Hep lure was Heddon's answer to the popular Mepps spinner.
Value: $20.00 – 30.00

Spinfin Kit SF-3
Date: c. 1957
Notes: This kit featured the popular single spinner Spinfin, a great river lure.
Value: $30.00 – 40.00

"Gamby Four" Kit
Date: c. 1957
Note: The Gamby was Heddon's answer to the weight-forward Paul Bunyan "66" Spinner.
Value: $30.00 – 40.00

Sonar-4 Kit
Date: c. 1959
Notes: These lures were designed to be cast into a school of fish or fished vertically in deep water.
Value: $30.00 – 40.00

Spinner Kit
Date: c. 1960
Notes: This kit featured the Hep & Toni spinners.
Value: $15.00 – 20.00

Tiny Trio Kit

Date: c. 1957

Notes: The rising popularity of spin fishing in America led a number of lure manufacturers to introduce spin kits. Heddon's kit featured small versions of the Lucky 13, the Tiny Torpedo, and the Runt.

Value: $30.00 – 40.00

C-Kit All Purpose Kit

Date: c. 1957

Notes: This is a kit organized for the spin fishermen casting to schooling fish.

Value: $30.00 – 40.00

LK-3 Lure Kit

Date: c. 1957

Notes: This kit featured small lures for spin fishing.

Value: $30.00 – 40.00

LK-3 Lure Kit

Date: 1957

Notes: This kit featured light lures designed for spin fishing.

Value: $30.00 – 40.00

Heddon Millionaires

Date: c. 1972

Notes: This interesting kit celebrates six Heddon lures with over 1 million each in sales. At the time, Heddon was owned by the Victor Comptometer Corporation.

Value: $60.00 – 90.00

It's ironic that when

a collector has a lot of money

to spend on lures, opportunities to buy

suddenly become nonexistent...

when he is low on funds, great

opportunities seem to be everywhere.

If an opportunity to buy

really good lures comes along at a cost

that exceeds his pocketbook,

the wise collector seeks help

among collector friends

to share in the purchase.

A percentage of something is

better than all of nothing.

Paw Paw Bait Co.
Paw Paw, Michigan

The minutes of the Board of Directors of the Paw Paw Bait Company show that it was in business in 1924, yet it was not incorporated until 1935. At that time Clyde C. Sinclair was elected president and Floyd A. Phelps, treasurer, with each man sharing equal ownership of 96% of the stock in the company. Mr. Phelps sold his interest in the company in 1944, but Mr. Sinclair kept his ownership and position as president of Paw Paw until 1963. The minutes show that in December of 1963, all stock was owned by Josephine Burns and A. F. Murch. From that time until 1970 when the manufacturing rights to the Paw Paw Bait Company were purchased by the Shakespeare Company, there was apparently little produced by Paw Paw. For just a short time the company name was kept alive with lures made under the name of "Paw Paw by Shakespeare," but soon the Paw Paw name was permanently dropped.

Paw Paw qualifies as one of the early bait manufacturers, yet compared to Heddon, Creek Chub, South Bend, Shakespeare or Pflueger, they were late comers. Like others, Paw Paw copied some lures from the product lines of other companies, but far and away most of their product line was comprised of lures of their own inventive style, design, and color pattern. Some Paw Paw lures would come and go, or be changed throughout the years such as their wobblers, their carved tail baits, torpedos, and injured minnows. However, they were always successfully offering something new and unique in either a bait design or an unusual color. For example, consider the highly collectible Wotta Frog, the beautiful Caster bait series, the odd looking Platterpuss and Bonehead series, and the jewel bedecked Plenty Sparkle, all produced and marketed between 1940 and 1960. This entire series of lures, the combination one-piece cup rig with diving lip, and the rainbow trout color pattern were all unique to Paw Paw. They were also an early marketer of plastic lures and offered their first Tenite bait in 1941.

Paw Paw spent little to advertise or to sell direct to the consumer, preferring to sell to jobbers, distributors, and other lure manufacturers. Therefore, documentation about their lures, in the form of catalogs, is difficult to find and sometimes makes identification of their lures more challenging. After the Great Depression era with the post-1940 lures, documentation is much more readily available and identification is much easier.

As a final bonus to those who appreciate the contributions of Paw Paw to lure manufacturing and to those who collect their beautifully painted and diverse line, the lures can usually still be found in great condition and at moderate prices... but better get on the bandwagon, this is changing fast!

David Stalnaker
Magnolia, Arkansas

Underwater Minnow #3300
Date: c. 1939
Length: 2⅝"
Notes: Although Paw Paw is not identified as being as involved in the production of Underwater Minnows as Heddon, Shakespeare, South Bend, and Pflueger, they nonetheless produced a few over the years, this being the last version.
Value: $24.00 – 30.00

"Belly Hook" Underwater Minnow
Date: c. 1939
Length: 3"
Notes: This lure is similar to the South Bend Nip-I-Diddee.
Value: $36.00 – 48.00

5-Hook Torpedo
Date: c. 1938
Length: 4"
Notes: This rare lure is the only 5-hook version of the Torpedo found to date.
Value: $180.00 – 240.00

Aristocrat Torpedo #2400
Date: c. 1958
Length: 3¾"
Notes: This lure is the standard 3-hook Torpedo.
Value: $20.00 – 25.00

Aristocrat Shiner #8500
Date: c. 1942
Length: 4"
Notes: The Aristocrat Shiner was made in both sinking and floating versions.
Value: $12.00 – 18.00

Little Shiner
Date: c. 1942
Length: 2¾"
Notes: This is a smaller version of the Aristocrat Shiner.
Value: $12.00 – 18.00

Pumpkinseed #1300 (top); Spinning Sunfish #1300
Date: c. 1940; c. 1960
Length: 2" each
Notes: These lures feature a high quality finish and tack eyes.
Value: $15.00 – 20.00

Strike Series Midget Spinner
Date: 1963
Length: 2"
Notes: Similar to the #1300 Series, this more recent lure has painted eyes and shows less overall craftsmanship.
Value: $8.00 – 15.00

Old Wounded Minnow #2500
Date: c. 1940s
Length: 3½"
Notes: This 2-treble hook lure predates the #1500 Young Wounded Minnow.
Value: $18.00 – 24.00

Young Wounded Minnow #1500
Date: c. 1941
Length: 3⅝"
Notes: Though similar, this lure has three trebles, in place of the two trebles on the Old Wounded Minnow.
Value: $18.00 – 24.00

Injured Minnow #1500
Date: c. 1940s
Length: 2¾"
Notes: Notice the side-mounted eyes as compared to the #1500 Young Wounded Minnow which had the eyes positioned on top.
Value: $18.00 – 24.00

Unknown Surface Bait
Date: c. 1940
Length: 2¾"
Notes: This is a floater similar to South Bend's Nip-i-Diddee.
Value: $45.00 – 60.00

Surface Minnow #3200
Date: c. 1946
Length: 3"
Notes: This is another floater like South Bend's Nip-i-Diddee.
Value: $24.00 – 30.00

Wounded Trout Caster
Date: c. 1941
Length: 3⅝"
Notes: This is a surface bait in Paw Paw's beautiful rainbow trout color.
Value: $180.00 – 240.00

Aristocrat Minnow
Date: c. 1946
Length: 3¼"
Notes: This bait has tentatively been identified as an Aristocrat Minnow. It has not been found in a catalog.
Value: $36.00 – 48.00

"Zaragossa Type"
Date: c. 1940
Length: 4⅜"
Notes: This bait is rare, but a few others have been found by collectors.
Value: $65.00 – 90.00

"Unknown Plunker Type"
Date: c. 1941
Length: 2½"
Notes: This fat Plunker features a scooped face similar to the CCBCO Skipper.
Value: $45.00 – 60.00

"Unknown Plunker"
Date: c. 1941
Length: 2½"
Notes: This is a paint style used only by Paw Paw.
Value: $45.00 – 60.00

Popper, older #2200 (top);
Popper, newer #2200
Date: c. 1940s
Length: 3" each
Value: $18.00 – 24.00; $12.00 – 18.00

Baby Popper #1200
Date: c. 1960s
Length: 2¼"
Notes: This is the smaller version of the #2200 Popper.
Value: $12.00 – 18.00

Frog Leg Flyrod Lure #73
Date: c. 1960
Length: 1¾"
Notes: Made from one leg of a Wotta-Frog, this lure was produced at the request of a fisherman and later added to Paw Paw's production line.
Value: $36.00 – 48.00

Darter #9200; J Jointed Darter #9200
Date: c. 1960s
Length: 3¾" (top); 3⅞" (bottom)
Notes: This bait is rare in the splatter finish.
Value: $12.00 – 18.00; $30.00 – 40.00

Plenty Sparkle #5500
Date: c. 1960
Length: 4"
Notes: This lure gets its name from the sparkling "rhinestones" set in the body. Sparkle Plenty was a character in the Dick Tracy comic strip.
Value: $15.00 – 18.00

Spinning Topper #9000 (in 3 colors)
Date: c. 1960
Length: 1½", 1½", 1⅜"
Value: $6.00 – 12.00

Spinning Torpedo #9900
Date: from 1960
Length: 1⅞"
Notes: This floater appears to be a competitor of Heddon's Tiny Torpedo.
Value: $5.00 – 10.00

Slim Jim Senior
Date: c. 1963
Length: 3¾"
Notes: This lure bears a strong resemblance to Smithwick's Devil's Horse.
Value: $6.00 – 9.00

The Bass Seeker
Date: c. 1938
Length: 4"
Notes: The cup head and wire line tie connection gave this bait a more lively action than any similar lure of the era.
Value: $20.00 – 25.00

Wobbler #4400
Date: c. 1940 through 1960s
Length: 3¾"
Note: This lure was also called Old Faithful.

Junior size Wobbler #4200
Date: c. 1941
Length: 2⅞"
Value: $18.00 – 24.00

Old Faithful #9400
Date: c. 1941
Length: 2⅜"
Notes: This is the smallest of the three Paw Paw Wobblers.
Value: $12.00 – 18.00

Mr. 13 Senior #1900
Date: c. 1960
Length: 3⅝"
Notes: Mr. 13 Senior is obviously a Lucky 13 copy.
Value: $12.00 – 15.00

Crawdad #500
Date: 1936
Length: 2¾"
Notes: This stylish lure is shown in the rare albino color.
Value: $30.00 – 45.00 in typical colors.

Bullhead #3500
Date: through 1930s, possibly 1940s
Length: 3⅞"
Notes: Brown flock is very rare, as is frog spot. Brown flock is a smaller size than normal.
Value: $120.00 – 180.00

Great Injured Minnow #3400
Date: 1930 – 1940s
Length: 4"
Notes: This lure was also called a Crippled Minnow.
Value: $90.00 – 120.00

Croaker (painted)
Date: c. 1940
Length: 3"
Notes: With side hooks and a painted finish, this is a very rare version of this lure.
Value: $300.00 – 350.00

Croaker #71
Date: c. 1940
Notes: This lure uses real frog skin stretched over the wood body.
Value: $200.00 – 300.00

Junior Wotta Frog #72; Senior Wotta Frog #73; Wotta Frog #73; Watta Frog #74

Date: 1960; c. 1960; c. 1941; c. 1941
Length: 2¾" (upper left); 3¾" (upper middle); 3¼" (lower middle); 4" (right)
Values: $30.00 – 45.00; $36.00 – 48.00; $36.00 – 48.00; $36.00 – 48.00

Musky Wotta-Frog

Date: c. 1941
Length: 5¼"
Notes: This is the true Musky Watta-Frog, measuring 5¼". Extremely rare.
Value: $500.00 – 700.00

Weedless Wow #600

Date: c. 1941
Length: 2¼"; 1¾"
Notes: These Weedless Wows are shown in the rare luminous paint finish.
Value: $75.00 – 90.00

Weedless Wow #75

Date: c. 1960
Length: 1¾"
Notes: This version of the Weedless Wow has rubber legs and is also called a Weedless Wotta Frog.
Value: $30.00 – 45.00

Mouse

Date: c. 1935
Length: 2½"
Notes: This Mouse is often confused with a similar lure made by the Mouse Bait Co., Ft. Worth, Texas.
Value: $100.00 – 150.00

Hair Mouse
Date: c. 1938
Length: 2½"
Notes: This plug was covered with deer skin with the hair left on.
Value: $150.00 – 200.00

Nature Mouse #40 (grey pearl, later called Minnie Mouse); Nature Mouse #50 (white suede); Nature Mouse #60 (white suede, flyrod size)
Date: c. 1940s
Length: 2⅜" (top); 2½" (bottom); 1⅞" (far right)
Value: $30.00 – 45.00; $30.00 – 36.00; $30.00 – 36.00

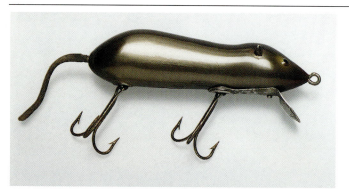

Musky Minnie Mouse
Date: uncatalogued
Length: 4⅛"
Notes: This beautiful lure has a high quality finish and terrific eye appeal.
Value: $300.00 – 360.00

Swimming Mouse #4600
Date: 1963
Length: 2¾"
Notes: This is Paw Paw's version of the Shakespeare Mouse.
Value: $12.00 – 15.00

Feather Tail Minnow #1200
Date: c. 1940s
Length: 2½"
Notes: This rare lure has a single hook within the feather tail.
Value: $30.00 – 45.00

River Go-Getter #800; River Go-Getter #900
Date: c. 1940
Length: 2⅝"
Notes: In different catalogs, Paw Paw listed the River Go-Getter as both #800 and #900.
Value: $18.00 – 24.00

#9300; #9300J
Date: c. 1950
Length: 3⅛" (top); 3¼" (bottom)
Notes: These were very popular lures with fishermen across the country.
Value: $12.00 – 15.00

#9100; #9100J
Date: c. 1950
Length: 2⅝" (top); 2¾" (bottom)
Notes: These lures are the smaller versions of the #9100 and #9100J.
Value: $12.00 – 15.00

Midget #7100; Feather Midget #7200
Date: c. 1960
Length: 1⅝; 1½"
Notes: These attractive lures were terrific fish catchers in streams and rivers.
Value: $9.00 – 12.00

Jig-a-Lure #2700
Date: 1940s – 1960
Length: 1⅜", 1⅝"
Notes: The top lure is the early version.
Value: $10.00 – 20.00

Trout Caster #7800L; Jointed Trout Caster #7800LJ
Date: c. 1940
Length: 4⅝"; 4¾"
Value: $60.00 – 90.00

Shiner Caster C-1100
Date: c. 1940
Length: 3⅝"
Notes: The Shiner Caster was a smaller version of the Trout Caster.
Value: $45.00 – 60.00

Bass Caster
Date: c. 1940
Length: 2¾"
Notes: This is the smallest of the Casters.
Value: $45.00 – 60.00

Jointed Chub Caster #C-900; Chub Caster #C-800
Date: c. 1940
Length: 3¾"; 3⅝"
Value: $45.00 – 60.00

Mud Minnow Caster #7000
Date: 1940
Length: 3⅞"
Notes: The Mud Minnow had a more rounded "catfish" tail than the other Caster lures.
Value: $60.00 – 90.00

Dace Caster

Date: c. 1940
Length: 4⅛"; 3½"
Notes: Featuring a pearlescent finish, the Dace Caster is the fattest of the Caster Series.
Value: $50.00 – 80.00

Perch Caster (3 trebles)

Date: c. 1940
Length: 5"
Value: $60.00 – 90.00

Pike Caster #6400L

Date: c. 1940
Length: 5⅛"; 5¼"
Notes: The fish-shaped "Caster" series lures are very desirable and beautifully finished.
Value: $60.00 – 90.00

Pike Caster, jointed #6400 LJ;
Pike Caster, jointed; #6400 SJ; Pike Caster #6400 S

Date: c. 1940
Length: 5½" (top); 3⅝" (middle); 3½" (bottom)
Value: $60.00 – 90.00; $45.00 – 60.00; $45.00 – 60.00

Spoon Belly Wobbler

Date: c. 1940
Length: 5⅜"
Notes: When produced as a lure without the painted body, the metal spoon portion of this bait was called the belly spoon.
Value: $210.00 – 240.00

Baby Sucker
Date: c. 1938
Length: 3⅞"
Notes: The body shape of this sleek lure is similar to the Dace Caster but without the fish-shaped tail.
Value: $120.00 – 150.00

Jointed Sucker
Date: c. 1938
Length: 4½"
Notes: This is the jointed version of the Sucker.
Value: $150.00 – 180.00

Pike Series #1000, early style; Pike Series #1000, jointed, early style
Date: c. 1940
Length: 4⅜" (top); 4½" (bottom)
Value: $18.00 – 24.00

Musky Pike #5100
Date: c. 1940
Length: 6¼"
Notes: This is the early version of the #5100 Musky Pike.
Value: $60.00 – 75.00

Dreadnought #5100J
Date: c. 1940s
Length: 6⅝"
Notes: Note the heavy hinge hardware.
Value: $90.00 – 120.00

Musky Pike #5100
Date: c. 1946
Length: 6¼"
Notes: Note the "scalloped" face of this late version of the #5100.
Value: $60.00 – 75.00

Musky Jointed Pike #5100J
Date: c. 1946
Length: 6⅝"
Notes: This is the jointed version of the #5100.
Value: $75.00 – 90.00

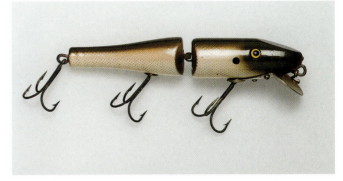

Frog Skin Pike
Date: c. 1940
Length: 4⅜"
Notes: This lure was covered with actual frog skin.
Value: $30.00 – 45.00

Junior Pike #1400
Date: 1940s – 1950s
Length: 3¼", 3⅜", 3¼"
Notes: These lures are shown in the order of their production, from top to bottom.
Value: $15.00 – 18.00

Baby Jointed Pike #2100
Date: 1940s, 1950s
Length: 3½"
Notes: Note the difference in head shape between these lures.
Value: $15.00 – 18.00

Pike #1600
Date: c. 1940, 1960s
Length: 4⅜", 4¼"
Notes: The clue to vintage is in the head shape. The top lure is the older of the two shown.
Value: $15.00 – 25.00

Baby Pike, regular (top)
Date: 1950s
Length: 3¾"
Notes: No lure number has been found for this bait.
Value: $15.00 – 18.00

Baby Pike, jointed (bottom)
Date: 1950s
Length: 3⅞"
Notes: No lure number has been found.
Value: $15.00

Deep Diver Piky – Get Um #2800
Date: 1950s
Length: 4⅜"
Notes: This lure features a deep diving lip and pink "rhinestone" eyes.
Value: $15.00 – 20.00

Famous Piky Getum #1000;
Jointed Piky Getum #2000
Date: c. 1960
Length: 4¼"; 4⅜"
Notes: These attractive lures feature a groove on each side of the head.
Value: $12.00 – 18.00

Jointed Pikaroon #9600
Date: 1963
Length: 2½"
Note: While the name is the same, this lure is not to be confused with Moonlight Bait Co. Pikaroon.
Value: $15.00 – 18.00

Clothes Pin Bait #2300
Date: c. 1940s
Length: 2½"
Notes: This is a fairly typical saltwater lure design.
Value: $12.00 – 18.00

"Saltwater Bait"
Date: c. 1940
Length: 2½"
Notes: This lure uses a #900 Go-Getter body and looks a lot like the Heddon Sea Runt, with two belly weights. It is found around the Texas coast more than anywhere else.
Value: $36.00 – 48.00

"No Eye Saltwater Fish"
Date: c. 1940
Length: 3¼"
Notes: This bait looks like the Heddon Little Job. It is weighted, probably for saltwater use.
Value: $36.00 – 48.00

"Saltwater Fish"
Date: c. 1940
Length: 2"
Notes: This bait looks similar to Heddon's Salt Water Special.
Value: $75.00 – 90.00

"Pencil Baits"
Date: c. 1950
Length: 4⅞"; 3⅝"; 2⅛"
Notes: Featuring a grooved head, it is obvious that these baits got their name from their slim pencil shape.
Value: $20.00 – 30.00

Go-Diva #3600
Date: c. 1940
Length: 3¾"
Notes: To quote the catalog, the Go-Diva "imitates a scampering minnow that tantalizes the fighters and makes them strike hard."
Value: $18.00 – 24.00

Split Tail Flap Jack #8900
Date: c. 1940s
Length: 3½"
Notes: One has to wonder if this lure was responsible for the design of Creek Chub's 1956 Nikie.
Value: $9.00 – 12.00

Flap Jack Phantom #3400
Date: c. 1941
Length: 3⅝"
Notes: This lure design is based on the Helin Flatfish.
Value: $12.00 – 18.00

Platypuss #3500
Date: c. 1941
Length: 3¾"
Notes: The Platypuss uses the same hook hardware as that on the Flapjack. Also called Platterpuss.
Value: $30.00 – 45.00

Lippy Joe
Date: c. 1949
Length: 2⅜"
Note: Lippy Joe is a Heddon River Runt look-alike.
Value: $10.00 – 20.00

PAW PAW BAIT CO.

Bonehead, Lazy Ike style
Date: c. 1960
Length: 3"
Notes: This is an uncatalogued Bonehead lure. The lure got its name from the textured "bonelike" paint finish.
Value: $30.00 – 40.00

Bonehead, Struttin' Sam
Date: 1959 – 1964
Length: 3⅝"
Notes: All Boneheads are hard to find.
Value: $60.00 – 90.00

Transparent Bass Seeker #300; Brilliant Bass Seeker #400
Date: c. 1950s; c. 1949
Length: 2¾" (top); 3" (bottom)
Notes: This lure was first called Zigger and was made both straight and jointed.
Value: $9.00 – 12.00

Woggle Bug #WB700
Date: c. 1963
Length: 2½"
Notes: The Woggle Bug owes a lot to the design of the Arbogast Jitterbug.
Value: $9.00 – 12.00

Wing Wobbler #3-P
Date: c. 1938
Length: 3½"
Notes: This wobbling spoon is white pearl with red wings and was also produced in a #3 copper and nickel version.

Sly Hawk #E16
Date: c. 1940
Length: 3¼"
Note: This lure appears to have been designed to pull through rushes and vegetation with little resistance.
Value: $15.00 – 18.00

Seagram's Lucky 7
Date: c. 1953
Length: 3"
Notes: This is an example of competition, selling both lures and whisky.
Value: $15.00 – 20.00

"Unknown"
Date: unknown
Length: 2⅞"
Notes: This splatter finish lure is reported to have come from Clyde Sinclair's estate (he was president of Paw Paw) and has Flap Jack hardware.
Value: $50.00 – 60.00

"Unknown Plunker or Popper type bait"
Date: unknown
Length: 3⅛"
Notes: This unknown bait has a black splatter Paw Paw finish.
Value: $20.00 – 25.00

"Unknown Darter type"
Date: unknown
Length: 4"
Notes: Another unknown with a black splatter finish.
Value: $20.00 – 25.00

PAW PAW BAIT CO.

Spearing Decoys

Date: c. 1930, 1940
Length: 7⅜", 5"
Notes: The top decoy shown is painted in the rare "Redhorse" pattern. The bottom decoy is typical Paw Paw splatter finish.
Value: $200.00 – 250.00

Jughead

Date: c. 1937
Length: 1¹¹⁄₁₆", ⅜"
Notes: This flyrod lure mimics Moonlight Bait Company's Trout Bob.
Value: $60.00 – 75.00

"Frog"

Date: c. 1940
Length: 1⅜" body
Notes: This beady-eyed frog has a shaped wooden body.
Value: $35.00 – 45.00

Flyrod Croaker

Date: c. 1940
Length: 1½"
Notes: This is the flyrod version of Paw Paw's #71 Croaker.
Value: $60.00 – 75.00

"Popper"

Date: c. 1946
Length: ¾" head
Notes: Bearing a strong resemblance to Heddon's Wilder-Dilg, this beautiful surface lure seems to beg for a bass to strike it.
Value: $30.00 – 40.00

McGinty
Date: c. 1940
Length: 1¾"
Notes: The McGinty was described in the catalog as "a spinning pickerel and bass lure."
Value: $10.00 – 20.00

Groove Head
Date: c. 1941
Length: 1⅝"
Notes: This lure design became common in the fishing lure industry after the South Bend Bait Co. introduced the Trout Oreno in 1920.
Value: $10.00 – 15.00

Flyrod Centipede
Date: c. 1946
Length: 1½"
Notes: This yellow lure is splattered with black paint and is typical of Paw Paw's unique "splatter paint" finish.
Value: $30.00 – 40.00

#71F largest size; mid-size #70F; smallest size #69F
Date: c. 1960
Length: 1³⁄₁₆" (left); ⁹⁄₁₆" (middle); ⅜" (right)
Value: $12.00 – 18.00

Pflueger (Enterprise Mfg. Co.)
Akron, Ohio

As E. F. Pflueger worked in his home with six employees in 1880, I am sure he would never have believed that over the next 60 years his endeavor would become the dominant tackle producer in the world. Over this 60-year period, Enterprise Manufacturing sold more fishing equipment than any other manufacturer.

Enterprise Manufacturing was always much more than a lure company. By 1940 there were approximately 390 items listed in their catalog, and less than a dozen were wooden bass lures. Even though their line of lures had shrunk, many of the lures were classics. It is hard to imagine how many Pal-O-Mines and Globes were sold. The company was still innovative, with lures like the Livewire and the Frisky, and with the unique "scramble" paint finish.

The movement away from glass-eyed baits to the less expensive pressed eye lures had begun. Enterprise had an extensive line of metal baits, rubber baits, and fly fishing lures. Also their line included rods, hooks, bobbers, sinkers, and a large group of additional accessories. Enterprise Manufacturing was a major supplier to a vast majority of hardware stores throughout the country.

By World War II the company had become the leader in the reel market. Their line of casting reels anchored by the Supreme were the dominant sellers. They also had a great line of salt water reels, and the Medalist fly reel was extremely popular. Over the next two decades the company became more and more dependent on the reel market. When the competing Ambassadeur 5000 hit the U.S. market in the 1960s, Enterprise took a fatal hit which led to the sale of the company in the early 1970s to Shakespeare.

When E. F. Pflueger first started making lures in 1880, I am sure he would never have imagined that for 90 years and many generations his family would be a major force in the tackle industry.

Drew Reese
Reeds Spring, Missouri

Neverfail Minnow #3100 (5 hook)
Date: c. 1940
Length: 3⅝"
Notes: The Neverfail was introduced c. 1907. The wood Pflueger baits covered in this chapter will be the painted pressed eye versions. Note early hook hangers.
Value: $120.00 – 180.00

Neverfail Minnow #3100 (3 hook)
Date: c. 1940
Length: 3"
Note: The hook hangers on this lure are the early Neverfail type discussed in *Fishing Lure Collectibles, Volume 1.*
Value: $120.00 – 130.00

Neverfail Minnow #3100 (3 hook)
Date: c. 1948
Length: 3"
Notes: This "Argyle socks" finished minnow features surface hook hangers and pressed eyes.
Value: $120.00 – 140.00

Neverfail Minnow #3100
Date: c. 1952
Length: 2¾", 2½"
Notes: This is a late version of the Neverfail without the older style side hooks. Note the incised gills.
Value: $30.00 – 36.00

Live Wire Minnow #9400
Date: c. 1931 – 1955
Length: 3¾"
Notes: This version of the Live Wire is made of wood; the early version was made of plastic with a plastic dorsal fin.
Value: $24.00 – 30.00

Scoop Minnow #9300; Baby Scoop #9300
Date: c. 1937
Length: 3⅝", 3"; 2"
Notes: The 3⅝" model was available in 1937, the 3" model was introduced in 1941. They are similar to the Creek Chub Injured Minnow and feature 3-blade props.
Value: $30.00 – 36.00

Globe Bait #3700
Date: c. 1930s – 1960s
Length: 5½", 3⅝", 2⅞"
Notes: The Globe was introduced in 1912 and remained in production into the 1960s.
Value: $15.00 – 20.00

Ballerina Minnow #5400
Date: c. 1952
Length: 4¼", 3⅜"
Notes: According to the 1952 Pflueger catalog, the Ballerina was designed as "a popping bait for salt water trout fishing."
Value: $15.00 – 25.00

Frisky Minnow #6100
Date: c. 1952
Length: 2¼"
Notes: An earlier "bottle nose" version of the Frisky was made in the 1930s.
Value: $15.00 – 25.00

Pal-O-Mine Minnow #5100
Date: c. 1948
Length: 4¼", 3¼"
Notes: Introduced in 1924, the Pal-O-Mine was a mainstay in the Pflueger catalog into the 1960s.
Value: $12.00 – 18.00

Pal-O-Mine Jointed Minnow #9000
Date: c. 1948
Length: 4¼", 3½"
Notes: Introduced in 1924, the jointed version of the Pal-O-Mine was very popular with fishermen.
Value: $12.00 – 18.00

Mustang Minnow #8900 (floating)
Date: c. 1937
Length: 4¼", 2¾"
Notes: Similar in looks to the Pal-O-Mine, the Mustang was produced in a wide variety of sizes. Floating and sinking versions were also available.
Value: $18.00 – 24.00

Mustang Underwater Popping Minnow #8600
Date: c. 1937
Length: 2½"
Value: $18.00 – 24.00

Mustang Jointed Minnow
Date: c. 1939
Length: 2½"
Notes: The Jointed Mustang appears to be uncatalogued.
Value: $30.00 – 35.00

Heavy Duty Mustang Minnow #9500
Date: c. 1939
Length: 5"
Notes: This is the largest catalogued Mustang and features metal plates on the back and belly.
Value: $25.00 – 30.00

Musky Mustang
Date: c. 1940
Length: 7¼"
Notes: This massive lure did not appear in any Pflueger catalogs. Note the multiple attachment line tie.
Value: $180.00 – 210.00

Musky Jointed Mustang
Date: c. 1940
Length: 7½"
Notes: This lure is the jointed version of the previous lure.
Value: $180.00 – 210.00

Poprite Minnow; Flyrod Poprite Minnow #8500
Date: c. 1948
Length: 3"; 1¼"
Notes: A 4" Poprite was first produced in 1935, the 3" model was shown in 1940, but by 1955, only the 3" remained in production.
Value: $15.00 – 30.00

Tantrum Minnow #8400
Date: c. 1952
Length: 4"
Notes: The Tantrum is basically a large, 3-treble hooked Poprite without a tail spinner.
Value: $18.00 – 25.00

Flocked Mouse; Spinning Mouse
Date: c. 1950
Length: 1⅝" (left); 2⅝" (right)
Notes: These rare little mice answered the need for small baits to be used with light tackle.
Value: $150.00 – 180.00

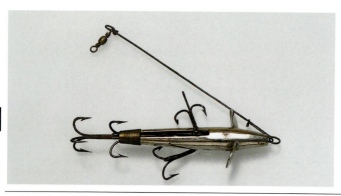

Breakless Devon #289
Date: c. 1897 – mid 1950s
Length: 2½"
Notes: Based on a late nineteenth century design by Archer Wakeman, the Breakless Devon was so named because the hooks and leader were made of wire and not of fragile gut common in the early years.
Value: $12.00 – 18.00

McMurray Spinner #40
Date: c. 1940
Length: 5⅜"
Notes: First appearing in Pflueger's catalog of 1894, the McMurray was still "going strong" in the 1952 catalog.
Value: $10.00 – 15.00

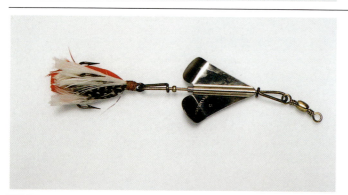

Black Bass Bait #116
Date: c. 1952
Length: 1⅝" blade
Notes: Based on an earlier Pflueger design of 1892, this bait was often used for surface "skittering" with a rapid retrieve.
Value: $18.00 – 24.00

Fluted Bait #108
Date: c. 1940
Length: 2⅛"
Notes: This is a standard fluted blade often used on early lures. Pflueger's 1892 catalog listed a bait using this fluted blade.
Value: $10.00 – 15.00

Kidney Pearl Bait #600
Date: c. 1940
Length: 2⅛₆" blade
Notes: With "blades made of genuine salt water pearl" shell, the Kidney was also made in a tandem version. Several pearl spinners were listed in the 1892 catalog.
Value: $15.00 – 20.00

Heart Bait #2600
Date: c. 1942
Length: 2¾"
Notes: Described as "especially killing for salmon," the Heart Bait was made in both painted and plated versions.
Value: $18.00 – 24.00

Indiana Spinner
Date: c. 1940
Length: 2¹⁄₁₆" blade
Notes: Pflueger made a variety of popular blade styles. The Indiana combined the thin qualities of the willow leaf blade with the more cupped and rounded Colorado blade.
Value: $10.00 – 15.00

Record Spoon #1800
Date: c. 1948
Length: 4⅝"
Notes: Similar to the Self Striker Spoon, the Record was highly touted as a salmon and salt water favorite.
Value: $5.00 – 10.00

Magic Spoon
Date: c. 1940
Length: 3"
Notes: This lure was later named the Scamper Wobbler.
Value: $10.00 – 15.00

Salamo Spoon #1500
Date: c. 1948
Length: 4½"
Notes: This large spoon featured a dressed treble hook and a highly polished finish.
Value: $10.00 – 15.00

Limper #7700
Date: c. 1948
Length: 3¹⁄₁₆"
Notes: Made in a wide variety of sizes, the Limper was designed to wobble erratically.
Value: $5.00 – 10.00

Harp Spinner
Date: c. 1937
Length: 1³⁄₁₆" blade
Notes: The Harp Spinner came with a paper pattern of a "frog" attached. The fisherman could use the pattern to cut his own pork rind trailers.
Value: $10.00 – 15.00

Luminous Tandem Spinner #3445;
Weighted Luminous Tandem Spinner #2945
Date: c. 1940
Length: 1⁹⁄₁₆" blade width
Notes: Pflueger began business as a manufacturer of luminous horse collars, then shifted to making lures, many of which featured luminous paint. The Tandem Spinner continued the luminous tradition into the post-WWII era.
Value: $5.00 – 10.00

Dragon Spinner #7342
Date: c. 1940
Length: 2" shaft
Notes: The "new and novel style" of the Dragon Spinner blade would probably appear to thread its way through the water like a screw.
Value: $10.00 – 15.00

O'Boy #4970
Date: c. 1930s
Length: 4" overall
Notes: The Weedless O'Boy spinner took its name from Pflueger's O'Boy minnow of 1924.
Value: $18.00 – 24.00

Pippin Wobbler
Date: c. 1940
Length: 2⅞"
Notes: The casting size Pippin was succeeded by a flyrod size which was often trolled behind deep diving lures.
Value: $18.00 – 24.00

Last Word Wobbler #2800;
Last Word Wobbler #5600
Date: c. 1946
Length: 3" (top); 2⅞" (bottom)
Notes: Using a metal fish-shaped body like the Pippen Wobbler, this lure was available either painted or plated.
Value: $10.00 – 15.00

Fan-Tail Squid
Date: c. 1940
Length: 2¼"
Notes: This slim celluloid plastic bait was designed for salt water fishing.
Value: $15.00 – 20.00

Zam #4800
Date: c. 1941
Length: 2⅛"
Notes: Similar to the Pippen Wobbler, the Zam was offered in both painted and plated finishes. A 1⅞" size Zam was also available.
Value: $15.00 – 25.00

Chum Spoon #7100
Date: c. 1946
Length: 2¹¹⁄₆₄"
Notes: Available in a variety of sizes and finishes, the Chum was popular enough to be produced and sold in great numbers.
Value: $5.00 – 10.00

Snapie Spinner #3370
Date: c. 1948
Length: 1¼" body
Notes: The attractive Snapie has a lot of eye appeal: unusual spinner blade shape, nicely painted triangular lead body, and bright hair weedguard.
Value: $15.00 – 20.00

Woopee Spinner #2300
Date: c. 1948
Length: 4¾" overall
Notes: The Woopee featured a spring-loaded device beneath the bucktail to keep tension on a pork rind strip.
Value: $15.00 – 25.00

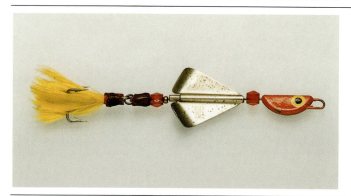

Cyclone Spinner #3000
Date: c. 1959
Length: 1⅛" blade
Notes: The weight-forward design of the Cyclone Spinner would allow the blade to spin when sinking or with a rapid retrieve.
Value: $15.00 – 20.00

The Frug
Date: c. 1965
Length: 1¾"
Notes: The Frug was a popular dance in the early 1960s. Pflueger attempted to equate the action of their "dance lures" to the movements of the dances that inspired them.
Value: $5.00 – 10.00

The Jerk
Date: c. 1965
Length: 3⅜", 4⅞"
Notes: The topwater Jerk is another of Pflueger's "dance lures."
Value: $5.00 – 10.00

The Watusi
Date: c. 1965
Length: 2⅝"
Notes: The Watusi is another "dance lure" named after the popular dance.
Value: $5.00 – 10.00

Gay Blade
Date: c. 1960
Length: 2"
Notes: The Gay Blade was a fantastic lure for schooling white bass. It was also made in a 1⁹⁄₁₆" size.
Value: $5.00 or less

Shiner Lure
Date: c. 1967
Length: 2¾"
Notes: The Shiner was also available in a 4" size.
Value: $5.00 or less

Pflueger Spin Kit #400
Date: c. 1959
Notes: The rising popularity of spin fishing in America led a number of lure manufacturers to introduce spin kits. Pflueger's kit featured downsized versions of their regular size metal lures.
Value: $20.00 – 25.00

Pflueger Spin Kit #405
Date: c. 1959
Notes: Like the #400 kit, the #405 features spin size versions of their regular lures.
Value: $20.00 – 25.00

PFLUEGER (ENTERPRISE MFG. CO.)

Collecting Tips And Observations #2

It has been said that

"knowledge is power,"

but how and where

does one gain knowledge?

Buy as many books as you can afford,

then read the words.

Study the pictures and

learn what they have

to tell you about

lure history and design.

It's the cheapest way to gain

the knowledge you need

to be a lure collector.

Wm. Shakespeare Co.
Kalamazoo, Michigan

The 1940s era represents over four decades of the Shakespeare Company's manufacturing of its "Fine Fishing Tackle." But Shakespeare would soon succumb to many significant changes. The lures that it currently produced were carry-overs from years past, and the development of new bait lines had come to a halt.

Like so many businesses in the early 1940s, normal production was forced to change in order to aid in the manufacturing of war materials and necessities. Although the war effort didn't greatly hinder the production of Shakespeare lures, the wartime period saw a drop of several lure styles. For a number of years after the war, we see a few of Shakespeare's more popular lures come back into the sales catalogs, but nowhere near the numbers and body styles sold just 10 years before.

In 1952, the Creek Chub Bait Company purchased Shakespeare and continued to manufacture the Shakespeare line until 1958. The entire Shakespeare/Creek Chub production line suddenly stopped at this time and would not start up for another 10 years. From then on, Shakespeare lures would no longer be made in the United States. Around 1968, the factory moved to Hong Kong and re-opened production, including a line of wood lures. Although the names and colors were completely new, the body styles shared a strong resemblance to the baits Shakespeare had manufactured 30 years before. Shakespeare continues to produce a full line of fishing tackle today.

Even though its handcrafted beginnings gave way to mass production and new technology, the quality, unique body styles, beautiful finishes, and fish-catching popularity keep Shakespeare Lures on top of the list among many collectors.

Dan Zemke
Robbinsdale, Minnesota

Submarine #6526

Date: 1940
Length: 3¾"
Notes: This basic lure was first introduced in 1907 as the #44 Submerged Wooden Minnow. Like most Shakespeare lures from this period, this lure has pressed eyes.
Value: $150.00 – 180.00

Rhode's Torpedo #6540

Date: c. 1934
Length: 3"
Notes: This lure is basically the Shakespeare #33 which was introduced in 1918.
Value: $90.00 – 120.00

Punkin-Seed 30P (floater)

Date: c. 1937
Length: 2½"
Notes: The Punkin-Seed was introduced in 1911 in floating and sinking versions.
Value: $48.00 – 60.00

Slim Jim #6552

Date: c. 1937
Length: 4¼"
Notes: The first Slim Jims were introduced in 1908 and had glass eyes. The later pressed eye version is shown.
Value: $24.00 – 36.00

McKinney Special

Date: c. 1950
Length: 3¾"
Notes: This is a special order Slim Jim made for McKinney Sporting Goods in Texas.
Value: $18.00 – 30.00

Slim Jim #6541

Date: c. 1940

Length: 3⅝"

Notes: Originally made with glass eyes in 1908, the Slim Jim was a mainstay in the Shakespeare line until the company was sold in 1952.

Value: $12.00 – 18.00

Spinning Slim Jim #6341

Date: c. 1950

Length: 2¼"

Notes: This is the smallest Slim Jim.

Value: $12.00 – 18.00

Jim Dandy Floater

Date: c. 1936

Length: 3¾"

Notes: This attractive floater was part of Shakespeare's economy Jim Dandy line of lures.

Value: $60.00 – 90.00

Nu-Crip Minnow #6510

Date: c. 1934

Length: 4⅛"

Notes: Introduced in 1934, the Nu-Crip was gone by the mid 1940s.

Value: $48.00 – 60.00

Shakespeare Special #6546

Date: c. 1939

Length: 3½"

Notes: The most obvious difference between this lure and Similar Dalton special is the notched rather than smooth face. The Shakespeare Special was also made in a larger 3-hook version.

Value: $12.00 – 18.00

Jerkin Lure #6567
Date: c. 1940
Length: 4"
Notes: A tail propeller was added to the Jerkin lure in the late 1940s.
Value: $9.00 – 15.00

Frogskin Bait #6505L
Date: c. 1940
Length: 3¾"
Notes: Originally a 1930 bait, real frogskin is stretched over the wooden body.
Value: $36.00 – 48.00

Frogskin Bait #6505S
Date: c. 1940
Length: 3"
Notes: This is a smaller version of the #6505L Frogskin Bait.
Value: $36.00 – 48.00

Baby Popper
Date: c. 1940
Length: 2⅛"
Notes: The overhanging mouth is a clue to identifying the Baby Popper.
Value: $30.00 – 45.00

Pop-I Bait #6574
Date: c. 1938
Length: 3⅝"
Notes: The Pop-I appears to have been in competition with the CCBCO Plunker.
Value: $45.00 – 60.00

WM. SHAKESPEARE CO.

Pop-I Bait #6575
Date: c. 1940
Length: 3⅛"
Notes: This is a later and more stocky version of the original Pop-I.
Value: $15.00 – 25.00

Spinning Pop-Eye #6375
Date: c. 1950
Length: 1⅞"
Notes: This is the smallest version of the Pop-I.
Value: $18.00 – 24.00

Bass-a-Lure #591
Date: c. 1939
Length: 3¾"
Notes: Originally made with glass eyes in 1923.
Value: $75.00 – 90.00

Kazoo Wobbler #6637
Date: c. 1940
Length: 4"
Notes: The earliest Kazoo Wobblers were glass eyed. The keel and ball tail hook hanger were later additions.
Value: $60.00 – 75.00

Egyptian Wobbler #6636
Date: c. 1940
Length: 5"
Notes: The Egyptian Wobbler was made with glass eyes in 1930.
Value: $60.00 – 75.00

Egyptian Wobbler Jr. #6635
Date: c. 1941
Length: 3¾"
Notes: This is a smaller version of the standard Egyptian Wobbler.
Value: $60.00 – 75.00

Jointed Egyptian Wobbler #6677
Date: c. 1935 – 1955
Length: 5"
Note: This lure is the jointed version of the Egyptian designed to give more radical action.
Value: $90.00 – 105.00

Jointed Egyptian Wobbler Jr. #6676
Date: c. 1940
Length: 4"
Notes: Shakespeare's catalog copy states that every Jointed Egyptian Wobbler was water-tested for action.
Value: $90.00 – 105.00

Kingfish Wobbler #6535
Date: c. 1940
Length: 5"
Notes: In 1935 the Kingfish Wobbler was made with glass eyes.
Value: $60.00 – 75.00

Striped Bass Wobbler
Date: c. 1940
Length: 6"
Notes: This large, strong lure is very rare.
Value: $95.00 – 150.00

"Striped Bass Special"
Date: c. 1940
Length: 6¼"
Notes: Dubbed "Striped Bass Special" by collectors, this lure appears to have been uncatalogued.
Value: $60.00 – 90.00

Tantalizer #6638
Date: c. 1940
Length: 4⅛"
Notes: The original 1928 Tantalizer had glass eyes.
Value: $45.00 – 55.00

Tantalizer Jr. #6638
Date: c. 1940
Length: 3⅝"
Notes: This is the small version of the standard Tantalizer.
Value: $45.00 – 55.00

Tarpalunge #6640
Date: c. 1938
Length: 5¾"
Notes: This lure features a special belly hook hanger and large single hooks.
Value: $150.00 – 180.00

Fisher Bait #6509
Date: c. 1940
Length: 3¾"
Notes: The Fisher Bait is basically an unjointed Tantalizer.
Value: $60.00 – 90.00

Junior Fisher Bait #6508

Date: c. 1940
Length: 2⅞"
Notes: This is the "little brother" to the standard Fisher Bait.
Value: $150.00 – 165.00

Sardinia #621

Date: c. 1936
Length: 3"
Notes: The rare Sardinia first appeared with glass eyes in 1925.
Value: $120.00 – 180.00

Jacksmith #6561

Date: c. 1940
Length: 4⅛"
Notes: Similar in appearance to the Heddon Basser, the Jacksmith features a keel and a cupped face.
Value: $75.00 – 90.00

Jack Jr. #6560

Date: c. 1940
Length: 2¾"
Notes: This is the smaller version of the Jacksmith lure.
Value: $75.00 – 90.00

Jointed Jacksmith

Date: c. 1940
Length: 4¼"
Notes: Resembling Heddon's Zig-Wag, the jointed Jacksmith appears to be uncatalogued and quite rare.
Value: $120.00 – 150.00

Buddy #6568

Date: c. 1937
Length: 4⅛"
Notes: Featured in the 1934 catalog, the plastic-lipped Buddy could be considered a forerunner of the Rapala.
Value: $12.00 – 24.00

River Pup #6564

Date: c. 1940
Length: 2½"
Notes: The 1934 version of the River Pup featured a stepped diving lip.
Value: $6.00 – 9.00

Glo-Lite Pup #6554

Date: c. 1940
Length: 2½"
Notes: This plastic version of the Glo-Lite Pup was guaranteed to glow four to five hours if exposed for three minutes to sunlight or flashlight.
Value: $6.00 – 9.00

Little Joe #6593

Date: c. 1940
Length: 2⅛"
Notes: "A super active wiggler that attracts the big ones," the 1934 Little Joe had glass eyes.
Value: $36.00 – 45.00

Baby Blitz #6550

Date: c. 1942
Length: 2"
Notes: This is a very lightweight lure with a lot of action in the water.
Value: $18.00 – 26.00

Swimming Mouse #6578
Date: c. 1940
Length: 3¼"
Notes: Like their living funny counterparts, Swimming Mice are everywhere.
Value: $12.00 – 18.00

Swimming Mouse Jr. #6580
Date: c. 1940
Length: 2¾"
Notes: The ubiquitous Swimming Mouse.
Value: $12.00 – 18.00

Baby Swimming Mouse #6577
Date: c. 1940
Length: 2½"
Notes: This is the smallest size casting mouse.
Value: $12.00 – 18.00

Glo Lite Mouse #6570
Date: c. 1940
Length: 2¾"
Notes: This plastic version of the Swimming Mouse was enhanced for night fishing and glowed in the dark.
Value: $6.00 – 9.00

Barbera Rat (Barbera Sport Swimming Mouse)
Length: 2¾"
Notes: Made as a specialty for Barbera Sport in San Antonio, Texas, this mouse has a hair tail instead of the usual string tail.
Value: $36.00 – 45.00

Spinning Mouse #6380
Date: c. 1950
Length: 2⅛"
Notes: This is the smallest of the many versions of the Swimming Mouse.
Value: $6.00 – 12.00

Muskie Pad'ler #6679; Bass Pad'ler #6678; Small Bass Pad'ler #6680
Date: c. 1936
Length: 4" (top); 3¼" (middle); 2⅞" (bottom)
Notes: The 1936 Paddler was a surface lure designed to represent a mouse or frog. The Muskie size is quite rare.
Value: $90.00 – 110.00; $90.00 – 110.00; $30.00 – 36.00

Dopey #6603
Date: c. 1911
Length: 1½"
Notes: Resembling the Keeling Tom Thumb of the 1920s, the little Dopey got its name from the movie "Snow White and the Seven Dwarfs."
Value: $6.00 – 12.00

Grumpy #6602
Date: c. 1941
Length: 1¾"
Notes: The Grumpy was named after one of the Seven Dwarfs from the "Snow White" movie.
Value: $6.00 – 12.00

Midget Spinner #6601
Date: c. 1940
Length: 1¾"
Notes: Early Midget Spinners had glass eyes.
Value: $30.00 – 45.00

Sea Witch #6531
Date: c. 1940
Length: 3⅞"
Notes: The 1930 Sea Witch was a glass-eyed bait.
Value: $12.00 – 18.00

Kasmiroski Special #562
Date: c. 1950
Length: 2⅛"
Notes: This lure was named for Louis Kasmiroski, a salesman for Shakespeare.
Value: $60.00 – 75.00

Wiggle Diver #6539; Wiggle Diver #6357
Date: c. 1940
Length: 4⅝" (top); 2¼" (bottom)
Notes: The Wiggle Diver was made both in wood and plastic.
Value: $9.00 – 18.00

Spintail #6303
Date: c. 1954
Length: 2¼"
Notes: Identical to the CCBCO Spoontail, this lure was produced after Creek Chub bought the Shakespeare Company in 1952. CCBCO continued to market Shakespeare lures but in red/blue instead of orange/blue boxes.
Value: $6.00 – 9.00

Spinning Bait Assortment #6300
Value: $60.00 – 90.00

Wm. Shakespeare Co.

Special Speedway Assortment
Value: $60.00 – 90.00

The authors offer: Free appraisal, identification and buying services. Call 818-763-9406.

Associate with other collectors. The

NFLCC and regional collectors clubs

offer great opportunities to increase

one's collection through trading, and

buying and selling.

Most veteran lure collectors have a

network of friends

and dealers who assist them

in locating and acquiring

lures they are seeking.

Meeting fellow collectors greatly

increases one's chance of finding

elusive lures and offers the

possibility for great friendships.

South Bend Bait Co.
South Bend, Indiana

The South Bend Bait Co. began in the kitchen of F. G. Worden of South Bend, Indiana. From that humble beginning, the Worden company was acquired by three businessmen and became the South Bend Bait Co. in 1909. Under the management of Ivar Hennings and with the popularity of the Bass-Oreno, South Bend became a popular manufacturer of high quality fishing lures and tackle. The lures included a full line based on the Bass-Oreno design. Like many other lure manufacturers, South Bend had a full line of underwater minnows, surface, fly rod, and musky baits. The company grew and at times supported 400 employees. The advent of World War II required the company to switch to war production, and the company received several awards for their war efforts.

The South Bend Bait Co. that emerged after World War II was not quite the same. It took several years to reach full production. Most underwater minnows were discontinued at the end of the 1930s, the last being the Panetella Minnow in 1942. Many new baits were introduced including the Nip-I-Diddees, Be-Bops, and many more plastic baits. By 1950, lure construction was simplified to include pressed eyes and the surface rig.

During this time period approximately 40 new colors were introduced, many brighter and more colorful. These included the "Firelacquer" colors which were advertised as being 500% to 800% brighter than standard finishes. The original Firelacquer colors were introduced in 1950 and were quickly modified a year later to add a Shadow-O-Wave.

The South Bend Bait Co. changed its name to the South Bend Tackle Co. in 1955. The company has gone through different ownerships since 1955.

Terry Wong
Phoenix, Arizona
Author, *South Bend Fishing Lures*

Underwater Minnow #905
Date: c. 1912 – 1939
Length: 3¾"
Notes: "Sidehook" minnows were part of the South Bend line of lures right from the beginning. The painted tack eyes shown here replaced glass eyes c. 1936.
Value: $100.00 – 125.00

Underwater Minnow #903
Date: 1912 – 1939
Length: 3"
Notes: This is the 3-hook version of the #905 Underwater Minnow. Painted cup hook rigging appears to be concurrent with painted tack eyes.
Value: $100.00 – 125.00

Midget Underwater Minnow #901
Date: c. 1920 – 1939
Length: 2½"
Notes: The smallest of South Bend's Underwater Minnows, the #901 is shown here with glass eyes and nickel plated cup hook rigging.
Value: $35.00 – 50.00

Panatella #915
Date: c. 1916 – 1942
Length: 4¼"
Notes: This attractive Panatella was competitive with the Heddon Torpedo and the Shakespeare Slim Jim.
Value: $100.00 – 125.00

Panatella Minnow #913
Date: c. 1912 – 1942
Length: 4½"
Notes: Available in side-mounted 5-hook and 3-hook versions, this version of the Panatella featured belly-mounted hooks similar to the Heddon Torpedo and Shakespeare Slim Jim.
Value: $30.00 – 45.00

Slim-Oreno #912

Date: c. 1933 – 1939
Length: 3 ¾"
Notes: The rare Slim-Oreno was South Bend's thinnest Underwater Minnow and was only made with painted eyes. The belly hook hanger is a staple style attachment.
Value: $50.00 – 60.00

Surf-Oreno #963

Date: c. 1916 – 1964
Length: 3¾", 3½"
Notes: The Surf Oreno went through numerous changes in body shape, hardware, and eye detail. This version has painted tack eyes and thru-wire line tie.
Value: $35.00 – 45.00

Surf-Oreno #963

Date: c. 1916 – 1964
Length: 3¾", 3½"
Notes: This is the "pressed eye" version of the Surf Oreno. This type of eye detail began in the early 1950s.
Value: $20.00 – 25.00

Midget Surf-Oreno #962

Date: 1916 – 1952
Length: 2¾"
Notes: This smallest version of the Surf-Oreno likely paved the way for the smaller Nip-I-Diddee.
Value: $50.00 – 60.00

Nip-I-Diddee #910

Date: c. 1948 – 1964
Length: 3"
Notes: Satisfying the demand by fishermen for smaller lures, the Nip-I-Diddee was a great fish producer.
Value: $10.00 – 15.00

Spin-I-Diddee #916
Date: c. 1952 – 1964
Length: 2¼", 2⅜"
Notes: Playing on the success of the Nip-I-Diddee, the Spin-I-Diddee offered fishermen the option of an even smaller lure for lighter tackle.
Value: $10.00 – 15.00

Wee-Nippee #T912
Date: c. 1952 – 1953
Length: 2⅜"
Notes: This is the smallest of the "Nippees."
Value: $10.00 – 15.00

Lunge-Oreno #966
Date: c. 1932 – 1942
Length: 7¼"
Note: The stately Lunge-Oreno featured thru wire construction and stainless steel props. The later versions used aluminum props as shown.
Value: $150.00 – 200.00

Lunge-Oreno #966
Date: c. 1932 – 1942
Length: 7¼"
Notes: The stainless steel props help identify this as an early Lunge-Oreno. This lure was also made with two propellers.
Value: $150.00 – 200.00

Midget Lunge-Oreno #965
Date: c. 1936 – 1939
Length: 3¾"
Notes: This is the smallest of South Bend's Lunge-Oreno line and featured a single propeller.
Value: $175.00 – 225.00

Truck-Oreno #936
Date: c. 1938 – 1939
Length: 9"
Notes: The massive Truck-Oreno was a hybrid of a Midget Lunge Oreno and a Whirl Oreno. Quite rare, a few forgeries have been seen over the years. Eye appeal? The "Truck" has it all.
Value: $600.00+

Whirl-Oreno #935
Date: 1929 – 1933, 1938 – 1940
Length: 3", 3½"
Notes: Basically a huge wooden propeller, the Whirl-Oreno was designed to be a floating "Buzz Bait."
Value: $90.00 – 120.00

Standard Woodpecker #923
Date: c. 1912 – 1942
Length: 4½"
Notes: One of South Bend's standbys, the Woodpecker remained in the catalog for about 30 years. Two-hook versions are rarer than the three-hookers.
Value: $80.00 – 100.00

Vacuum Bait #1
Date: c. 1921 – 1938
Length: 2½"
Notes: Based on Professor Howe's 1909 patent, the Vacuum Bait appeared both with and without eye detail. Both glass and painted tack eyes were used.
Value: $150.00 – 200.00

Bass-Oreno #973
Date: c. 1916 – 1964
Length: 3½", 3¾"
Notes: The Bass-Oreno was South Bend's most successful lure. A wide range of colors were available, making the Bass-Oreno a very popular collectible.
Value: $5.00 – 10.00

Babe-Oreno #972
Date: c. 1916 – 1964
Length: 2¾"
Notes: Smaller than the Bass-Oreno, the Babe-Oreno was equally popular with bass fishermen.
Value: $5.00 – 10.00

Midge-Oreno #968
Date: c. 1933 – 1964
Length: 2¼"
Notes: Based on the original Bass-Oreno design, the Midge-Oreno was a very popular lure for ponds and streams.
Value: $5.00 or less

Spin-Oreno #967
Date: c. 1953 – 1964
Length: 2"
Notes: The Spin-Oreno answered the demand for a small spinning size Bass-Oreno.
Value: $5.00 or less

Musk-Oreno #976
Date: c. 1916 – 1942
Length: 4½"
Notes: Designed for musky fishing, the Musk-Oreno featured heavy-duty treble hooks and a soldered tail hook hanger.
Value: $10.00 – 15.00

Better Bass-Oreno #73
Date: c. 1934 – 1942
Length: 3½"
Notes: The design for the Better Bass-Oreno is credited to long-time South Bend production manager and lure designer, Louis Chappleau. The hooks were affixed to an aluminum thru-body plate.
Value: $20.00 – 25.00

Better Babe-Oreno #72
Date: c. 1934 – 1942
Length: 3"
Notes: This Louis Chappleau design featured an aluminum plate inset into the body which provided attachments for hooks and line tie.
Value: $20.00 – 25.00

King Bass-Oreno #977
Date: c. 1950 – 1952
Length: 4⅝"
Note: This lure design allowed the hooks to "break away" from the body to prevent a hooked fish from using the lure as leverage to "throw" the lure.
Value: $30.00 – 40.00

King Andy #975
Date: c. 1951 – 1953
Length: 4⅝"
Notes: The nickel-plated back strip makes the King Andy easy to identify.
Value: $30.00 – 40.00

Coast-Oreno #985
Date: c. 1923 – 1942
Length: 4⅝"
Notes: The stylish Coast-Oreno was one of many large single hooked South Bend saltwater lures. A more thorough exploration of the various sizes and styles can be seen in *Fishing Lure Collectibles Volume 1*.
Value: $200.00 – 250.00

Wiz-Oreno #967
Date: c. 1925 – 1929
Length: 3"
Notes: This lure is basically a Babe-Oreno body with an extended/spinnered belly hook and a tail clip for pork rind, etc.
Value: $50.00 – 60.00

Bass-Obite #1973
Date: c. 1938 – 1942
Length: 3¾"
Notes: Made of plastic, the Bass-Obite featured molded eye detail and a hook-mounting screw running from the lip to the tail.
Value: $30.00 – 40.00

Bass-Obite (Baby) #1972
Date: c. 1938 – 1942
Length: 2⅞"
Notes: This is the small Bass-Obite referred to by collectors as the Baby version. Production of the Bass-Obite lures ceased after WWII.
Value: $30.00 – 40.00

Two-Oreno #975
Date: c. 1937 – 1942
Length: 3¾"
Notes: This lure features a Bass-Oreno lip at one end and a Pike-Oreno lip at the other, allowing two different actions in one lure.
Value: $50.00 – 60.00

Baby Two-Oreno #974
Date: c. 1937 – 1942
Length: 3"
Notes: This is the small version of the Two-Oreno.
Value: $50.00 – 60.00

Two-Obite #1975
Date: c. 1938 – 1942
Length: 3¾"
Notes: Having already made a plastic Bass-Oreno, the Bass-Obite, South Bend produced the Two-Oreno in plastic as well. The result was the Two-Obite, a classy and attractive lure when found in excellent condition.
Value: $30.00 – 40.00

Two-Obite (Baby) #1974
Date: c. 1938 – 1942
Length: 2¾"
Notes: This is the small version of the #1975 Two-Obite.
Value: $30.00 – 40.00

Pike-Oreno #957
Date: c. 1922 – 1952
Length: 4¼"
Notes: The Pike-Oreno name was used for 30 years to describe this diving lure which was made in several body shapes. The lure shown is from the early 1940s.
Value: $20.00 – 30.00

Jointed Baby Pike-Oreno #2956
Date: c. 1941 – 1953
Length: 4", 3⅜"
Notes: This lure follows the trend of a number of the large companies to make a jointed version of a lure already in production, in this case the Baby Pike-Oreno.
Value: $15.00 – 20.00

Big Pike-Oreno #958
Date: 1932 – 1942
Length: 5⅜"
Notes: The big Piko-Oreno was made in both 5⅜" and 6" lengths.
Value: $25.00 – 30.00

Li'l Rascal #955
Date: c. 1950 – 1953
Length: 2¼", 2¾"
Notes: The Li'l Rascal is the smallest unjointed Pike-Oreno type lure that South Bend made. It was scaled down for spin fishing.
Value: $10.00 – 15.00

SOUTH BEND BAIT CO.

105

Jointed Midget Pike-Oreno #2955
Date: c. 1941 – 1942
Length: 2¼"
Notes: This very small and infrequently found jointed lure is essentially a scaled-down Jointed Pike-Oreno.
Value: $35.00 – 45.00

Giant Jointed Pike-Oreno #960
Date: c. 1936 – 1942
Length: 6¾"
Notes: This is the largest of the Pike-Orenos.
Value: $45.00 – 55.00

Panatella Wobbler #921
Date: c. 1935 – 1938
Length: 4"
Notes: This is one of South Bend's Best-O-Luck line of lures, their economy line. Sleek and handsome, the Panatella Wobbler uses simple screw eyes instead of cup hook rigging and features a restyled lip shape.
Value: $30.00 – 40.00

Dive-Oreno #954
Date: c. 1941 – 1952
Length: 3¼", 4"
Notes: The #954 was designed as a deep diver and was a very popular lure for fishing impounded lakes with steep underwater banks, ledges, and drop-offs.
Value: $10.00 – 20.00

Dive-Oreno #952
Date: c. 1941 – 1952, 1962 – 1964
Length: 2¼", 3¼"
Notes: Like the #954 Dive-Oreno, this smaller version was modeled after the Pike-Oreno.
Value: $10.00 – 15.00

Fish-Oreno #953
Date: c. 1926 – 1952
Length: 3½"
Notes: Originally produced with glass eyes, the Fish-Oreno came with a printed guarantee stating that it would catch fish. This lure might be considered a heavily weighted Bass-Oreno. Note the plated cast metal plate at the head.
Value: $40.00 – 50.00

Fish-Oreno #953 (pressed eye)
Date: c. 1926 – 1952
Length: 3½"
Notes: This is the last version of the Fish-Oreno and features pressed eyes. Note the belly hook cup and line tie are surface type hook hangers.
Value: $30.00 – 40.00

Baby Teas-Oreno #939
Date: c. 1931 – 1950
Length: 3¼"
Notes: Featuring painted cup hook rigging and painted talk eyes, the #939 maintains the thick body shape of the early Teas-Oreno.
Value: $30.00 – 40.00

Baby Teas-Oreno #939
Date: 1931 – 1950
Length: 3½"
Notes: This version of the Baby Teas-Oreno has a thin, flat-bellied body shape and features a long tail hook hanger for extra strength.
Value: $25.00 – 35.00

Midget Teas-Oreno #936
Date: c. 1941 – 1950
Length: 2¾", 2⅞"
Notes: Using the new thin body shape, the Midget Teas-Oreno is the smallest of the wood Teas-Orenos.
Value: $20.00 – 30.00

Super Snooper #1960
Date: c. 1950 – 1952
Length: 2⅞"
Notes: Made of plastic, the Super-Snooper followed in the footprints of the Midget Teas-Orenos.
Value: $15.00 – 20.00

Min-Oreno #926
Date: c. 1933 – 1939
Length: 3½"
Notes: The flatsided Min-Oreno design was perfectly suited for imitating sunfish and perch.
Value: $20.00 – 30.00

Min-Oreno #927
Date: c. 1933 – 1939
Length: 4½"
Notes: Referred to by collectors as the "pike size" Min-Oreno, this lure features painted tack eyes and painted cup hook hardware.
Value: $20.00 – 30.00

"Depression Era" Min-Oreno
Date: c. 1939
Length: 3½"
Notes: The identity of this lure is based on comparison of the body shape, body size, and unmarked yellow box. Speculation regarding the Depression Era is based on the known fact that other lure makers attempted to remain in production by using components already in existence.
Value: $90.00 – 100.00

Plug-Oreno #959
Date: c. 1932 – 1942
Length: 2"
Notes: This unusual weedless "chunk bait" was made originally with glass eyes. The lure shown has talk eyes and is painted in the rare "frog splotch" finish. Plug-Orenos have a lot of eye appeal and are highly sought after by collectors.
Value: $150.00 – 200.00

Plunk-Oreno #929 (old style)
Date: c. 1929 – 1932
Length: 3⅞"
Notes: This paint-eyed version of the Plunk-Oreno considerably pre-dates the chronology of this book but is included as a reference for the new style Plunk-Oreno. The earliest Plunk-Orenos had glass eyes.
Value: $60.00 – 80.00

Plunk-Oreno #929 (new style)
Date: c. 1937 – 1942
Length: 2¼" (top); 2⅛" (middle); 1" (bottom)
Notes: This is the "new style" Plunk-Oreno as revised in 1937. During the five years it was in production, this lure underwent changes in size and in the slant of the face.
Value: $55.00 – 70.00

Mouse-Oreno #949; Flyrod Mouse-Oreno #948
Date: c. 1932 – 1942
Length: 2¾"; 1⅝"
Notes: The handsome Mouse-Oreno was made in both casting and flyrod sizes. Three colors were made: gray flocked, black, and pearl, as shown.
Value: $50.00 – 70.00

Entice-Oreno #991
Date: c. 1938 – 1939
Length: 2⅝"
Notes: The Entice-Oreno appears to have been put into production to compete with Heddon's River Runt and Shakespeare's River Pup.
Value: $30.00 – 40.00

Tex-Oreno Sinker #995
Date: c. 1938 – 1939
Length: 2¾"
Notes: Designed for sea trout fishing off the Texas Coast, the Tex-Oreno featured a flush-fitting metal weight beneath the head.
Value: $70.00 – 90.00

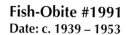

Fish-Obite #1991
Date: c. 1939 – 1953
Length: 2⅜"
Notes: Another lure in the competitive River Runt/River Pup market, the Fish-Obite had a distinctive raised ring around the tail into which the words "The Bait that's Right" were encouragingly stamped.
Value: $10.00 – 15.00

Peach-Oreno #500
Date: c. 1941 – 1942
Length: 3¼", 2½"
Note: The Peach-Oreno was made in seven sizes, the largest being 4⅞". The name Peach-Oreno came from the 1890s slang term "peachoreno," used to give high praise.
Value: $20.00 – 25.00

Frog-Oreno #560
Date: c. 1937 – 1942
Length: 2⅝"
Notes: Featuring a painted lead head with deer hair body and legs, the Frog-Oreno could easily have been altered to create a Crayfish imitation.
Value: $20.00 – 30.00

Old Cabin Still Bait
Date: c. 1955
Length: 3⅝"
Notes: While the authors are unaware of the existence of this lure in any company catalogs, the lure shown was found mint in the South Bend box. Possibly South Bend made the lure for a limited promotion of Old Cabin Still Whiskey.
Value: $50.00 – 60.00

Be Bop #903
Date: c. 1950 – 1952
Length: 4½", 3⅜"
Notes: The Be Bop was a surface hook rigged floater along the lines of the Heddon Zaragossa and remained in production for three years. Two sizes were made.
Value: $10.00 – 15.00

Go Plunk #2929
Date: c. 1950 – 1952
Length: 3⅛"
Notes: This "Plunker" had extra surface action because it was jointed.
Value $5.00 – 10.00

Explorer #920
Date: c. 1951 – 1952
Length: 3¾"
Note: The deep diving Explorer was also made in a jointed model.
Value: $10.00 – 15.00

Fin-Dingo #1965
Date: 1952 – 1953
Length: 1½"
Notes: Packaged in a plastic tube, the Fin-Dingo was produced in a wide variety of colors. Designed to maintain an upright position in the water, this lure got its swimming action from its fins.
Value: $20.00 – 30.00

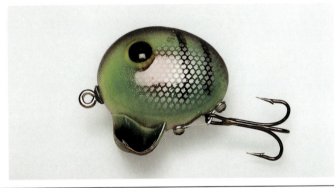

Optic #677
Date: c. 1959 – 1962
Length: 2¼"
Note: Based on the Bayou Boogie shape, the Optic was so named because of the interior "movement" of lines within the ridged body, the same physical effect which makes the eyes on some dolls seem to move when the head is turned. A "moving eye" Optic was also made.
Value: $10.00 – 15.00

Rock Hopper #675 & #676
Date: 1959
Length: 2⅛" (top); 1⅝" (bottom)
Notes: Appearing for only one year, the Rock Hopper featured a unique "through the lip" line tie attachment on the belly.
Value: $5.00 – 10.00

Itsaduzy #543
Date: 1951 – 1953
Length: 1" body
Note: The Itsaduzy is a slightly similar version of the old Dart-Oreno but with a weedguard and plastic eyes.
Value: $15.00 – 20.00

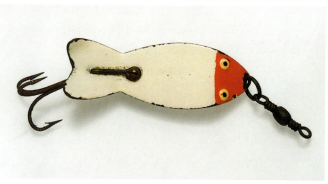

Flash-Oreno #506
Date: c. 1927 – 1942
Length: 3"
Notes: The Flash-Oreno had a large semi-spherical plated weight on the belly for balance.
Value: $18.00 – 24.00

Sun Spot Spoon
Date: c. 1941 – 1942
Length: 2¼", 1¼"
Notes: Made in 10 sizes from 1¼" to 5", the Sun Spot Spoon was perforated to allow light to shine through the colored plastic.
Value: $10.00 – 15.00

Metal Wobbler #581
Date: 1934 – 1953
Length: 3⅝"
Notes: Nicely finished, this lure has raised eyes, made in four sizes from 1¼" to 3½".
Value: $15.00 – 20.00

Spoon-Oreno #586
Date: 1932 – 1943
Length: 2½"
Notes: The Spoon Oreno was produced in both polished and painted finishes.
Value: $5.00 – 10.00

Trix-Oreno #593 – 599
Date: c. 1931 – 1953
Notes: The Trix-Oreno was made in a variety of colors and sizes and featured a thick plate at the head for balance.
Value: $5.00 or less

Flipit #625
Date: 1959
Length: 2½"
Notes: Available in five sizes and three colors.
Value: $5.00 or less

Super-Duper #509
Date: c. 1953 – 1964
Length: 2¼"
Notes: The Super-Duper was made in a variety of polished and painted finishes.
Value: $5.00 or less

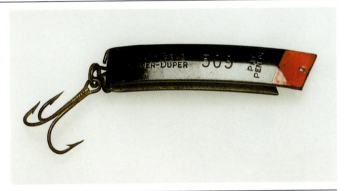

Select-Oreno #1950
Date: c. 1942
Notes: Available only in 1940, the clever Select-Oreno kit contained four interchangeable Popper bodies which could be combined to make 16 different color combinations. Clint Brown's Select-A-Bait was the model for the Select-Oreno.
Value: $125.00 – 175.00

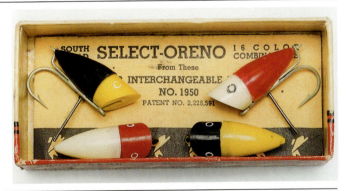

Spinning Lure Kit #475
Date: c. 1952
Notes: Keeping up with the spin fishing trend, South Bend offered the Spinning Lure kit which featured downsized versions of their lures.
Value: $70.00 – 90.00

South Bend Lure Assortment #269
Date: c. 1968
Notes: This spinning lure kit featured Super-Dupers and Flipits.
Value: $25.00 – 35.00

Miscellaneous Lures

They came in droves and right on the heels of the big lure companies. The notion of designing a "better mouse trap" has always appealed to mankind and when accompanied by the idea of making money, formed a compelling combination which America's curious and entrepreneurial lure inventors simply could not resist. Interestingly, the "bigs" could ill afford to rest upon their laurels for the "smalls" were always pushing, innovating, and sometimes copying their products. By the end of WWII, the genealogical family tree of fishing lures was sprouting new branches faster than history would be able to record.

Being a "big" carried a lot of responsibility, a lot of overhead, and a lot of pressure to research and develop new and effective lures. Being the pace setter is not easy... run faster, run better, don't stop to rest or you will be passed by. Lateral moves represent a lost dynamic. There are only two directions that avoid the static: fall back or move ahead. One must work continually to move forward, for falling behind sets you on the bench where you can only watch the other players in the game. Competition underscores the free enterprise system and as free people, Americans have always embraced a good game.

While the "bigs" were producing beautiful lures in a dozen or so locations in the country, new lure makers were popping up all over the land. Sometimes the small company products rivaled their large competitors but often they lacked finish, showing sanding marks, rough paint, and other imperfections, characteristics that collectors today embrace for their desirable human qualities as opposed to an impersonal, machine-made look.

Frequently rare and difficult to find, the efforts of the "smalls" figure prominently in the overall picture of the lure collecting hobby. Fishermen have always appreciated cleverly designed lures, and today's lure collectors seek and desire such innovations. Within the hobby the term "miscellaneous" is used to describe the lures of the small companies, so when a collector states that they collect miscellaneous lures, they are saying that their interests differ from those seeking the "bigs." They are taking the path less traveled in an unending search of the elusive and rare.

Dudley Murphy
Springfield, Missouri

Bayou Boogie
A.D. Manufacturing Co., Monroe, Louisiana
Date: c. 1955
Length: 3"; 1½"
Notes: The Bayou Boogie was one of the first and best vibrating lures ever produced.
Value: $5.00 or less

Adamson Multi-Use Fish Lure
A & H Products Co., Holyoke, Colorado
Date: c. 1956
Length: 1¾" body
Notes: This wild creature featured a wooden body with painted thumbtack eyes, marabou feather wings, and a leather skirt.
Value: $15.00 – 20.00

Go-Getter "Minnow"
Abbey & Imbrie, New York, New York
Date: c. 1938
Length: 4"
Notes: The fish-shaped body and tail gave this lure collectible eye appeal.
Value: $50.00 – 55.00

Go-Getter "Wobbler"
Abbey & Imbrie, New York, New York
Date: c. 1938
Length: 2⅝"
Notes: This lure features a typical Abbey & Imbrie paint job.
Value: $10.00 – 15.00

Go-Getter Crab
Abbey & Imbrie, New York, New York
Date: c. 1938
Length: 2½"
Notes: This cute lure features painted tack eyes and a crawdad-type tail.
Value: $20.00 – 25.00

Cigar Lure
Abel Quality Products, Camarillo, California
Date: c. 1998
Length: 6"
Notes: Known for making high-quality fly reels, Abel shows a sense of humor and an interest in cigars (Abel owned a cigar company).
Value: $5.00 or less

Dozey Boy
Accepted Lures Hasand, Inc., Cleveland, Ohio
Date: c. 1960
Length: 2⅜"
Notes: With tremendous eye appeal, the Dozey Boy featured an unusual lip and user-activated "hook set."
Value: $35.00 – 50.00

River Devil
Tony Accetta & Son, Cleveland, Ohio
Date: c. 1936
Length: 1½" body
Notes: The River Devil is an Al Foss "look-alike" with similar action and fish attracting qualities.
Value: $5.00 – 10.00

Jigolet
Tony Accetta & Son, Cleveland, Ohio
Date: c. 1940
Length: 2½"
Notes: This plastic lure and the similar weedless version were the only floaters in the Accetta line. Tony Accetta, a famous tournament caster, was known for spoons and spinners.
Value: $10.00 – 15.00

Jigolet (Snagless)
Tony Accetta & Son, Cleveland, Ohio
Date: c. 1940
Length: 2½"
Notes: This lure is the weedless version of the standard Jigolet.
Value: $10.00 – 15.00

Hobo
Tony Accetta & Son, Cleveland, Ohio
Date: c. 1940
Length: 2¼"
Notes: The card says it all. This Al Foss style lure was a great surface and underwater bait.
Value: $15.00 – 20.00

Bug Spoon
Tony Accetta & Son, Cleveland, Ohio
Date: c. 1940
Length: 1⅝"
Notes: The 1939 version of this bait was also called the Bug Spoon and features an attached front section with short pointed wings like those on the River Devil.
Value: $15.00 – 20.00

Pet Spoon
Tony Accetta & Son, Cleveland, Ohio
Date: c. 1942
Length: 3¼"
Notes: The Pet Spoon was made in a great variety of sizes and weights.
Value: $5.00 or less

Spin Dodger
Tony Accetta & Son, Cleveland, Ohio
Date: c. 1942
Length: 2¼"
Notes: The Spin Dodger is similar in design to the Hobo Spoon.
Value: $5.00 – 10.00

Weed Dodger
Tony Accetta & Son, Cleveland, Ohio
Date: c. 1946
Length: 2⅝"
Notes: This is a larger version of the Spin Dodger, produced without a front spinner.
Value: $5.00 – 10.00

Wacky

Tony Accetta & Son, Cleveland, Ohio
Date: c. 1946
Length: 1½"
Notes: The Wacky is a spinning spoon which was heavy for its small size.
Value: $5.00 or less

Live Action Frog

Action Frog Corporation, Long Beach, California
Date: c. 1960
Length: 5½" overall
Notes: On retrieve, water pressure against the "fan blade" propeller causes this fantastic plastic frog lure to kick his legs.
Value: $90.00 – 120.00

Hi-Yo

Activated Lure Co., Barberton, Ohio
Date: c. 1947
Length: 1⅝" body
Notes: Using dry ice in the rubber-capped body, the Hi-Yo would dart forward as gas was pushed out the tail.
Value: $20.00 – 25.00

Roto-Fli Poppa No. 7

Pop Adam, Ponca City, Oklahoma
Date: c. 1935
Length: 1¼" body
Notes: Patented by Pop Adam in 1930, this lure became the Bass Pop when True-Temper hired Pop to design lures in 1939.
Value: $5.00 – 10.00

Roto Fli

Pop Adam, Ponca City, Oklahoma
Date: c. 1936
Length: 1" blade
Notes: This pair of weight-forward spinners feature heart-shaped spinners and unusual conical heads.
Value: $5.00 – 10.00

Loose Caboose
Advance Tackle Co., Youngstown, Ohio
Date: c. 1950
Length: 1¾"
Notes: The Loose Caboose was a very high-quality lure. One of its best features was the custom-formed clear teatite plastic box.
Value: $15.00 – 20.00

AL & W Waterwitch; AL & W Favorite
Allcock, Laight & Westwood Co., Ltd., Canada
Date: c. 1950
Length: 2¼"; 1⅝"
Notes: These are typical AL&W spoons of plated and painted metal, with the addition of beads and plastic tail.
Value: $5.00 or less

Potbelly
Gale Allen, Silver Springs, Maryland
Date: c. 1974
Length: 3⅝"
Notes: The Potbelly was a regional effort to approximate the fish-catching success of the Big O and Balsa B.
Value: $25.00 – 30.00

Ambrose Bait
Ambrose Baits, Arkansas
Date: c. 1950
Length: 3½"
Notes: Mr. Ambrose was a river guide in the Arkansas and Missouri Ozarks. He made many of his lures while guiding customers down Ozark streams. Lures painted while on the water were always white. Lures made at home featured more complicated paint jobs.
Value: $10.00 – 15.00

Lucky Bunny
American Rod & Gun, Stamford, Connecticut
Date: c. 1954
Length: 3½"
Notes: The Lucky Bunny featured a molded plastic body and an actual rabbit's foot.
Value: $25.00 – 30.00

Lucky Bunny
American Rod & Gun, Stamford, Connecticut
Date: c. 1954
Length: 2⅝"
Notes: This is the small size Lucky Bunny, also featuring a real rabbit's foot.
Value: $20.00 – 25.00

Tennessee Shad — "Top Secret"
Boots Anderson, Maryville, Tennessee
Date: c. 1966
Length: 3"
Notes: This is the earliest handcarved version of the Tennessee Shad. All Tennessee Shad lures are made from balsa wood with stainless steel line ties and hook hangers.
Value: $100.00 – 120.00

Tennessee Shad — "Top Secret"
Boots Anderson, Maryville, Tennessee
Date: c. 1970
Length: 3"
Notes: Second version of the Tennessee Shad. Name appears on the lip with a ® mark.
Value: $60.00 – 90.00

Tennessee Shad — "Hammerhead Minner"
Boots Anderson, Maryville, Tennessee
Date: c. 1965 – 1968
Length: 3½"
Notes: This is an early Boots Anderson lure with no name on the lip.
Value: $100.00 – 120.00

Tennessee Shad — "Chugger"
Boots Anderson, Maryville, Tennessee
Date: c. 1966
Length: 2½"
Notes: This neat little surface bait is very simple with a notched face.
Value: $100.00 – 120.00

Tennessee Shad — "Big Mo"
Boots Anderson, Maryville, Tennessee
Date: c. 1970
Length: 3½"
Notes: Allegedly Fred Young based the design for his "Big O" on this lure.
Value: $120.00 – 150.00

Tennessee Shad — "Pond Minner"
Boots Anderson, Maryville, Tennessee
Date: c. 1970
Length: 2"
Value: $120.00 – 150.00

Tennessee Shad — "Florida Minner"
Boots Anderson, Maryville, Tennessee
Date: c. 1970
Length: 4¾"
Notes: Only a few of these large baits were made.
Value: $120.00 – 150.00

Tennessee Shad — "Creek Minner"
Boots Anderson, Maryville, Tennessee
Date: c. 1965 – 1972
Length: 3"
Notes: The early versions of this lure had no name on the lip.
Value: $100.00 – 120.00

Tennessee Shad — "Little Lonnie"
Boots Anderson
Date: c. 1972
Length: 3¼"
Notes: Lip is marked Tennessee Shad ®, and the back is slightly flattened on this version.
Value: $65.00 – 100.00

MISCELLANEOUS LURES

Tennessee Shad — "Signature Plug"
Boots Anderson, Maryville, Tennessee
Date: 2001
Length: 3⅛"
Notes: These new lures are occasionally available with Boots Anderson's signature on the side.
Value: $10.00 – 25.00

Anderson Minnow
Anderson Bait Co., Chicago, Illinois
Date: c. 1949
Length: 3⅝
Notes: This lure featured a long spring-loaded hook which would release when struck by a fish.
Value: $25.00 – 30.00

Weedless Wonder
Anderson & Son, Inc., Hope Valley, Rhode Island
Date: c. 1969
Length: 2¹⁵⁄₁₆"
Notes: By pushing the hook toward the front, locking the lever, this lure was designed to fish weedless until tripped by a striking fish.
Value: $25.00 – 30.00

Pretz-L-Lure
An-O-Mated Lure Co., North Hollywood, California
Date: c. 1960
Length: 3¼"
Notes: Wind the legs, tightening a rubber band, and fix with a pretzel. When the pretzel softened in the water, the rubber band unwound and the legs went wild!
Value: $35.00 – 45.00

Buzzter Boy
Aqua-Sonic, Phoenix, Arizona
Date: c. 1960
Length: 3¾"
Notes: The battery-powered Buzzter Boy emitted a buzzing sound in the water.
Value: $30.00 – 35.00

Aquasonic Lil' Noisy; Deep Baby Noisy
Aquasonic Lures, Inc., Cibolo, Texas
Date: c. 1993
Length: 3" overall each
Notes: This is a typical crank bait design with the exception of the ultrasonic feature which created an enticing sound underwater.
Value: $5.00 or less

Aquasonic "Boogie"
Aquasonic Lures, Inc., Cibolo, Texas
Date: c. 1993
Length: 2¼" each
Notes: This lure is similar to the Bayou Boogie. Water passing through the hole in the face and out exit holes in the body would create a fish attracting sound.
Value: $5.00 or less

Jitterbug (wood)
Fred Arbogast, Akron, Ohio
Date: c. 1938 – 1940
Length: 2¾"
Notes: This is the first version of the Jitterbug. Made of wood, this version has an unusual "half bowl" hook hanger design referred to as Style 1.
Value: $55.00 – 60.00

Jitterbug (wood, single hook)
Fred Arbogast, Akron, Ohio
Date: c. 1940 – 1942
Length: 2⅛"
Notes: This little Jitterbug features a single treble hook and a Style 2 hook hanger which had a flat "flap" to prevent hook tangles. Blue and white is a rare and desirable Jitterbug color.
Value: $55.00 – 60.00

Jitterbug (wood, peanut size)
Fred Arbogast, Akron, Ohio
Date: c. 1942 – 1946
Length: 2¼"
Notes: This version of the wood Jitterbug used a Style 3 hook hanger similar to the Style 1 "half bowl." The wood body with the plastic lip (as shown) was introduced around 1942 but was quickly discounted because of poor action.
Value: $45.00 – 50.00

Musky Jitterbug (wood)
Fred Arbogast, Akron, Ohio
Date: c. 1940 – 1942
Length: 4½"
Notes: The largest of the Jitterbugs, the musky size was originally made with two treble hooks. Around 1942, this lure was discontinued only to be reintroduced around 1947 as a three-hook model with side hooks.
Value: $55.00 – 60.00

Jitterbug (plastic)
Fred Arbogast, Akron, Ohio
Date: c. 1958
Length: 2½"
Notes: Arbogast appears to have stopped making wood Jitterbugs around 1943 in favor of plastic. Wartime metal shortages prompted a return to the plastic lip attached to a plastic body. Eventually the Jitterbug was made only in plastic with an aluminum lip as we see it today. Blue head is somewhat rare.
Value: $5.00 – 10.00; blue $30.00 – 35.00

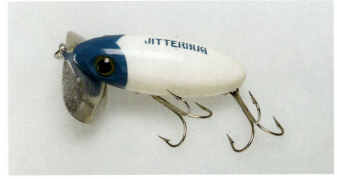

Jitterbug Group
Fred Arbogast, Akron, Ohio
Date: 1978
Length: 2⅝"
Notes: This series of plastic Jitterbugs featured natural colors: Redwing, Blackbird, Sparrow, Mouse, and Chipmunk.
Value: $20.00 – 25.00

Jointed Jitterbug
Fred Arbogast, Akron, Ohio
Date: c. 1960s
Length: 2⅝"
Notes: The action-packed Jitterbug became even more animated with a jointed body.
Value: $5.00 or less

Jitterbug (plastic)
Fred Arbogast, Akron, Ohio
Date: c. 1960s
Length: 1¾"
Notes: This small two-hook version of the Jitterbug represents the final stage of the lure's development.
Value: $5.00 or less

Jitterbug (spinning)
Fred Arbogast, Akron, Ohio
Date: c. 1960s
Length: 1½"
Notes: This lightweight Jitterbug featured a single treble hook and was designed for spin fishing.
Value: $5.00 or less

Jitterbug (weedless)
Fred Arbogast, Akron, Ohio
Date: c. 1960s
Length: 2¼"; 2"
Notes: Although not perfectly weedless, the upturned hooks on this model Jitterbug tended to avoid hangups much better than the two treble hook models.
Value: $5.00 or less

Jitterbug (flyrod size)
Fred Arbogast, Akron, Ohio
Date: c. 1960s
Length: 1⅛"
Notes: This baby of the Jitterbug family featured a hard foam body molded to a plastic lip.
Value: $10.00 – 15.00

Hula Popper
Fred Arbogast, Akron, Ohio
Date: c. 1948
Length: 2¼"
Notes: New in 1948, the Hula Popper brought to the surface the fish-catching success the Hawaiian Wigglers had established underwater: the rubber skirt, destined to become a feature on many Arbogast lures. The lures shown in flocked/regular mouse and redwing blackbird are from the 1970s. The spinning Hula Popper is included as a size reference.
Value: $5.00 or less

Hula Popper (spinning)
Fred Arbogast, Akron, Ohio
Date: c. 1955
Length: 1½"
Notes: This small version of the Hula Popper came with a belly treble hook. An optional tail hook could be slipped on to catch short strikers.
Value: $5.00 or less

Hula Popper (ultra lite)
Fred Arbogast, Akron, Ohio
Date: c. 1960s
Length: 1⅛"
Notes: Often misidentified as a flyrod size Hula Popper, this is actually a small spinning size with the elongated profile of the original 2¼" casting model.
Value: $5.00 – 10.00

Hula Popper (flyrod size)
Fred Arbogast, Akron, Ohio
Date: c. 1940
Length: ⅝" – ¾"
Notes: Six stages are shown here in profile to describe changes in the design of the flyrod Hula Popper. From left to right: 1. Flat and thin in profile, eyes top and bottom (2 lures); 2. Similar to #1 but with a notched face and two eyes; 3. Notched mouth, fatter than #2, unpainted raised eyes on bottom; 4. Like #3, no raised eyes on bottom; 5. Fat, notched face; 6. Latest body shape, flat slanted face.
Value: $10.00 – 40.00

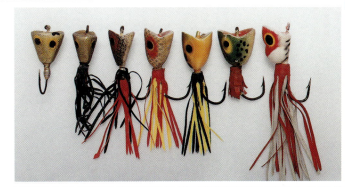

Hula Dancer
Fred Arbogast, Akron, Ohio
Date: c. 1954
Length: 1½"
Notes: Originally supplied in a white two-piece cardboard picture box, the Hula Dancer was an attractive sinking lure which caught a lot of fish.
Value: $5.00 or less

Arbo-Gaster
Fred Arbogast, Akron, Ohio
Date: c. 1960
Length: 1¾"
Notes: Fatter than the Hula Dancer, the Arbo-Gaster was designed to run deep.
Value: $5.00 or less

Sputterbug
Fred Arbogast, Akron, Ohio
Date: c. 1960
Length: 3⅛"
Notes: The Sputterbug and later the smaller Sputterbuzz were floating "Buzz Bait" surface plugs utilizing the patented hula skirt and a large aluminum spinner.
Value: $5.00 or less

Hustler
Fred Arbogast, Akron, Ohio
Date: c. 1965
Length: 3⅝" overall
Notes: Arbogast called the deep-diving Hustler "revolutionary." Notice the metal reinforcement beneath the lip.
Value: $5.00 or less

Tipsy
Fred Arbogast, Akron, Ohio
Date: c. 1979
Length: 2½"
Notes: The Tipsy was designed to float on its side and dive on retrieve.
Value: $5.00 – 10.00

Dorado
Fred Arbogast, Akron, Ohio
Date: c. 1979
Length: 4½"
Notes: The slender Dorado was designed to be a mid-depth lure.
Value: $5.00 or less

Arby "Hanger"
Fred Arbogast, Akron, Ohio
Date: c. 1984
Length: 5"
Notes: The deep-diving Hanger was designed to dive deep and suspend.
Value: $5.00 or less

Fred's Frog
Fred Arbogast, Akron, Ohio
Date: c. 1995
Length: 2⅜"
Notes: Fred's Frog is an attractive surface lure with leather legs and a single upturned hook.
Value: $5.00 – 10.00

Snooker
Fred Arbogast, Akron, Ohio
Date: c. 1995
Length: 4¼"
Notes: The Snooker was designed for saltwater fishing.
Value: $5.00 or less

Phred's Phydeaux
Fred Arbogast, Akron, Ohio
Date: c. 1995
Length: 5⅝"
Notes: Phred's Phydeaux was designed for saltwater fishing.
Value: $5.00 – 10.00

#1 Hawaiian Wiggler (runs deep)
Fred Arbogast, Akron, Ohio
Date: c. 1938
Length: 1¼"; 1¼"; 1¼"; ⅞"
Notes: Fred Arbogast's patent application for his rubber hula skirt was granted in 1938. The c. 1934 shaker featured a bucktail dressed hook and provided the design for the skirted Hawaiian Wiggler. Spinners were made both as singles and tandems. Weed-guards often featured "Tin Liz" tail spinners. The lure on the right is of recent manufacture.
Value: $5.00 or less

#1 Hawaiian Wiggler (runs medium)
Fred Arbogast, Akron, Ohio
Date: c. 1938
Length: 1⅜" head
Notes: The flattened head allowed this lure to plane upward and sink slowly.
Value: $5.00 or less

#2 Hawaiian Wiggler (runs shallow)
Fred Arbogast, Akron, Ohio
Date: c. 1938
Length: 1" head; 1½" head
Notes: The wide, flat head allowed this lure to plane upward for near surface action. The top lure is a recent unnumbered version.
Value: $5.00 or less

Sputter Fuss
Fred Arbogast, Akron, Ohio
Date: c. 1947
Length: 1⅛"
Notes: The flat, wide head of the Sputter Fuss allowed a surface "Buzz Bait" action while the weedguard allowed it to be fished in lily pads and rushes.
Value: $5.00 – 10.00

Fly Rod Hawaiian
Fred Arbogast, Akron, Ohio
Date: c. 1938
Length: ¾" head
Notes: Made of lightweight aluminum, this little lure could be fished shallow or "skittered" on the surface.
Value: $15.00 – 20.00

Hawaiian #4
Fred Arbogast, Akron, Ohio
Date: c. 1965
Length: 1¼" blade
Notes: Bearing faint resemblance to the Hawaiian series, this recent vintage example nonetheless bears the family name.
Value: $5.00 or less

Mopar Dart
Fred Arbogast, Akron, Ohio
Date: c. 1963
Length: ⅞" head
Notes: This version of the Hawaiian was made especially to publicize the Mopar Dart automobile, which was new in 1963.
Value: $5.00 – 10.00

Twin Liz
Fred Arbogast, Akron, Ohio
Date: 1950
Length: 1¾" bodies
Notes: Arbogast received a patent for the Tin Liz in 1930. The Twin Liz is basically a Tandem version of the original, without glass eyes.
Value: $20.00 each

Spinning Tin Liz
Fred Arbogast, Akron, Ohio
Date: c. 1950
Length: 1¾"
Notes: This little bait is basically a Tin Liz with a hula skirt instead of a tail-shaped spinner.
Value: $5.00 – 10.00

Tin Liz, flyrod size
Fred Arbogast, Akron, Ohio
Date: c. 1950
Length: 1¹⁄₁₆"; 1½"; 1¹³⁄₁₆"
Notes: Made of thin stamped aluminum, the flyrod sized Tin Liz could also be used for ultra light spinning.
Value: $10.00 – 15.00

Hum-Bug
Fred Arbogast, Akron, Ohio
Date: c. 1958
Length: 1⅜" blade
Notes: The Hum-Bug is a "single spinner" using the popular "Abu-style" blade.
Value: $5.00 – 10.00

Dekalb Lure
Fred Arbogast Company, Inc., Akron, Ohio
Date: c. 1974
Length: 2¼"
Notes: Arbogast made this novelty lure as a promotional item for Dekalb.
Value: $25.00 – 30.00

Mud Bug
Fred Arbogast, Akron, Ohio
Date: c. 1975
Length: 2⅛", 1⅝"
Notes: The Mud Bug is a deep-running crankbait with crawfish action.
Value: $5.00 or less

Hopalong
Arnold Tackle Co., Paw Paw, Michigan
Date: c. 1946
Length: 2⅝"
Notes: The metal plate spanning the tail section of this top water lure caused it to waddle and hop from side to side.
Value: $20.00 – 30.00

Cool Ripple Frog
Associated Specialties, Chicago, Illinois
Date: c. 1947
Length: 1½" body
Notes: The Cool Ripple Frog featured a soft rubber body and nylon fiber legs. The propeller on this particular lure was installed backwards at the factory.
Value: $25.00 – 35.00

Trip Lure
Atomic Fishing Tackle, Div. S. & G. Products Inc.,
Bogota, New Jersey
Date: c. 1946
Length: 2"
Notes: A spring-activated shaft allowed the side hooks to open out when a fish struck.
Value: $30.00 – 35.00

Oscar the Frog
T.F. Auclaire and Associates Inc., Detroit, Michigan
Date: c. 1947
Length: 4¾"
Notes: Made of hinged metal legs on a painted wood body, Oscar swims on retrieve. Very rare.
Value: $175.00 – 250.00

Bang-O-Lure 1, 2, 3, 4
Jim Bagley Bait Co., Winter Haven, Florida
Date: c. 1962
Length: 5"; 4", 2½", 1¾"
Notes: The 5" Bang-O-Lure was Jim Bagley's first bait. The brass wire hook hanger was replaced with screw eyes in a strip of hardwood in 1982.
Value: $10.00 – 15.00

Deep Bang-O-Lure
Jim Bagley Bait Co., Winter Haven, Florida
Date: c. 1985
Length: 4⅞"
Notes: A Bang-O-Lure with a reinforced plastic deep diving lip.
Value: $5.00 – 10.00

Bang-O-Lure Suspend
Jim Bagley Bait Co., Winter Haven, Florida
Date: c. 1991
Length: 5"
Notes: The lead weight under the chin of this recent lure could be trimmed to achieve neutral buoyancy.
Value: $5.00 – 10.00

"dub'l – 07"
Jim Bagley Bait Co., Winter Haven, Florida
Date: c. 1968
Length: 5"; 3½"
Notes: Made with and without a tail spinner, this was a buoyant surface lure designed to float with the nose in a near-vertical position.
Value: $15.00 – 20.00

Balsa Go-Devil
Jim Bagley Bait Co., Winter Haven, Florida
Date: c. 1968
Length: 3½"
Notes: The metal lip on this lure was intended to be bent to adjust the depth. The body is basically a reversed dub'l – 07 weighted to run deep.
Value: $15.00 – 20.00

Poor Penny
Jim Bagley Bait Co., Winter Haven, Florida
Date: c. 1968
Length: 1"; ¾"
Notes: Fishing with Jim Bagley's Poor Penny is said to have influenced Tom Mann to develop the Mann's Little George Bait. Jim Bagley began his tackle business in 1951 by selling pork rinds and soft plastic baits before focusing on balsa lures. The Poor Penny was never put in production.
Value: $25.00 – 35.00

Balsa B4
Jim Bagley Bait Co., Winter Haven, Florida
Date: c. 1970
Length: 4"
Notes: This is the largest of the early Balsa Bs. The first version of the Balsa B featured square diving lips and brass wire hook hangers. The lures could be adjusted easily by bending the brass wire line tie.
Value: $40.00 – 50.00; $25.00 – 30.00

Balsa B1; B2; B3
Jim Bagley Bait Co., Winter Haven, Florida
Date: c. 1970 – 1974
Length: 2"; 2¼"; 3"
Notes: Called the "Big-B" in Bass Pro Shop's first catalog (1974). The Balsa B followed the footsteps of the Tennessee Shad and the Big-B to become an all-time great fish catcher.
Value: $15.00 – 20.00

Honey B
Jim Bagley Bait Co., Winter Haven, Florida
Date: c. 1975
Length: 1½"
Notes: The Honey B is the smallest Balsa B. The lure shown is a special order finish and was among the first Balsa Bs stocked in the original fishing tackle section area of Johnny Morris's father's liquor store. The complete stock sold out to eager fishermen in 20 minutes.
Value: $15.00 – 20.00

Diving B1; B2; B3
Jim Bagley Bait Co., Winter Haven, Florida
Date: c. 1975
Length: 1⅞"; 2¼"; 3"
Notes: These lures were the first diving Balsa Bs and featured a lead "anchor" to secure the wire harness to the lip.
Value: $5.00 – 10.00

Deep Honey B; Deep Killer B1
Jim Bagley Bait Co., Winter Haven, Florida
Date: c. 1976 – 1978
Length: 1½"; 1¾"
Notes: These lures feature brass wire line tie and extended diving lips.
Value: $5.00 – 10.00

Killer B2; B3

Jim Bagley Bait Co., Winter Haven, Florida
Date: c. 1976
Length: 2¾"; 2¼"
Notes: The Killer B2 and B3 were introduced before the Killer B1. Note the body shape is slimmer than the Balsa B.
Value: $5.00 – 10.00

Deep Killer BII; BIII

Jim Bagley Bait Co., Winter Haven, Florida
Date: c. 1976 – 1980
Length: 2½"; 2¾"
Notes: The lures shown have reinforced plastic lips and stainless steel screw eyes. The presence of screw eyes indicates a wooden (not balsa wood) lure body.
Value: $5.00 – 10.00

Rat Fink

Jim Bagley Bait Co., Winter Haven, Florida
Date: c. 1975
Length: 2¼"
Notes: The stylish Rat Fink had brass hook hangers, balsa buoyancy, and a tail spinner.
Value: $20.00 – 25.00

Balsa Shiner

Jim Bagley Bait Co., Winter Haven, Florida
Date: c. 1976
Length: 2½"
Notes: Beginning as the Balsa Shiner, this lure was later named the Pin-Fish, and even later the Bagley Shiner. The lure was actually made of hardwood.
Value: $10.00 – 15.00

Sink-N-Swim Bang-O-B

Jim Bagley Bait Co., Winter Haven, Florida
Date: c. 1978
Length: 3"
Notes: A handwritten number on the belly indicates the model number and color.
Value: $5.00 – 10.00

Diving Bang-O-B6
Jim Bagley Bait Co., Winter Haven, Florida
Date: c. 1978
Length: 5¼"
Notes: This is a deep-diving lure designed for "really big fish." The body is made of hardwood to withstand sharp teeth.
Value: $5.00 – 10.00

Diving Bang-O-B8
Jim Bagley Bait Co., Winter Haven, Florida
Date: c. 1978
Length: 8"
Notes: A larger version of the Bang-O-B6, this hardwood lure also features a Lexan diving lip.
Value: $5.00 – 10.00

Small Fry: Rainbow Trout; Natural Shad; Baby Bass; Crappie; Spring Bream
Jim Bagley Bait Co., Winter Haven, Florida
Date: c. 1979
Length: 3"; 3"; 2¾"; 2¾"; 2⅜"
Notes: This series of lures has fantastic eye appeal for the collector and great action for the fisherman.
Value: $5.00 – 10.00

Small Fry: Copper Foil Craw; Bitty Craw
Jim Bagley Bait Co., Winter Haven, Florida
Date: c. 1979 – 1982
Length: 2⅛"; 1⅞"
Notes: These attractive crawfish were part of Bagley's Small Fry series of lures. The brass wire hook hangers on the top lure identify it as the earlier model.
Value: $5.00 – 10.00

B Flat 2
Jim Bagley Bait Co., Winter Haven, Florida
Date: c. 1982
Length: 2½"
Notes: This lure was first made in 1978 with brass wire hook hangers. The screw-eye model shown was introduced in 1982.
Value: $5.00 – 10.00

Stick-Up
Jim Bagley Bait Co., Winter Haven, Florida
Date: c. 1983
Length: 4¾"
Notes: This lure was first produced in 1982 without the bucktail tail hook.
Value: $15.00 – 25.00

Finger Mullet – Deep Sinker
Jim Bagley Bait Co., Winter Haven, Florida
Date: c. 1983
Length: 3¼"
Notes: The Finger Mullet series was made of hardwood. The model with the line tie beneath the chin is called a Jumpin-Mullet.
Value: $5.00 – 10.00

Finger Mullet – Shallow Sinker
Jim Bagley Bait Co., Winter Haven, Florida
Date: c. 1990
Length: 4"
Notes: Designed for saltwater fishing, the Finger Mullet series was made of hardwood.
Value: $5.00 – 10.00

Diving Smoo
Jim Bagley Bait Co., Winter Haven, Florida
Date: c. 1987
Length: 3"
Notes: Bagley also offered a 2¼" size Smoo and a 5" model Deep Smoo. The Smoo was made in both deep and shallow models.
Value: $5.00 – 10.00

ET3
Jim Bagley Bait Co., Winter Haven, Florida
Date: c. 1988
Length: 3"
Notes: Named after the extra terrestrial visitor in the movie, ET was also made in a 2⅜" size.
Value: $5.00 – 10.00

Fat Cat
Jim Bagley Bait Co., Winter Haven, Florida
Date: c. 1989
Length: 1¾"
Notes: Bagley also made a Mama Cat at 3".
Value: $5.00 – 10.00

ICU
Jim Bagley Bait Co., Winter Haven, Florida
Date: c. 1993
Length: 4"
Notes: The ICU was also made in a 3" size in 1994.
Value: $5.00 – 10.00

Hustle Bug
Jim Bagley Bait Co., Winter Haven, Florida
Date: c. 1994
Length: 2¼"
Notes: The painted eye model is less desirable than the bead-eyed model shown.
Value: $10.00 – 15.00

Rattlin Twitcher
Jim Bagley Bait Co., Winter Haven, Florida
Date: c. 1996
Length: 4¼"
Notes: This is a topwater lure designed to allow fishermen to create a "Zig-Zag" action on retrieve.
Value: $5.00 – 10.00

Weed Hog
Bailey Weedless Company, Ohio
Date: c. 1948
Length: 2" rubber body
Notes: Positioned within a wire frame and acting as a weedguard, the hollow rubber chamber also provided floatation for this unusual lure.
Value: $20.00 – 25.00

Laddie #2
Bill Baker Baits, Maramec, Oklahoma
Date: c. 1980
Length: 2⅜"
Notes: This wood lure features an inserted plastic diving lip and was a late runner in the balsa crank bait "rush" of the 1970s.
Value: $5.00 – 10.00

Balsa Boogie; Dagerboard Boogie
Balsa Baits Company, Springfield, Missouri
Date: 1976
Length: 3"; 2⅜"
Notes: A 3⅜" Balsa Boogie was also made.
Value: $5.00 – 8.00

Slo-Poke
Barbee Bait Co., Fort Wayne, Indiana
Date: c. 1955
Length: 1¼"
Notes: This lure was also made in two larger sizes. Barbee Bait Co. made a Weedless Wizard which was similar but had a dressed trailer instead of chamois like the Slo-Poke.
Value: $10.00 – 20.00

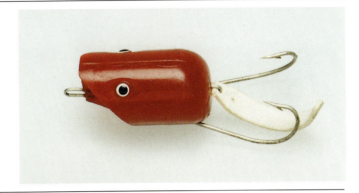

Reel Shad
E.R. Barber, Raceland, Kentucky
Date: c. 1960
Length: 2¼"
Notes: The deep diving Reel Shad was designed for Kentucky's deep impoundments.
Value: $10.00 – 15.00

Bass Bird
Bass Bird Lure Co., Bloomington, Illinois
Date: c. 1984
Length: 2⅛"
Notes: The Bass Bird was designed to leap out of the water when twitched, like a struggling bird.
Value: $5.00 – 8.00.

MISCELLANEOUS LURES

139

Uncle Buck's Buzzer
Bass Pro Shops, Springfield, Missouri
Date: c. 1983
Length: 1⅛" blade
Notes: Named after Uncle Buck, uncle of Bass Pro Shops founder and owner Johnny Morris. This in-line spinner evokes memories of the 1852 J.T. Buel Arrowhead Spinner.
Value: $5.00 – 10.00

Fanny Bates
Bates Baits, La Crosse, Wisconsin
Date: c. 1941
Length: 2⅝"
Notes: This plastic lure was produced after Bates purchased the Lauby Bait Co. in 1939. The original Lauby design was retained. Bates sold out to Paul Bunyan in the mid 1940s.
Value: $10.00 – 20.00

Tweedler
Bear Creek Bait Co., Kaleva, Michigan
Date: c. 1948
Length: 2¼"
Notes: Known for its ice-spearing decoys, Bear Creek's wooden Tweedler is chunky and attractive, bearing some resemblance to the Arbogast Jitterbug.
Value: $20.00 – 25.00

Sucker Minnow
Bear Creek Bait Co., Kaleva, Michigan
Date: c. 1950
Length: 3⅝"
Notes: The plastic Sucker Minnow is reminiscent of the style of ice-spearing decoys the company made.
Value: $10.00 – 15.00

Old Fighter
Beaver Bait Co., Ambridge, Pennsylvania
Date: c. 1950
Length: 3"
Notes: Two banks of beads and spinners gird this lipped lure. Made in several colors, the Old Fighter is collectible, if for no other reason than its competitive name.
Value: $35.00 – 40.00

Eager Beaver #1
Beaver Creek Tackle, Inc., Leetonia, Ohio
Date: c. 1960
Length: 3"
Notes: This deep-running member of the "Beaver Better Baits" family features a hair-dressed weedguard with an overtied rubber base. The spoon is made of anodized aluminum.
Value: $10.00 – 15.00

Beetle Bug ("Clam Shell")
Beetle Bug Co., Detroit, Michigan
Date: c. 1935 – 1936
Length: 1⅞" body
Notes: This rare lure features a "scissors" weedless hook system held open by a spring. A fish biting the lure would be exposed to the hooks. The company was sold to Millsite c. 1937.
Value: $50.00 – 55.00

Beetle Bug with Spinner
Beetle Bug Co., Detroit, Michigan
Date: c. 1935 – 1936
Length: 1¼" body
Notes: This bug was stamped from sheet brass and featured an Al Foss style spinner.
Value: $35.00 – 40.00

Torpedo Ray
John Irving Bell, Royal Oak, Michigan
Date: c. 1948
Length: 3⅝"
Notes: The barbed wires protruding from the wood body are unique among fishing lures. Coupled with a stationary single tail hook and eccentric moveable spinning attachment, the Torpedo Ray was an active and efficient lure.
Value: $25.00 – 35.00

Honest John
Berea Bait Manufacturing Co., Berea, Kentucky
Date: c. 1967
Length: 4¾"
Notes: The no-eyed Honest John joins the legions which were influenced by the Rapala.
Value: $10.00 – 15.00

Biek "Paddle Bait"
Biek Manufacturing Co., Dowagiac, Michigan
Date: c. 1941
Length: 2⅞"
Notes: This lure must have made considerable commotion with its flat face creating a wake and the large paddles thrashing the water.
Value: $40.00 – 50.00

Agitator
Biek Manufacturing Co., Dowagiac, Michigan
Date: c. 1941
Length: 2⅝"
Notes: Like the Biek "Paddle Bait," the Agitator was born in Dowagiac, Michigan, right under the nose of James Heddon's Sons. Curiously, neither company produced lure designs that were stylistically competitive with one another.
Value: $30.00 – 35.00

Hairwing Adult Dragonfly
William F. Blades, Chicago, Illinois
Date: c. 1948
Length: 1⁵⁄₁₆"
Notes: A native of England, Blades was born in Sheffield in 1884 and immigrated to America shortly after the turn of the century.
Value: $90.00 – 110.00

Grasshopper
William F. Blades, Chicago, Illinois
Date: c. 1948
Length: ⅞" hook
Notes: Blades thought of his flies as "natural imitations" to realistically match the natural organism. Nearly all Blades' flies utilize natural materials with the exception of the head cement.
Value: $75.00 – 100.00

Hard Body Crayfish
William F. Blades, Chicago, Illinois
Date: c. 1948
Length: 1½"
Notes: Blades tied flies for himself and a few friends but never offered his work for sale.
Value: $90.00 – 110.00

Mayfly, Hexagenia Munda
William F. Blades, Chicago, Illinois
Date: c. 1948
Length: ⅞" hook
Notes: Rectangular paper identification tags are found on some Blades flies and increase their value and provenance considerably.
Value: $90.00 – 110.00.

Damselfly Nymph
William F. Blades, Chicago, Illinois
Date: c. 1948
Length: ¾" hook
Notes: Blades wrote his first book, *Fishing Flies and Fly Tying*, in the late 1940s. The book was published in 1951. Two subsequent editions were also published.
Value: $75.00 – 100.00

Damselfly
William F. Blades, Chicago, Illinois
Date: c. 1948
Length: ¾" hook
Notes: This Damselfly has legs made from the quill of a feather with the hackle trimmed away. Hand coloring enhances the realistic appearance.
Value: $90.00 – 110.00

Adult Damselfly
William F. Blades, Chicago, Illinois
Date: c. 1948
Length: ⅞"
Notes: The flies of Bill Blades established a new benchmark for realism that has only recently been met by the ultra-realistic flies of David Martin (see the chapter on Contemporary Lures).
Value: $90.00 – 110.00

Stonefly Nymph
William F. Blades, Chicago, Illinois
Date: c. 1948
Length: 1¹⁵⁄₁₆" hook
Notes: With eye appeal consisting of extreme detail, exact proportion, and high craftsmanship, it is no wonder that Blades' flies are sought after by serious collectors and jealously guarded by those who own them.
Value: $100.00 – 120.00

Stonefly Nymph
William F. Blades, Chicago, Illinois
Date: c. 1948
Length: 1¼"
Notes: Another Stonefly pattern that looks real enough to crawl.
Value: $90.00 – 110.00

Caddis Larvae with Case
William F. Blades, Chicago, Illinois
Date: c. 1948
Length: 1" hook
Notes: Typical of Blades' attention to detail is the inclusion in these flies of actual river gravel to make the larvae case, just like the real thing.
Value: $75.00 – 100.00

Dragonfly Nymph
William F. Blades, Chicago, Illinois
Date: c. 1948
Length: 1¹⁄₁₆"
Notes: Blades often tied imitations of nymphs in different stages of development, as in this example.
Value: $75.00 – 100.00

Dragonfly Nymph
William F. Blades, Chicago, Illinois
Date: c. 1948
Length: 1⅜" hook
Notes: Like the previous example, one can see a particular stage of development depicted by this Dragonfly Nymph.
Value: $90.00 – 110.00

Dragonfly
William F. Blades, Chicago, Illinois
Date: c. 1948
Length: 2¼"
Notes: This large Dragonfly uses hackle feathers for its impressionistic wings.
Value: $120.00 – 150.00

Injured Baby Sunfish

William F. Blades, Chicago, Illinois
Date: c. 1948
Length: 2¼"
Notes: This is a bass-sized deer hair sunfish with trimmed fins and a feather tail.
Value: $90.00 – 110.00

Cork-Bodied Squirrel Tail Frog

William F. Blades, Chicago, Illinois
Date: c. 1948
Length: 1¼"
Notes: The sleek shape of this lure reflects Blades' stylistic interpretation of a small frog.
Value: $60.00 – 75.00

Blaz-O-Lure

Blaz-O-Lure Manufacturing Co., Los Angeles, California
Date: c. 1954
Length: 3⅜"
Notes: This very plain-looking lure used batteries to power a bulb inside.
Value: $10.00 – 20.00

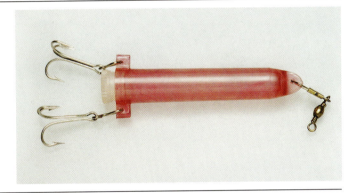

Squeaky Mr. Mouse

Blimp's Fishing Tackle Co., Manchester, Kentucky
Date: c. 1970
Length: 3¼"
Notes: The spinning head on this mouse was designed to squeak when retrieved. The natural rodent squeaking sound was thought to attract bass.
Value: $15.00 – 25.00

Bobopen

Bobopen Co., Colorado
Date: c. 1962
Length: 2"
Notes: Other than a dental plate, it is hard to tell what this unusual lure was designed to imitate. Its novel shape gives this bait collectibility.
Value: $10.00 – 15.00

Hand Made Bomber
Bomber Bait Co., Gainesville, Texas
Date: c. 1942
Length: 2¾"
Notes: Totally handmade, this Bomber features red bead eyes. However, bead eyes were never produced. Extremely rare.
Value: $300.00 – 350.00

Bomber – No Eye
Bomber Bait Co., Gainesville, Texas
Date: c. 1944 – 1946
Length: 2⅝"
Notes: This lure features a handmade lip and line tie. The cup hardware is made of shoelace eyelets (either black or brown). #500 series shown. Also made in #400 and #600.
Value: $100.00

Bomber
Bomber Bait Co., Gainesville, Texas
Date: c. 1944 – 1946
Length: 2¾"
Notes: The black pupil within the yellow eye is typical of Bombers with eyes and handmade line ties. #500 series shown, but came also in the #400 and #600.
Value: $90.00 – 110.00

#400; #500; #600 Bomber – No Eye
Bomber Bait Co., Gainesville, Texas
Date: c. 1946
Length: 2½"; 2¾"; 3⅛"
Notes: This Bomber version has no eyes and features a Luxon line tie. Nickel-plated flat cup hardware.
Value: $30.00 – 35.00

#500 Bomber
Bomber Bait Co., Gainesville, Texas
Date: c. 1947 – 1949
Length: 3"
Notes: This beautifully painted lure features a Luxon line tie with a "Small X." The "Small X" line continued until 1951 when the "Large X" line tie usage began. The eyes have returned but are now orange with a black pupil.
Value: $15.00 – 20.00

1949 Plastic Bombers #600; #500; #400

Bomber Bait Co., Gainesville, Texas
Date: c. 1949
Length: counter-clockwise: 4"; 3¾"; 3¼" overall
Notes: Entirely made of molded plastic, this lure was in production for less than two years.
Value: $20.00 – 30.00

Fly Rod Bomber

Bomber Bait Co., Gainesville, Texas
Date: c. 1950
Length: 1¼"
Notes: Only six of these little lures are known to exist. This is probably a prototype or experimental bait.
Value: $250.00 – 300.00

Bomber #200; #300; #400; #500; #600

Bomber Bait Co., Gainesville, Texas
Date: c. 1952
Length: 1¾"; 2⅛"; 2⅜"; 2¾"; 3"
Notes: This is the last version of wooden Bombers. Production of wood Bombers was discontinued after 1971. All the lures shown here except the #400 are special order colors.
Value: $10.00 – 15.00 standard; $45.00 – 50.00 special order

Heavy Duty Bomber

Bomber Bait Co., Gainesville, Texas
Date: c. 1953
Length: 3¼"
Notes: Heavy duty "L rig" hook rigging and oversize line tie are added to a #600 body to produce this light saltwater Bomber.
Value: $30.00 – 35.00

Knothead #1300; #1200

Bomber Bait Co., Gainesville, Texas
Date: c. 1948
Length: 3⅜"; 2¼"
Notes: The Knothead was produced for only about three years.
Value: $90.00 – 100.00

Bomberette #800; #700; Midget Bomberette #2700
Bomber Bait Co., Gainesville, Texas
Date: c. 1948
Length: counterclockwise: 2⅝"; 2⅛"; 1¾"
Notes: The #800 and #700 Bomberettes were discontinued in 1954. The #2700 Midget Bomberette was made until the end of 1971.
Value: $55.00 – 75.00

Top Bomber #4000; #6000
Bomber Bait Co., Gainesville, Texas
Date: c. 1951
Length: 2⅜"; 3¼"
Notes: In production for just 3 or 4 years, the Top Bomber was only produced with a tail prop.
Value: $75.00 – 100.00

Waterdog – #1700; #1600; #1500
Bomber Bait Co., Gainesville, Texas
Date: c. 1955
Length: 4"; 3"; 2⅛"
Notes: The slender Waterdog was an especially deep-running lure.
Value: $5.00 – 10.00

Lipless Waterdog
Bomber Bait Co., Gainesville, Texas
Date: c. 1968
Length: 4"
Notes: This lure uses a Waterdog body with fore and aft propellers. Very limited production; special order only.
Value: $175.00 – 300.00

Lipless Waterdog
Bomber Bait Co., Gainesville, Texas
Date: c. 1960s
Length: 4"
Notes: Similar to the previous lure, but without propellers.
Value: $175.00 – 300.00

#7200 Baby Spinstick; #7300 Spinstick Bomber
Bomber Bait Co., Gainesville, Texas
Date: c. 1954
Length: 2⁵⁄₁₆"; 3½"
Notes: The Spinstick was discontinued in 1989, and a new version was added in 1997.
Value: $10.00 – 15.00

#7400 Stick
Bomber Bait Co., Gainesville, Texas
Date: c. 1954
Length: 3¾"
Notes: Made in one size only, the Stickbait remained in production until 1981.
Value: $5.00 – 10.00

Looboyle Special
Bomber Bait Co., Gainesville, Texas
Date: c. 1953 – 1956
Length: 3⅛"
Notes: Designed and produced for Looboyle in Tulsa, Oklahoma, this rare Bomber was in production for only a few years.
Value: $180.00 – 240.00

Glass-Eyed Bomberette #800
Bomber Bait Co., Gainesville, Texas
Date: c. 1949
Length: 3"
Notes: Bomber occasionally experimented with glass-eyed lures but never put them into production. This lure is extremely rare. The frog paint pattern is unusual.
Value: $360.00+

Experimental Bomber #500
Bomber Bait Co., Gainesville, Texas
Date: c. 1963
Length: 2¾"
Notes: This lure uses a #500 Bomber body and features a Waterdog lip and spinner. Very rare. Made with and without spinner.
Value: $75.00 – 100.00

Bomber Jerk #4500; #4400; #4300
Bomber Bait Co., Gainesville, Texas
Date: c. 1953
Length: 4⅛"; 3½"; 3"
Notes: A light saltwater lure, the Jerk bait features heavy duty "L rig" hook hangers.
Value: $20.00 – 30.00

Bushwacker
Bomber Bait Co., Gainesville, Texas
Date: c. 1953
Length: ¾" body
Notes: This is one of the first production safety pin-style spinnerbaits. This bait came in a ¼ oz. #5300 and a ½ oz. #5400. Also came with twin spinners, ¼ oz. #6300 and ½ oz. #6400.
Value: $5.00 or less

Gimmick
Bomber Bait Co., Gainesville, Texas
Date: c. 1952
Length: ¾" body
Notes: This neat little spinner was a competitor of the popular Paul Bunyan 66 lure. This lure also came in a ¼ oz. #3400 and a ½ oz. #3500.
Value: $5.00 or less

Slab Spoon
Bomber Bait Co., Gainesville, Texas
Date: c. early 1960s
Length: 1½"
Notes: Available in five sizes, the Slab Spoon was designed for vertical jigging.
Value: $5.00 or less

The Needlefish (underwater)
Boone Bait Company, Winter Park, Florida
Date: c. 1957
Length: 5⅜", 4⅜"
Notes: The Needlefish was made in two styles — underwater and topwater.
Value: $5.00 – 10.00

The Needlefish (surface)
Boone Bait Company, Winter Park, Florida
Date: c. 1957
Length: 3¾"
Notes: Like the underwater version, the surface Needlefish maintains its gar-like appearance with the addition of a tail spinner.
Value: $5.00 – 10.00

Wavefish
Broadson Tackle, Saline, Michigan
Date: c. 1950
Length: 2⅞"
Notes: The wire hook harness on this lure can be moved to different positions for different actions.
Value: $10.00 – 20.00

Gaylure
Braidwood Stamp Co., New Jersey
Date: c. 1938
Length: 2⅜" plastic body
Notes: This lure is very attractively made and features a spoon/hook that attaches to an open loop on the belly, allowing great jointed action.
Value: $25.00 – 30.00

Brooks Double O
Brooks Baits, R-Jay Industries, Inc., Cuyahoga Falls, Ohio
Date: c. 1939
Length: 3⅛"
Notes: Without the tail, this attractive bait was named the "O."
Value: $10.00 – 15.00

Brooks Buzzer
Brooks Baits, R-Jay Industries, Inc., Cuyahoga Falls, Ohio
Date: c. 1940
Length: 2⅞"
Notes: The Buzzer is basically a Double O without the diving lip.
Value: $15.00 – 20.00

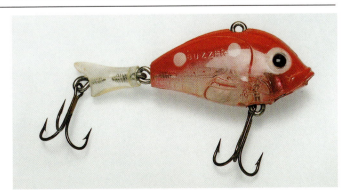

Brooks Jointed Digger, JO series
Brooks Baits, R-Jay Industries, Inc., Cuyahoga Falls, Ohio
Date: c. 1947 – 1954
Length: 3¼"
Notes: This jointed, deep diving lure came in eight colors.
Value: $5.00 – 10.00

Brooks Reefer
Brooks Baits, R-Jay Industries, Inc., Cuyahoga Falls, Ohio
Date: c. 1947 – 1954
Length: 4"
Notes: This lure came in four types: Reefer, 3" (unjointed); Baby Reefer, 2¼"; Jointed Reefer, 4"; and Baby Jointed Reefer.
Value: $5.00 – 10.00

Brooks Jointed Top Water, JTW Series
Brooks Baits, R-Jay Industries, Inc., Cuyahoga Falls, Ohio
Date: c. 1947 – 1954
Length: 3½", 2¼"
Notes: These fish-tailed surface lures feature minimal design and efficient function.
Value: $10.00 – 15.00

Brooks Popper Type Plug, No. SP-5
Brooks Baits, R-Jay Industries, Inc., Cuyahoga Falls, Ohio
Later, Division of Harrison Industries, Inc., Newark, New Jersey
Date: c. 1947 – 1954
Length: 1⅜"
Notes: The baby of the Brooks line, this little lure features Brooks' attractive eye detail.
Value: $10.00 – 15.00

Brooks No. 7 Weedless
Brooks Baits, R-Jay Industries, Inc., Cuyahoga Falls, Ohio
Date: c. 1941
Length: 1½" body
Notes: This skirted and spinnered plastic lure was made in two sizes and six colors.
Value: $5.00 – 10.00

Brooks Fluttertail Spoon
Brooks Baits, R-Jay Industries, Inc., Cuyahoga Falls, Ohio
Date: c. 1954
Length: 3¼" overall
Notes: A nickel metal flasher body with the same type plastic tail as the jointed top water lure.
Value: $5.00 – 10.00

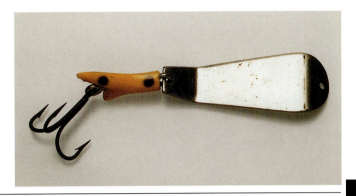

Bug-N-Bass
Buckeye Bait Corporation, Council Bluff, Kansas
Date: c. 1965
Length: 3½"
Notes: This bug-chasing plunker had an open mouth and "flow-thru" gills for a realistic look and action.
Value: $5.00 – 10.00

Spoonplug
Buck's Baits, Hickory, North Carolina
Date: 1960
Length: c. 3¾", 2⅛"
Notes: Designed by Buck Perry, the Spoonplug was formed from flat metal sheet and painted attractively. Buck Perry's structure fishing discoveries revolutionized bass fishing as described in his book, *Spoonplugging*.
Value: $5.00 – 10.00

Bucktail "Spinner"
Bucktail Paint Co., Waco, Texas
Date: c. 1941
Length: 1" head
Notes: The technique of spinning and shaping deer hair on a hook was the basis for this company's lures.
Value: $40.00 – 50.00

Bucktail "Bass Bait"
Bucktail Bait Co., Waco, Texas
Date: c. 1941
Length: 4½"
Notes: Tied on a twisted wire attached to a treble hook, this large Bucktail bait features a diving lip.
Value: $40.00 – 50.00

Electro-Lure
Paul Bunyan, Minneapolis, Minnesota
Date: c. 1938
Length: 4"
Notes: This lure could be unscrewed to insert a battery which would light up a bulb in the head. The Electro-Lure was originally marketed by the Lloyd Co.
Value: $30.00 – 35.00

Transparent Dodger (No. 900), Artful Dodger
Paul Bunyan, Minneapolis, Minnesota
Date: c. 1939
Length: 3⅝", 1⅜"
Notes: The Dodgers were very thin baits designed for a wide wobble. The Artful Dodger gets its name from the character in Charles Dickens' *Oliver Twist.*
Value: $15.00 – 20.00

Brookland Dodger
Paul Bunyan, Minneapolis, Minnesota
Date: c. 1939
Length: 3⅝"
Notes: This lure is the same basic lure as the Transparent Dodger, but with the addition of metal wings.
Value: $15.00 – 20.00

Double Action Twirl Bug
Paul Bunyan, Minneapolis, Minnesota
Date: c. 1940
Length: 2¾"
Notes: The Twirl Bug series features components reflecting outstanding craftsmanship, a carryover from the original Lloyd Co. lures. The lure shown has a prop and a wiggling lip, thus double action.
Value: $20.00 – 25.00

Twirl Bug
Paul Bunyan, Minneapolis, Minnesota
Date: c. 1940
Length: 3" shaft
Notes: This version of the Twirl Bug had plastic wings and a nose-mounted prop.
Value: $20.00 – 25.00

MISCELLANEOUS LURES

Twirl Bug Wiggler

Paul Bunyan, Minneapolis, Minnesota
Date: c. 1940
Length: 3"
Notes: The most minimal of the Twirl Bugs, this version only had plastic wings for action.
Value: $20.00 – 25.00

Paul Bunyan Minnow; Paul Bunyan Minnow; Silver Shiner

Paul Bunyan, Minneapolis, Minnesota
Date: c. 1940
Length: 3⅝" (large); 1⅞" (small); 1⅞"
Notes: These attractive, minnow-shaped lures were very tastefully designed. The flyrod size could be purchased with a diving lip or with a front spinner.
Value: $20.00 – 30.00

Centipede Spinner

Paul Bunyan, Minneapolis, Minnesota
Date: c. 1940
Length: 6¼" overall
Notes: The long, revolving Centipede Spinner body is stamped from a single piece of metal. The U-shaped head is attached with a split ring.
Value: $30.00 – 35.00

Floating Weaver

Paul Bunyan, Minneapolis, Minnesota
Date: c. 1941
Length: 2⅞"
Notes: The Weavers were Paul Bunyan's entries into the River Runt market.
Value: $5.00 – 10.00

Weaver (deep)

Paul Bunyan, Minneapolis, Minnesota
Date: c. 1941
Length: 2⅜"
Notes: The Deep Weaver had an extended diving lip.
Value: $5.00 – 10.00

Ladybug Diver
Paul Bunyan, Minneapolis, Minnesota
Date: c. 1946
Length: 3¼"
Notes: Showing its evolution from the Lauby and Bates lures, this version of the Ladybug was weedless.
Value: $15.00 – 20.00

Paul Bunyan "66"
Paul Bunyan, Minneapolis, Minnesota
Date: c. 1948
Length: 1½" shaft
Notes: The weight-forward "66" was especially popular with fishermen who liked to fish drop-offs in large impoundments.
Value: $5.00 or less

Chunker #2011
Burke Flexo-Products Co., Traverse City, Michigan
Date: c. 1966
Length: 3⅝"
Notes: Burke was a manufacturer of soft baits. The flex plug line of lures capitalized on their soft lure technology by creating lures that landed on the water naturally and felt natural to a striking fish.
Value: $5.00 or less

Ol' Twitch #2013
Burke Flexo-Products Co., Traverse City, Michigan
Date: c. 1966
Length: 2⅝"
Notes: This is the "Baby Lucky 13" of soft baits.
Value: $5.00 or less

Big Dig #2015
Burke Flexo-Products Co., Traverse City, Michigan
Date: c. 1966
Length: 3¼"; 2½"
Notes: The deep diving Big Dig was made in two sizes. Note the large buoyant rear end which would slow down the wobbling action.
Value: $5.00 or less

Wee Gillie #2012
Burke Flexo-Products Co., Traverse City, Michigan
Date: c. 1966
Length: 2"
Notes: The Wee Gillie was a soft vibrational-type lure.
Value: $5.00 or less

Aqua-Bat
F.S Burroughs and Co., Inc., Dover, New Jersey
Date: c. 1947
Length: 2⅞"
Notes: Designed to hold a special aqua tab inside the spring-loaded mouth, this bait would bubble violently when it contacted the water.
Value: $25.00 – 30.00

The Croaker
F.S Burroughs and Co., Inc., Ledgewood, New Jersey
Date: c. 1955
Length: 2½"
Notes: This neat little frog was designed to float and jump upward when twitched on retrieve.
Value: $15.00 – 20.00

The Tad-Pole
F.S Burroughs and Co., Inc., Ledgewood, New Jersey
Date: c. 1958
Length: 3¼"
Notes: This beautiful Tad-Pole features a jointed body and a natural-looking transparent tail.
Value: $30.00 – 35.00

Buzz-Saw
Buzz-Saw Tackle Company, Detroit, Michigan
Date: c. 1958
Length: 4¹⁄₁₆"
Notes: The Buzz-Saw features two revolving "saw blades" positioned at 90 degrees. Water pressure against the blades would cause them to spin on retrieve.
Value: $35.00 – 45.00

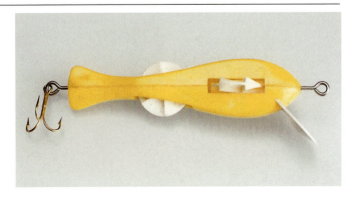

Litl-Liz
C&G Tackle Co., Tulsa, Oklahoma
Date: c. 1960
Length: 2⅛"
Notes: The Litl-Liz is a deep diver featuring cup hook hardware and clear glass eyes.
Value: $10.00 – 15.00

Lady Bug Kit (4 lures)
Cabella's, Sidney, Nebraska
Date: c. 1999
Length: 1¾"
Notes: This cute set of bugs may be ordered through Cabella's catalog.
Value: $11.00 + shipping

Scootin' Annie
Lucky Cameron, Pittsburgh, Pennsylvania
Date: c. 1937
Length: 4¼"
Notes: The Scootin' Annie was produced in only one size and one color. The example shown was never painted.
Value: $30.00 – 35.00

Lulu
Captivated Lures, Inc., Jacksonville, Florida
Date: c. 1947
Length: 6⅛"
Notes: This large plastic lure featured a battery-powered propeller at the nose and a line tie on the tail.
Value: $30.00 – 35.00

Catch-All
Catch-All, Inc., Hiles, Wisconsin
Date: c. 1955
Length: 2½", 1⅜"
Notes: The Catch-All was manufactured for only about 2½ years.
Value: $30.00 – 35.00

MISCELLANEOUS LURES

158

Adjustable Wing Lure
Challenge Tackle, Inc., Meadville, Pennsylvania
Date: c. 1952
Length: 2⅛"
Notes: The wings on this lure were adjustable for different actions.
Value: $10.00 – 20.00

Spinner Spoon
Challenge Tackle Co., Meadville, Pennsylvania
Date: c. 1952
Length: 3⅞"
Notes: This lightweight plastic lure featured two spinners in the body for surface buzzing action.
Value: $10.00 – 20.00

"Artie" Mack's Magic Minnow
F.E. Chester Manufacturing Co., Bellefont, Rhode Island
Date: c. 1940
Length: 3½"
Notes: The Magic Minnow design must have changed ownership several times as evidenced by the various published company names and addresses. The lure shown was found in a two-piece cardboard box with the above information printed on top. The lure is made of German silver.
Value: $45.00 – 50.00

Dazzler
F.E. Chester, Rhode Island
Date: c. 1938
Length: 2¼"
Notes: The jewelled Dazzler also featured a stamped "engraved" pattern. Similarities in this concept can be found in English lures of the late 1800s.
Value: $10.00 – 15.00

King Chub
Chicago Tackle Co., Chicago, Illinois
Date: c. 1952
Length: 3⅜"
Notes: Two smaller sizes of the King Chub were made: 2" and 2½". The jointed head is a unique feature.
Value: $10.00 – 15.00

Christensen Frog
O. Christensen, Minnesota
Date: c. 1936
Length: 1½" body
Notes: Small wire springs exert outward pressure on the legs of this frog. When retrieved, the legs come together as shown. The feet are broken off in the example shown.
Value: $120.00 – 125.00

Max Weesner's Casting Spinner
Cincinnati Bait Co., Cincinnati, Ohio
Date: c. 1940
Length: 1" blade
Notes: The metal head of this bait was slightly convex on the underside, causing it to fall slowly and plane to the surface on retrieve.
Value: $5.00 or less

#300 Water Scout (left, floater; right, sinker)
C.A. Clark Bait Company, Springfield, Missouri
Date: c. 1938
Length: 2¼"; 2"
Notes: By 1938, the Water Scout had undergone changes from no eye detail to dent eye and finally to this third version with tack eyes. Sinkers had a red dot painted on or near the tail.
Value: $35.00 – 45.00

#1000 Little Eddie
C.A. Clark Bait Company, Springfield, Missouri
Date: c. 1946
Length: 1⅝"
Notes: The Little Eddie was available in #1000 sinking or #2000 floating models. This lure was named after Charlie Clark's son Ed.
Value: $20.00 – 30.00

#600 Duck Bill
C.A. Clark Bait Company, Springfield, Missouri
Date: c. 1937
Length: 2¼"
Notes: This deep-diving bait with tack eyes was also made in a smaller version called the Duckling.
Value: $30.00 – 40.00

#500 Duckling
C.A. Clark Bait Company, Springfield, Missouri
Date: c. 1946
Length: 2"
Notes: Developed by C.A. Clark's son, Ed, the Duckling is a scaled-down version of the Duck Bill.
Value: $40.00 – 60.00

Deep Diving Water Scout
C.A. Clark Bait Company, Springfield, Missouri
Date: c. 1935
Length: 3⅛"
Notes: This was either a limited production model or an experimental bait.
Value: $80.00 – 100.00

#700 Popper Scout
C.A. Clark Bait Company, Springfield, Missouri
Date: c. 1945
Length: 2½"
Notes: The #700 Popper Scout was also made in a smaller Popper Scout Junior #1700.
Value: $20.00 – 30.00

#900 Darter Scout
C.A. Clark Bait Company, Springfield, Missouri
Date: c. 1945
Length: 2⅞"
Notes: Made in a larger and a smaller size, this lure is often referred to as a Top Scout.
Value: $30.00 – 40.00

#25 Dwarf Deamon
C.A. Clark Bait Company, Springfield, Missouri
Date: c. 1958
Length: 2"
Notes: This is the very rare small version of the Darter Scout.
Value: $80.00 – 100.00

#2600 Goofy Gus
C.A. Clark Bait Company, Springfield, Missouri
Date: c. 1948
Length: 3⅛"
Notes: This bait has a distinctive "waist" and has also been found with only a nose propeller.
Value: $50.00 – 60.00

Baby Goofy Gus
C.A. Clark Bait Company, Springfield, Missouri
Date: c. 1958
Length: 2⅛"
Notes: This very small and rare version of the Goofy Gus features tack eyes and oval propellers.
Value: $80.00 – 100.00

#800 Streamliner
C.A. Clark Bait Company, Springfield, Missouri
Date: c. 1946
Length: 2¼"
Notes: The Streamliner is a narrow plastic variation of the Water Scout.
Value: $20.00 – 30.00

#1500 Jointed Duck Bill
C.A. Clark Bait Company, Springfield, Missouri
Date: c. 1946
Length: 2¾"
Notes: Made of plastic, the Jointed Duck Bill is an interesting variation on the basic Clark design.
Value: $20.00 – 30.00

Convert-A-Lure
Convert-A-Lure Co., Rockford, Illinois
Date: c. 1960
Length: 3⅛"
Notes: Packaged three to an orange cardboard "kit box," this lure featured interchangeable bodies to create a more affordable variety of lure color combinations.
Value: $75.00 – 100.00

Cook's Goldblume

F.W. Cook Company, Inc., Evansville, Indiana
Date: c. 1965
Length: 3⅞"
Notes: Made of hollow plastic, the Cook's Goldblume is a great addition to a novelty lure collection.
Value: $35.00 – 45.00

Cook's 500

F.W. Cook Company, Inc., Evansville, Indiana
Date: c. 1965
Length: 4"
Notes: The hollow plastic Cook's 500 pays tribute to the Indianapolis 500 race. A great novelty bait.
Value: $35.00 – 45.00

Flutter Jack

L.B. Cook Bait Manufacturing Co., Shreveport, Louisiana
Date: 1947
Length: 1½" body
Notes: The Flutter Jack is a terrific surface buzz bait. The example shown is early and appears to have been silver plated. A Flutter Jack, Jr. was also made.
Value: $10.00 – 15.00

Gene Cooper Lure

Cooper Lures, Chicago, Illinois
Date: c. 1951
Length: 2" body
Notes: This inventive lure uses cloth legs and a wiggling lip to achieve the action of a swimming fish.
Value: $20.00 – 25.00

Ubangi

Forrest Allen, Stamford, Connecticut
Date: c. 1955
Length: 2"
Notes: This deep-diving floater features a cupped face and long lip.
Value: $10.00 – 15.00

Big-O
Cotton Cordell, Hot Springs, Arkansas
Date: c. 1978
Length: 3½" overall
Notes: This is the plastic version of the Big-O.
Value: $5.00 or less

Commemorative Big-O
Cordell Bait Company, Hot Springs, Arkansas
Date: c. 1992
Length: 3⅛"
Notes: The plastic lure was commissioned by the Bass Angler's Sportsman Society for their 25th anniversary.
Value: $20.00 – 25.00

The Prez
Cordell Tackle, Inc., Hot Springs, Arkansas
Date: c. 1980
Length: 2¼"
Notes: Made during the Carter administration, The Prez is often referred to by collectors as the Jimmy Carter lure.
Value: $5.00 or less

Dragonfly
Coronado Tackle Company
Date: c. 1954
Length: 2⅞"
Notes: The plastic Dragonfly is a buzzing surface lure similar in design to the flying Helgramite of 1883.
Value: $20.00 – 25.00

Bullcat
Crank Bait Corporation
Date: c. 1981
Length: 3"
Notes: This great-looking catfish is molded of a hard foam plastic.
Value: $5.00 or less

"Deep Shad"
Crank Bait Corporation
Date: c. 1981
Length: 5"
Notes: This hard foam bait features a long, deep-diving lip.
Value: $5.00 or less

Cast-Atem
Creme Lure Company, Akron, Ohio; Tyler, Texas
Date: c. 1965
Length: 3"
Notes: The Cast-Atem draws heavily on the design of the Dalton Special.
Value: $5.00 – 10.00

Cheeta
Creme Lure Company, Akron, Ohio; Tyler, Texas
Date: c. 1965
Length: 2⅝"
Notes: The deep-diving Cheeta features a distinctive joint design.
Value: $5.00 – 10.00

"Spin Tail"
Creme Lure Company, Akron, Ohio; Tyler, Texas
Date: c. 1970
Length: 1⅝"
Notes: Apparently not catalogued, the Spin Tail has been credited by collectors to Creme during the latter years.
Value: $5.00 – 10.00

Flash Minnow
Bill Crowder Bait Company, Newark, New Jersey
Date: c. 1958
Length: 2½"
Notes: The Flash Minnow features a flat, textured metal body with a diving lip and tufts of nylon to represent pectoral fins.
Value: $15.00 – 20.00

Big Jerk
Bill Crowder Bait Company, Newark, New Jersey
Date: c. 1958
Length: 1⅝"
Notes: Bill Crowder lures are all small casting-size baits.
Value: $10.00 – 15.00

Do Wee Gee
Bill Crowder Bait Company, Newark, New Jersey
Date: c. 1958
Length: 1½"
Notes: The Do Wee Gee features a similar body shape to that of
the Big Jerk.
Value: $10.00 – 15.00

Crutch's Lizzard
W.O. Crutchfield, Elizabethton, Tennessee
Date: c. 1958
Length: 5½"
Notes: While this lure was patented in 1958, Crutch's Lizzards
were being made by hand in the late 1940s. The eyes are necklace
beads.
Value: $25.00 – 30.00

Ed's Hula Hula
Ed Cumings, Inc., Flint, Michigan
Date: c. 1937
Length: 3¾"
Notes: Two similar lures for saltwater fishing, the Waikiki (9") and
the Honolulu Belle (9" and 14") were also made.
Value: $30.00 – 35.00

D.A.M. Killer Wobbler
D.A.M., Germany
Date: c. 1950
Length: 4"
Notes: Attractive paint finishes are typical on D.A.M. lures even
during the painted-eye period as shown.
Value: $50.00 – 55.00

D.A.M. Pike, double joint
D.A.M., Germany
Date: c. 1950
Length: 6"
Notes: This nicely finished pike features two joints and handpainted tail and eyes. A plastic pike bearing the D.A.M. trademark is currently available through Cabella's.
Value: $40.00 – 50.00

Pike, single joint
D.A.M., Germany
Date: c. 1950
Length: 4¾"
Notes: The earliest D.A.M. lures had glass eyes.
Value: $35.00 – 40.00

L.E.P. (Light Emitting Plug)
Danon Company, Washington, Missouri
Date: c. 1983
Length: 3"
Notes: This lure employs two small batteries to power a small light bulb in the tail.
Value: $5.00 – 10.00

Trigger-Fish
Davis Tackle Manufacturing Company, Detroit, Michigan
Date: c. 1948
Length: 3½"
Notes: The treble hook locks when compressed against a spring inside the body of this lure. A striking fish activating the back plate would release the hook. The example shown is an uncatalogued color.
Value: $50.00 – 55.00

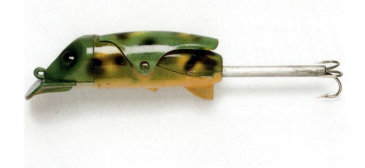

Whitmore Shrimp
Deception Lures, Australia
Date: c. 1995
Length: 2½"
Notes: This is a deep-diving Australian shrimp imitation crankbait.
Value: $5.00 – 10.00

Bass Caller
Detroit Bait Company, Detroit, Michigan
Date: c. 1939
Length: 3½"
Notes: Made of wood with a depression on the head, the Bass Caller is a tough bait to find with perfect paint finish.
Value: $40.00 – 50.00

Duck Bill Wriggler
Bill De Witt Baits, Auburn, New York
Date: c. 1939
Length: 3⅝"
Notes: This stylized hollow lure is made from two pieces of molded plastic glued together at the edge.
Value: $25.00 – 35.00

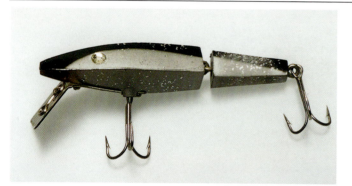

Diamond Jim
Diamond Jim Tackle Company, Evanston, Illinois
Date: c. 1955
Length: 3½"
Notes: The Diamond Jim has "diamond" eyes and is diamond-shaped in cross section.
Value: $5.00 – 10.00

Bleeding Minnow
Dick Products, Detroit, Michigan
Date: c. 1962
Length: 2¾"
Notes: With bleeding tablets inserted beneath the white hinged gill, this minnow would bleed for 25 – 35 minutes.
Value: $15.00 – 20.00

Killer Diller
Dillon-Beck Manufacturing Co., Irvington, New Jersey
Date: c. 1941
Length: 3¼"
Notes: If ever a lure had a pleasant expression, the rare Killer Diller is it.
Value: $25.00 – 35.00

Boomerang
Downunder Lures Pty. Ltd., Australia
Date: c. 1995
Length: 2½"
Notes: The Boomerang is a deep-diving Australian crankbait.
Value: $5.00 or less

Bull Nose Frog
Eger Bait Manufacturing Co., Bartow, Florida
Date: c. 1937
Length: 3"
Notes: Eger is a highly collectible lure company, and this frog with its bulbous head and hand painted detail is one of the tough Eger baits to find.
Value: $55.00 – 60.00

Bull Nose Frog
Eger Bait Manufacturing Co., Bartow, Florida
Date: c. 1937
Length: 3"
Notes: This version of the previous lure is covered with real frog skin. Eger also covered several of their lures and a couple for Shakespeare with frog skin.
Value: $45.00 – 50.00

Eger Darter 1500 Series
Eger Bait Manufacturing Co., Bartow, Florida
Date: c. 1941
Length: 3⅞"
Notes: Eger Darters are often found covered with frog skin.
Value: $25.00 – 30.00

Junior Dillinger 200 Series
Eger Bait Manufacturing Co., Bartow, Florida
Date: c. 1941
Length: 3⅜"
Notes: The Dillinger Series included larger 3- and 5-hook versions.
Value: $15.00 – 20.00

Baby Dillinger 0 Series
Eger Bait Manufacturing Co., Bartow, Florida
Date: c. 1941
Length: 2"
Notes: The paint style shown is commonly associated with Eger.
Value: $10.00 – 15.00

Sea Dillinger 400 Series
Eger Bait Manufacturing Co., Bartow, Florida
Date: c. 1941
Length: 4"
Notes: A saltwater bait, the Sea Dillinger is basically a 3-hook Dillinger without the propellers.
Value: $10.00 – 15.00

Sea Sargeant
Eger Bait Manufacturing Co., Bartow, Florida
Date: c. 1941
Length: 4¾"
Notes: This attractive fish-shaped Eger lure is rare and desirable.
Value: $50.00 – 55.00

Electrolure
Electrolure Co., Chicago, Illinois
Date: c. 1947
Length: 3⅜"
Notes: This lure uses a battery-lighted bulb and a flashy tail prop to attract fish.
Value: $40.00 – 50.00

Electralure
Electralure, Mentor, Ohio
Date: c. 1995
Length: 2½"
Notes: The Electralure is a recent attempt to catch fish using a lighted bulb. Water apparently acted as a conductor to turn on the light.
Value: $5.00 – 10.00

Jumping Jo
Electronic Units Co., Dayton, Ohio
Date: c. 1946
Length: 3¾"
Notes: Jumping Jo is made of thin metal stamped in two parts and soldered together. As the name would imply, Jo would indeed jump on retrieve.
Value: $25.00 – 35.00

Queen Bingo
Doug English Lure Company, Corpus Christi, Texas
Date: c. 1960
Length: 2⅝"
Notes: The Queen Bingo was a popular Texas saltwater lure.
Value: $5.00 – 10.00

Dardevle; Dardevlet
Lou J. Eppinger, Detroit, Michigan
Date: c. 1906 – present
Length: 3½"; 2¾"
Notes: The Dardevle, one of the all-time bestselling lures, is found in a variety of shapes and sizes. The shape shown is the same as the 1906 Osprey Spoon.
Value: $5.00 – 10.00

Klinker
Lou J. Eppinger, Detroit, Michigan
Date: c. 1930
Length: 1⅞" body
Notes: The unusual Klinker is one of the more difficult Dardevles to find.
Value: $10.00 – 15.00

Winged Husky Devle
Lou J. Eppinger, Detroit, Michigan
Date: c. 1930
Length: 4"
Notes: The sure-hooking Winged Husky Devle is relatively rare. When searching for a more imaginative name for his bait than the Osprey, Lou Eppinger decided on Daredevil but feared negative public response to the word "devil." Thus, the change in spelling to "devle."
Value: $20.00 – 25.00

Eppinger Osprey No Tangle Casting Spinner
Lou J. Eppinger, Detroit, Michigan
Date: c. 1930
Length: 1¼" blade
Notes: This spinner features a hook release for changing hooks.
Value: $10.00 – 15.00

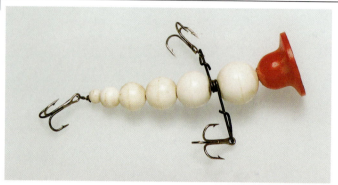

Helga-Devil
Etchen Tackle Co., Detroit, Michigan
Date: c. 1946
Length: 3¾"
Notes: This unusual lure was designed as a floating "plunker" — perhaps the white beads offered a sonic quality.
Value: $20.00 – 25.00

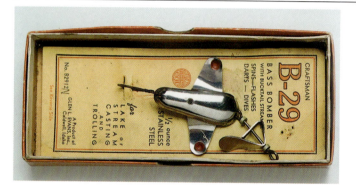

B-29 Bass Bomber
Glen L. Evans, Inc., Caldwell, Idaho
Date: c. 1946
Length: 2" body
Notes: This post-WWII lure pays tribute to the U.S. Air Corps B-29 Bomber.
Value: $15.00 – 20.00

Atomic Bass Buster
Glen L. Evans, Inc., Caldwell, Idaho
Date: c. 1946
Length: 4½" overall
Notes: After WWII ended, the word "atomic" was popular in everyday usage and in advertising, implying a hi-tech attitude. Perhaps Glen Evans thought "atomic" would make fish bite?
Value: $15.00 – 20.00

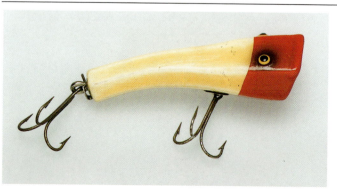

Blooper
Glen L. Evans, Inc., Caldwell, Idaho
Date: c. 1948
Length: 3¼"
Notes: The five-sided Blooper is an attractive and somewhat rare lure.
Value: $30.00 – 40.00

Sashay Minnow
Glen L. Evans, Inc., Caldwell, Idaho
Date: c. 1968
Length: 4"
Notes: The Sashay Minnow was designed to compete with the popular Rapala.
Value: $10.00 – 15.00

Gad-About
Glen L. Evans, Inc., Caldwell, Idaho
Date: c. 1968
Length: 1" body
Notes: The Gad-About featured a wobbling lip and a dressed treble hook.
Value: $5.00 – 10.00

Shyster
Glen L. Evans, Inc., Caldwell, Idaho
Date: c. 1968
Length: 1" body
Notes: The Shyster was a close competitor of the Abu Spinner.
Value: $5.00 or less

Weed Queen
Evans Walton Company, Detroit, Michigan
Date: c. 1936
Length: 2⅝"
Notes: This lure has spring hooks designed to release when a fish strikes.
Value: $40.00 – 50.00

The Ewelure
Ewell Parker Co., Amarillo, Texas
Date: c. 1958
Length: 1⅞"
Notes: The stubby Ewelure features a jointed tail and a solid plastic body.
Value: $15.00 – 20.00

Twinkle Bug
F.M.F. Lures, Gadsden, Alabama
Date: c. 1960
Length: 3¾"
Notes: This is a battery-powered lighted lure which would spin on retrieve, causing a loose BB inside to make and break the battery contact, causing the light bulb to flicker.
Value: $25.00 – 30.00

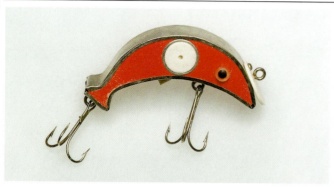

Bubble Minnie
Fair Play Industries, Detroit, Michigan
Date: c. 1948
Length: 3⅛"
Notes: A bubble tablet inserted into the side of this lure would foam and bubble when the lure contacted the water.
Value: $20.00 – 25.00

Bubble Sally
Fair Play Industries, Detroit, Michigan
Date: c. 1948
Length: ¾"
Notes: Like the Bubble Minnie, this lure used a special tablet to cause a fish-attracting bubbling action in the water.
Value: $15.00 – 20.00

Pop-Eye
Fetchi-Lure Company, Kansas City, Missouri
Date: c. 1954
Length: 3⅛"
Notes: The appropriately-named Pop-Eye came in a fitted cardboard box with a plastic lid.
Value: $5.00 – 10.00

Dizzy Diver
Fishathon Bait Manufacturing Co., Okmulgee, Oklahoma
Date: c. 1947
Length: 2⅛"
Notes: This Oklahoma-made diver was designed to run deep and was popular for fishing in the state's large impoundments.
Value: $10.00 – 15.00

Dizzy Crawdad
Fishathon Bait Manufacturing Co., Okmulgee, Oklahoma
Date: c. 1947
Length: 2⅛"
Notes: The Dizzy Crawdad is basically a Dizzy Diver with bead eyes on the tail end.
Value: $20.00 – 25.00

Dizzy Floater
Fishathon Bait Manufacturing Co., Okmulgee, Oklahoma
Date: c. 1947
Length: 3¾"
Notes: This lure copied the design of Heddon's Lucky 13 and was often fitted with a prop at the tail.
Value: $10.00 – 15.00

Dalton Special
Florida Fishing Tackle Co., St. Petersburg, Florida
Date: c. 1948
Length: 3¾"
Notes: P.P. Dalton filed a patent application for this prolific fish catcher in 1939. After an unsatisfactory relationship with Shakespeare, who made the lure for a time, he sold his rights to the Dalton Special to the Florida Fishing Tackle Co.
Value: $5.00 – 10.00

Fly Boy
Fly Boy Lures, Inc., Shawnee Mission, Kansas
Date: c. 1974
Length: 3"
Notes: This innovative deep diver has adjustable wings which can be locked in place with a belly-mounted set screw, giving a variety of depth options.
Value: $15.00 – 20.00

Rocket Racer
Foster Enterprises, Wayne, Michigan
Date: c. 1960
Length: 3¼"
Notes: The Rocket Racer featured a removable cap at the rear which allowed a live minnow to be inserted.
Value: $5.00 – 10.00

Fury

Fury Manufacturing Co., Brighton, Michigan
Date: c. 1948
Length: 2⅝"; 2"; 1⅛"
Notes: Interchangeable bodies/hooks were a big selling point for the Fury. A variety of sizes and colors were available.
Value: $5.00 – 10.00

Gene's Gem

G.G. Bait Company, Flint, Michigan
Date: c. 1949
Length: 3⅜"
Notes: This plastic lure featured BBs inside the body to create a fish-attracting rattle.
Value: $5.00 – 10.00

Twin Dancer

Gardner Specialty Company, Gardner, Massachusetts
Date: c. 1948
Length: 3"
Notes: The lip on this lure could be swiveled 180° to alter the action.
Value: $15.00 – 20.00

Genalure

Genalure Co., St. John, Indiana
Date: c. 1986
Length: 2¼"
Notes: This lure design features a small propeller-driven generator inside which powers a light bulb when pulled through the water.
Value: $30.00 – 35.00

Magnetic Weedless

General Tool Company, St. Paul, Minnesota
Date: c. 1947
Length: 3"
Notes: This lure features an easily tripped magnetic weedguard.
Value: $15.00 – 20.00

Spoon Fin
General Tool Company, St. Paul, Minnesota
Date: c. 1947
Length: 2¾"
Notes: This good-looking lure features glass eyes and moveable fins.
Value: $15.00 – 20.00

The Gen-Shaw Bait (2 joints)
Gen-Shaw Bait Company, Kankakee, Illinois
Date: c. 1950 – 1953
Length: 3½"
Notes: Most Gen-Shaws found by collectors are made of plastic. The example shown is an early wood version.
Value: $35.00 – 40.00

The Gen-Shaw Bait (1 joint)
Gen-Shaw Bait Company, Kankakee, Illinois
Date: c. 1950 – 1953
Length: 3"
Notes: This is a single-joint version of the previous lure and shows the larger eye used in the plastic versions.
Value: $60.00 – 70.00

The Gen-Shaw Bait (2 joints)
Gen-Shaw Bait Company, Kankakee, Illinois
Date: c. 1950 – 1953
Length: 3½"
Notes: This is the common plastic version of the Gen-Shaw bait which features large eyes.
Value: $15.00 – 20.00

Paddle Popper
Gi-Gi Lure Company, Fort Worth, Texas
Date: c. 1966
Length: 2¼"
Notes: The "arms and hands" actually appear to swim when this lure is retrieved.
Value: $15.00 – 20.00

Bass Bird
J.J. Gill & Associates, Huntington Park, California
Date: c. 1946
Length: 3¾"
Notes: Made with a hollow aluminum body, this surface lure has characteristics of several surface lures from the late 1800s and early 1900s.
Value: $30.00 – 35.00

The Jumper
Gilmore Tackle Company, Lurton, Arkansas
Date: c. 1974
Length: 4"
Notes: The Jumper is still a very popular surface bait in the Ozarks.
Value: $5.00 or less

The Hoodler
Gilmore Tackle Company, Lurton, Arkansas
Date: c. 1974
Length: 4"
Notes: The floating/diving Hoodler still catches a lot of fish in Ozark lakes.
Value: $5.00 or less

Saf-T-Lure
Glenwillow Products, Cleveland, Ohio
Date: c. 1947
Length: 2⅛"
Notes: The treble hook could be retracted into the body of this lure so that it could be safely carried in a pocket.
Value: $30.00 – 35.00

Saf-T-Lure
Glenwillow Products, Cleveland, Ohio
Date: c. 1947
Length: 4½"
Notes: This is the largest Saf-T-Lure and features the same "no-tangle" hook storage design as the small version. A middle-size model was also made.
Value: $55.00 – 60.00

The Gopher
Gopher Baits, Sheboygan, Wisconsin
Date: c. 1960
Length: 5¾"
Notes: Originally made with glass eyes, this is a large lure with a lot of surface action designed to attract large fish.
Value: $25.00 – 30.00

Captive Catch
Gourmet Lures, Inc., Shawnee Mission, Kansas
Date: c. 1990
Length: 3⅜"; 1⅜"
Notes: These lures are recent wiggling versions of the glass minnow tubes in use in the early 1900s.
Value: $5.00 – 10.00

Bumble Bug
Gowen Manufacturing Co., Gowen, Michigan
Date: c. 1950
Length: 2⅞"
Notes: Originally made of wood, this plastic lure had a metal apparatus which moved when the prop turned. Pork rind clamped in metal clips would wiggle in the water like frog legs.
Value: $10.00 – 15.00

We-D-Fyer (surface)
Great Lakes Bait Co., Detroit, Michigan
Date: c. 1958
Length: 2¾"
Notes: This is a surface lure with a single hook hidden in the body, making it weedless until a fish touching the notched "backbone" released the hook.
Value: $20.00 – 25.00

We-D-Fyer (diver)
Great Lakes Bait Co., Detroit, Michigan
Date: c. 1958
Length: 2¾"
Notes: This is the diving version of the We-D-Fyer and uses the same touch controlled weedless design.
Value: $20.00 – 25.00

Blockhead Frog Surface Lures
Earl Gresh, St. Petersburg, Florida
Date: c. 1940
Length: 3⅝"
Notes: Ear Gresh was a Florida boat builder, artist, and woodworker in addition to being a lure maker. Gresh's well-crafted lures are highly sought after by collectors.
Value: $125.00 – 150.00

No. 1 Laminated Wood "6-Pack" Lure
Earl Gresh, St. Petersburg, Florida
Date: c. 1940
Length: 4½"
Notes: Made especially for packaging in a "6-Pack" presentation box (see page 364), this beautiful lure is made of laminated mahogany.
Value: $125.00 – 175.00

No. 4 Potbelly "6-Pack" Lure
Earl Gresh, St. Petersburg, Florida
Date: c. 1940
Length: 3⅝"
Notes: This attractive surface lure features two spinners and a nice paint finish.
Value: $125.00 – 150.00

No. 5 "6-Pack" Top Water Lure
Earl Gresh, St. Petersburg, Florida
Date: c. 1940
Length: 3¼"; 3¾"
Notes: The bottom lure shows Earl Gresh's unusual "sawtooth scale" finish.
Value: $125.00 – 150.00

No. 6 Octagon "6-Pack" Lure
Earl Gresh, St. Petersburg, Florida
Date: c. 1940
Length: 3"
Notes: This attractive floater features double props and Gresh's wonderful sense of proportion.
Value: $200.00 – 250.00

Surface Bass Dalton Special Type Lures
Earl Gresh, St. Petersburg, Florida
Date: c. 1940
Length: 4⅛"
Notes: These lathe-turned and hand-shaped lures are basic surface designs. Note the two sets of eyes on the middle lure, giving the appearance of two fish.
Value: $200.00 – 250.00

Bill's Lucky-Strike Minnow
W.J. Grube, Delaware, Ohio
Date: c. 1940
Length: 1⅝"
Notes: This is a small, stout rubber lure with clever and attractive design features. Grube was also a maker of rubber insects.
Value: $30.00 – 35.00

Nimble Nose
Gudebrod Bros. Silk Co., Inc., Philadelphia, Pennsylvania
Date: c. 1975
Length: 2⅞"
Notes: Made in several sizes, the Nimble Nose features several common Gudebrod characteristics: transparent body with foil insert, scale texture, and large, realistic eyes.
Value: $5.00 – 10.00

Bippie
Gudebrod Bros. Silk Co., Inc., Philadelphia, Pennsylvania
Date: c. 1975
Length: 2"
Notes: This chunky floater features a tail spinner and a wide-grooved mouth.
Value: $5.00 – 10.00

Basspirin
Gudebrod Bros. Silk Co., Inc., Philadelphia, Pennsylvania
Date: c. 1975
Length: 2"
Notes: A 2¾" Basspirin was also made.
Value: $5.00 – 10.00

Bump 'n' Grind; Sinner Spinner; Blabber Mouth
Gudebrod Bros. Silk Co., Inc., Philadelphia, Pennsylvania
Date: c. 1975
Length: 1⅝"; 1⅝"; 1¾"
Notes: These beautiful little spinning lures were also made in casting sizes.
Value: $5.00 – 10.00

Easy-Boy Plug with Strip-Teaser Jackets
H & H Plug Co., Waterloo, Iowa
Date: c. 1954
Length: 2⅛"
Note: Different color jackets could be slipped onto this lure to quickly change colors.
Value: $35.00 – 40.00

Halik Frog "Senior"
The Halik Co., Moose Lake, Minnesota
Date: c. 1949
Length: 2¼"
Notes: Upon returning from WWII and at the suggestions of his friend Carl Meyers, Ike Boekenoogen scrapped the notion of making toys in favor of making this mechanical frog.
Value: $30.00 – 35.00

Halik Frog "Junior"
The Halik Co., Moose Lake, Minnesota
Date: c. 1949
Length: 1¾"
Notes: This is the small version of the Halik Frog.
Value: $30.00 – 35.00

"H.J.S." Wiggler Bait
Hardy Brothers, Alnwick, England
Date: c. 1936
Length: 3½"
Notes: Historically, Hardy has played a prominent part in the development of fishing tackle dating into the 1800s. This attractive lure is made of wood and features removable belly weights.
Value: $55.00 – 65.00

Cat's Paw Weedless Casting Bait
Wilson W. Hargrett, Detroit, Michigan
Date: c. 1940
Length: 3¼"
Notes: The metal plate under this bait acts as a lever to open up two single hooks when a fish bites the lure.
Value: $25.00 – 35.00

Bill Plummer's Frog (Superfrog)
Harrison-Hoge Industries, St. James, New York
Date: c. 1960 – present
Length: 2" body, 1⅜" body
Notes: Bill Plummer's Frog features an unusual weedguard for fishing the soft, natural-looking bait in heavy weeds.
Value: $5.00 – 10.00

Weighted Finned Minnow
Jim Harvey/Local Industries, Inc., Lakeville, Connecticut
Date: c. 1942
Length: 3"
Notes: Way ahead of his time, Jim Harvey coated his lures with a heavy lacquer finish, giving them the look of today's epoxy flies.
Value: $25.00 – 30.00

McLeod's Universal
Irving Haug, Detroit, Michigan
Date: c. 1947
Length: 3"
Notes: This "screw-apart" bait could be fished as is or with a live minnow inside. Note the adjustable aluminum wings.
Value: $20.00 – 25.00

Bombardier
Hawk Fish Lure Corp., St. Louis, Missouri
Date: c. 1949
Length: 1½"
Notes: Olan Lavern Hawk and his son Dave began this company and after changing ownership several times, resumed production in Arkansas where they also made the Lucky Bug.
Value: $5.00 – 10.00

Lucky Bug
Cap't & Dave Fish Lure Co., Harrison, Arkansas
Date: c. 1949
Length: 2⅛"
Notes: The large number of color patterns produced give the Lucky Bug an attractive and inexpensive display potential. This design was named the Hawk when it was made in St. Louis.
Value: $10.00 – 15.00

Injured Shad
Dave Hawk Lure Co., Harrison, Arkansas
Date: c. 1950
Length: 2"
Notes: This wooden lure is often confused with the plastic Phillips #300 Crippled Killer.
Value: $15.00 – 25.00

Multilure
Boyd Hayden & Co., Watertown, Massachusetts
Date: c. 1950
Length: 3¾"
Note: The Multilure featured interchangeable color inserts.
Value: $5.00 – 10.00

Multi-Zig
Boyd Hayden & Co., Watertown, Massachusetts
Date: c. 1950
Length: 3⅛"
Notes: Similar to the Multilure, the Multi-Zig featured side-mounted treble hooks.
Value: $5.00 – 10.00

Flatfish
Helin Tackle Co., Detroit, Michigan
Date: patented September 12, 1933
Length: 3⅜"
Notes: Charles Helin advertised the Flatfish as being the world's bestselling lure.
Value: $5.00 – 10.00

Swimmerspoon

Helin Tackle Co., Detroit, Michigan
Date: c. 1960
Length: 2⅝" overall
Notes: This lure has a painted plastic body to give a more colorful three-dimensional quality.
Value: $10.00 – 15.00

Fishcake

Helin Tackle Co., Detroit, Michigan
Date: c. 1956
Length: 2¼"
Notes: Made in several sizes, the Fishcake was a forum for Charles Helin's political ideals — the black spinners turned right and the red spinners (red as in Communist) to the left.
Value: $10.00 – 15.00

Bag-O-Mad Jr.

Bill Herington Bait Co., Green City, Missouri
Date: c. 1935
Length: 2¾"
Notes: This wood lure had two holes in the face which exited out holes on each side, an interesting and early "flow-thru" design.
Value: $40.00 – 50.00

Herb's Dilly

J.M. Herbert, Indiana
Date: c. 1940
Length: 1¾"
Notes: This is an early "Buzz Bait" featuring an off-balance blade design.
Value: $10.00 – 15.00

Herter's Guide Minnow

Herter's Inc., Waseca, Minnesota
Date: c. 1965
Length: 3"
Note: Herter's catalog was a dream book for a lot of fishermen who still chuckle about the "world famous" phrase which was often used to describe their versions of existing lures. Nonetheless, Herter's numerous lures make them an enjoyable and inexpensive collectible.
Value: $5.00 or less

Herter's Canadian Otter
Herter's Inc., Waseca, Minnesota
Date: c. 1965
Length: 3"
Notes: Like the Guide Minnow, this fur-trimmed lure design is based on the Lazy Ike.
Value: $5.00 or less

Herter's Leprechaun
Herter's Inc., Waseca, Minnesota
Date: c. 1965
Length: 2¾"
Notes: This "Lazy Ike" design features a metal diving bill.
Value: $5.00 or less

Herter's Injured Minnow
Herter's, Inc., Waseca, Minnesota
Date: c. 1965
Length: 2¾"
Notes: This handsome side-floating minnow appears to be an original Herter's design.
Value: $5.00 or less

Herter's Mouse
Herter's Inc., Waseca, Minnesota
Date: c. 1965
Length: 2¾"
Notes: Similar to the CCBCO and Shakespeare Mice, this version is flatter and wider in profile.
Value: $5.00 or less

Herter's Famous Texas Big Eye
Herter's Inc., Waseca, Minnesota
Date: c. 1965
Length: 3¼"
Notes: This lure was made to compete with the "Bingo style" Texas lures.
Value: $5.00 or less

Herter's Moselle Lure

Herter's Inc., Waseca, Minnesota
Date: c. 1968
Length: 1½" shaft
Notes: Herter's often had their metal lures made in Japan. This lure has no place of manufacture stamped on it. Clearly it was made to compete with the multitude of French spinners flooding the American lure market.
Value: $5.00 or less

Herter's Swiss Spoon; Herter's Spoon; Herter's Indian Mouse; Herter's French Canadian

Herter's Inc., Waseca, Minnesota
Date: c. 1968
Length: 2"; 1¾"; 1⅞"; 1⅝"
Notes: This is a small selection of Herter's Spoons which were made in Japan.
Value: $5.00 or less

Herter's India Mahseer Spoon

Herter's Inc., Waseca, Minnesota
Date: c. 1968
Length: 1¾"
Notes: This design mimics Pflueger's Chum Spoon. Herter's loved to add spinners to give the effect of moving fins.
Value: $5.00 or less

Herter's Snake Tail

Herter's Inc., Waseca, Minnesota
Date: c. 1968
Length: 2½"
Notes: This multiple spinner lure has" Made in Japan" stamped in ink on the underside.
Value: $5.00 or less

Herter's Thor Spoon

Herter's Inc., Waseca, Minnesota
Date: c. 1964
Length: 2⅜"
Notes: Thor is an attractive bead-eyed spoon which was made in Japan.
Value: $5.00 or less

Herter's Atlas
Herter's, Inc., Waseca, Minnesota
Date: c. 1968
Length: 2¼"
Notes: The Atlas looks like a version of Pflueger's Limper Spoon.
Value: $5.00 or less

Herter's Authentic Russian Spoon
Herter's, Inc., Waseca, Minnesota
Date: c. 1968
Length: 3⅝"
Notes: This nicely painted spoon has yellow glass bead eyes.
Value: $5.00 or less

Herter's Red Eye
Herter's Inc., Waseca, Minnesota
Date: c. 1968
Length: 1⅞"
Notes: Like its predecessor, the Red Eye Wiggler, this spoon has red glass eyes.
Value: $5.00 or less

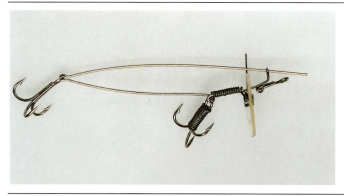

Herter's Hook Harness
Herter's, Inc., Waseca, Minnesota
Date: c. 1955
Length: 4"
Notes: Herter's Hook Harness appears to be their own design and was touted as having been outlawed on some waters because it was so deadly when a live minnow was impaled upon it.
Value: $5.00 or less

Wonder Bug
Mike Hildreth, Gunnison, Colorado
Date: c. 1963
Length: 2¾"
Notes: This handmade lure was copied from a bug Mike Hildreth discovered in Mexico c. 1927. Only one color was available.

Hinkle Lizard
Joe B. Hinkle, Louisville, Kentucky
Date: c. 1946
Length: 6"
Notes: This plastic three-piece lizard had a lot of surface action and featured natural paint finishes.
Value: $30.00 – 35.00

Bon-Net Lure
W.H. Hobbs Supply Co., Eau Claire, Wisconsin
Date: c. 1952
Length: 3⅝"
Notes: This large 6-hook surface lure is similar in looks to Heddon's #300 but uses surface hook rigging.
Value: $40.00 – 50.00

Red Eye Wiggler
The Hofschneider Corp., Rochester, New York
Date: c. introduced in 1928
Length: 3"
Notes: The Red Eye Wiggler featured red glass bead eyes and a highly polished surface.
Value: $5.00 or less

Red Eye Junior
The Hofschneider Corp., Rochester, New York
Date: c. 1954
Length: 1⅜" blade
Notes: This is a spinning version of the Red Eye Wiggler mounted on a shaft.
Value: $5.00 or less

Butch; Sourpuss
Holdenline Co., Cleveland, Ohio
Date: c. 1937
Length: 2¾"; 3"
Notes: These clear plastic lures featured somewhat realistic inserts sealed inside. Ribs cut into the plastic added to the lure's realism.
Value: $10.00 – 15.00

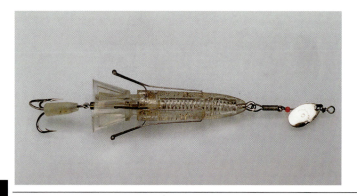

Missile-Lure
Holiday Products, Amarillo, Texas
Date: c. 1965
Length: 3"
Notes: The weedguard design makes this lure look like a rocket or missile, thus the name.
Value: $15.00 – 20.00

Skipper
Hom-Art Bait Co., Akron, Ohio
Date: c. 1946
Length: 2½"
Notes: Looking very much like an Arbogast Jitterbug with holes in the lip, the Skipper had a diving sibling named the Dipper.
Value: $20.00 – 25.00

Hoot Spinner
Hoot Spinner Co., Los Angeles, California
Date: c. 1939
Length: 1¾"
Notes: The card for this lure says it all.
Value: $10.00 – 15.00

Shmoo Plug-Bait
Horrocks-Ibbotson Co., Utica, New York
Date: c. 1950
Length: 2⅞"
Notes: This little wood novelty bait was named after the happily prolific little character in the Lil' Abner comic strip.
Value: $60.00 – 100.00

The Twiggler Bait
F.H. Horvath, Little Workshop, Westminster West, Vermont
Date: c. 1954
Length: 2⅞"
Notes: This little surface buzzer had a lot of splash and action.
Value: $15.00 – 20.00

Houser Hell Diver

The House of Houser, St. Louis, Missouri
Date: c. 1950
Length: 6" box width
Notes: The Hell Diver is considered by many to be the first large blade spinner bait. It was produced with either Colorado or Willowleaf blades.
Value: $5.00 – 10.00

Rattalur

Hubs Chub, Arcadia, Indiana
Date: c. 1980
Length: 3⅞"
Notes: The Rattalur featured interior rattles and angled cuts along the side for surface action.
Value: $5.00 or less

The Byonic Lure

Invader Lure Co., Highland, California
Date: c. 1970
Length: 3½"
Notes: It seems logical that a Byonic Lure would accompany the technological age and the Bionic Man.
Value: $30.00 – 35.00

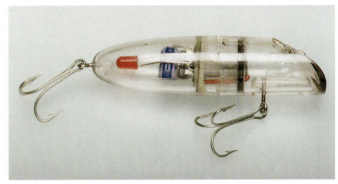

Jack's Dual Spinner

Jack's Lures, Columbus, Indiana
Date: c. 1940
Length: 1½"
Notes: This lure gave the appearance of a crawfish when fished on ledges and drop-offs in deep impoundments.
Value: $5.00 or less

Rip-L-Lure

Jack's Tackle Mfg. Co., Oklahoma City, Oklahoma
Date: c. 1948
Length: 3"
Notes: This lure is well crafted and features a swiveling "lip" and gorgeous paint job.
Value: $30.00 – 35.00

Jointed Wig-L-Lure
Jack's Tackle Mfg. Co., Oklahoma City, Oklahoma
Date: c. 1948
Length: 3¾"
Notes: This is the jointed version of the Rip-L-Lure.
Value: $30.00 – 35.00

Pogo Stick
Jack's Tackle Mfg. Co., Oklahoma City, Oklahoma
Date: c. 1955
Length: 3¾"
Notes: The plastic Pogo Stick is a surface lure which features a long "keel."
Value: $5.00 – 10.00

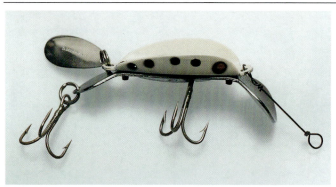

Jack's Luck-E-Lure
Jack's Tackle Mfg. Co., Oklahoma City, Oklahoma
Date: c. 1955
Length: 2⅜" overall
Notes: This neat little metal bait has a double lip similar to the Shakespeare Dopey.
Value: $5.00 – 10.00

Jacobs Polly-Frog
E.L. Jacobs, Vicksburg, Michigan
Date: c. 1942
Length: 2"
Notes: The handmade Polly-Frog has great comic character and eye appeal. It is relatively rare.
Value: $35.00 – 40.00

Beetle-Plop
The W.J. Jamison Co., Chicago, Illinois
Date: c. 1938
Length: 1¾"
Notes: The Coaxer-like Beetle-Plop was one of Jamison's early efforts at making a plastic lure.
Value: $25.00 – 30.00

MISCELLANEOUS LURES

Jamison Wig-L-Twin
The W.J. Jamison Co., Chicago, Illinois
Date: c. 1939
Length: 2½"
Notes: The strange looking Wig-L-Twin has great eye appeal with its nice paint, drooping nose, and trailing spinners.
Value: $15.00 – 20.00

Jamison Quiverlure
The W.J. Jamison Co., Chicago, Illinois
Date: c. 1940
Length: 3"
Notes: Containing twisted pieces of flat wire that quivered when the lure moved, this lure was made in three sizes and was also later manufactured by the Dillon Beck Mfg. Co.
Value: $20.00 – 25.00

Twin Spinner
The W.J. Jamison Co., Chicago, Illinois
Date: c. 1940
Length: 4¼" overall
Notes: Jamison popularized the Twin Spinner when they introduced it in 1915.
Value: $5.00 – 0.00

Shannon Spoon
The W.J. Jamison Co., Chicago, Illinois
Date: c. 1940
Length: 1¾"
Note: Part Spoon, part Twin Spin, this lure featured a slotted body, bucktail dressed hook, and a trailing spinner.
Value: $5.00 – 10.00

Bottle Bass Popper – Miller
The W.J. Jamison Co., Chicago, Illinois
Date: c. 1946
Length: 3"
Notes: This Popper makes a great addition to a novelty lure collection. Lone Star and Blatz Beer versions were also made.
Value: $20.00 – 25.00

Bottle Bass Popper – Blatz
The W.J. Jamison Co., Chicago, Illinois
Date: c. 1946
Length: 3"
Notes: This lure is a great addition to a novelty collection.
Value: $20.00 – 25.00

Jamison Super-Twin
The W.J. Jamison Co., Chicago, Illinois
Date: c. 1954
Length: ¾" body
Notes: This is a spinning size Twin-Spin weighted to sink fast and deep.
Value: $5.00 – 10.00

Jarrett Beetle
Jarrett Bait Co., Oklahoma
Date: c. 1950
Length: 1¾" body
Notes: This solid plastic lure features attractive paint and removable legs.
Value: $5.00 – 10.00

Jemco Sonic Lure
Jemco Bait Co., East Gary, Indiana
Date: c. 1956
Length: 2¾"
Notes: A sound is produced by the rotating head when this lure is retrieved.
Value: $20.00 – 25.00

Frog Legs (wood)
Jensen Distributing Co., Waco, Texas
Modern Sporting Goods, Austin, Texas
Date: c. 1940
Length: 1¾"
Notes: This is the first version of the interesting Frog Legs lure. When the line tie is pulled, the legs extend.
Value: $55.00 – 60.00

Jensen Frog Legs (plastic)
Jensen Distributing Co., Waco, Texas
Date: c. 1946
Length: 1½"
Notes: The yellow color is rare in this plastic version of Frog Legs.
Value: $25.00 – 30.00

Jensen Kicker
Jensen Distributing Co., Waco, Texas
Date: c. 1950
Length: 1⅞" body
Notes: This is a surface plunking version of Frog Legs with the same mechanical leg action.
Value: $20.00 – 30.00

Jensen Midget Kicker
Jensen Distributing Co., Waco, Texas
Date: c. 1950
Length: 1⅛"
Notes: This small underwater swimmer had Jensen's kicking legs for great natural action.
Value: $25.00 – 30.00

Jensen Wiggler
Jensen Distributing Co., Waco., Texas
Date: c. 1950
Length: 1¼" body
Notes: This lure looks identical to the standard Jensen Wiggler but has no wiggling lip. Lone Star and Blatz Beer were also made.
Value: $20.00 – 25.00

Cripple Critter Crawfish
Joe-Bob Mfg. Co., Oklahoma City, Oklahoma
Date: c. 1947
Length: 4⅛"
Notes: This impressive crawfish has a plastic body, rubber band legs, bead eyes, and a jointed body. . . a lot of eye appeal.
Value: $15.00 – 20.00

Cripple Critter Diver
Joe-Bob Mfg. Co., Oklahoma City, Oklahoma
Date: c. 1947
Length: 2¼"
Notes: This lure appears to be made from the front section of the Cripple Critter Crawfish with an added lip.
Value: $10.00 – 15.00

MISCELLANEOUS LURES

Johnson Automatic Striker
Carl A. Johnson, Chicago, Illinois
Date: c. 1935
Length: 2¼" body
Notes: This is the smallest of the three Automatic Strikers. Glass eyes, a mechanical apparatus, and great paint combine to give this lure eye appeal and collectibility.
Value: $90.00 – 120.00

Silver Minnow
Louis Johnson Company, Chicago, Illinois
Date: c. 1928
Length: 2⅞", 1⅛"
Notes: The Johnson Silver Minnow was, and still is, a fantastic fish catcher in weedy water. Always well crafted, the drop forged Silver Minnow was either silver, black, or gold plated.
Value: $5.00 or less

Weedless Triple Hook
Louis Johnson Co., Chicago, Illinois
Date: c. 1938
Length: 2½"
Notes: This is a variation on the Silver Minnow using a weedless treble hook.
Value: $5.00 or less

Lujon
Louis Johnson Co., Chicago, Illinois
Date: c. 1947
Length: 1½"
Note: The Lujon was made in a wide variety of sizes. The example shown is one of the smallest.
Value: $5.00 or less

Jordan's Dirigible Minnow
F. Jordan, Mfg., New York, New York
Date: c. 1940
Length: 3¾"
Notes: "Try Diriging" suggests the box for this rare lure. Metal fins in the sides give the lure swimming action.
Value: $60.00 – 90.00

Judge's Jaw Breaker
Judge's Bait Shop, Mt. Vernon, Missouri
Date: c. 1956
Length: 3½"
Notes: This lure was also made in a 2½" length and is a rare lure highly sought after by Missouri collectors.
Value: $30.00 – 35.00

Jet Jiggler
KO Plug Co., Yonkers, New York
Date: c. 1960
Length: 3"
Notes: A serpentine opening runs the length of this lure, creating a jet of water on retrieve.
Value: $25.00 – 30.00

Splash King
Kala Lure Company, Detroit, Michigan
Date: c. 1948
Length: 3¼"
Notes: The wooden Splash King uses two clear plastic lips to give the lure both wiggle and splash.
Value: $25.00 – 30.00

Bass Charger
Katchmore Bait Co., Indiana
Date: c. 1955
Length: 2" body
Note: This is a surface frog type lure which resembles the Comstock Weedless Chunk of 1926. An attachment system was provided for securing pork rind or chamois strip.
Value: $20.00 – 25.00

Flying Fish Lure
Kentucky Bait Co., Kentucky
Date: c. 1960
Length: 3¼"
Notes: This lure has wings that fold back into the body when the line
tie is pulled. Evidence exists suggesting that these lures were painted by the Fred Rinehart Co., makers of the Jinx lure.
Value: $15.00 – 20.00

Fish Call
Keys and Jones Mfg. Co., Ltd., Mountain Home, Arkansas
Date: c. 1969
Length: 3½"
Notes: Water passing through this lure produces a honking sound.
Value: $10.00 – 15.00

Trail-A-Bait
Kringfisher Company, Inc., Mountain View, California
Date: c. 1957
Length: 3"
Notes: The hollow body of this lure is open at each end, allowing scented material, cheese, etc. to be inserted.
Value: $10.00 – 15.00

Keen Kicker Frog
Herman Otto Kuehn
Date: c. 1935
Length: 3"
Notes: This clever mechanical lure was patented in 1932 and was marketed in the mid to late 1930s. A pull on the line
tie causes the legs to kick, and a wobbling motion is provided by the diving lip.
Value: $400.00+

Wiggle Worm
L & L Bait Co., Van Dyke, Michigan
Date: c. 1955
Length: 3¼"
Notes: Usually found in half-red/half-white or solid red, the Wiggle Worm had a lazy wobbling action.
Value: $15.00 – 20.00

Bassmaster; Panfish Master

L & S Bait Company, Bradley, Illinois
Date: c. 1948
Length: 3"; 2½"
Notes: Made first from wood and then plastic, these L & S lures are quite collectible. The top lure features early opaque eyes.
Value: $5.00 or less

Baby Cat

L & S Bait Company, Bradley, Illinois
Date: c. 1950
Length: 3¼"
Notes: The Baby Cat has great eye appeal with its realistically shaped head and attractive eyes.
Value: $5.00 or less

Mirrolure 2M

L & S Bait Company, Bradley, Illinois; Clearwater, Florida
Date: c. 1952
Length: 2"
Notes: L & S adopted the term Mirrolure to describe the reflective material within the clear plastic body.
Value: $5.00 or less

Spin Mirrolure

L & S Bait Company, Bradley, Illinois; Clearwater, Florida
Date: c. 1955
Length: 2", 1½", 1⅜"
Notes: These little lures are great river lures for smallmouth bass.
Value: $5.00 or less

Mirrolure TT18

L & S Bait Company, Bradley, Illinois; Clearwater, Florida
Date: c. 1955
Length: 3½"
Notes: This is a saltwater lure with a speckled Mirrolure finish.
Value: $5.00 or less

Surface Mirrolure 12 MBT
L & S Bait Company, Bradley, Illinois; Clearwater, Florida
Date: c. 1957
Length: 2⅞"
Notes: The MBT code designates this jointed topwater lure as having a bucktail rear hook.
Value: $5.00 or less

"Invertable Saltwater Lure" #99M28
L & S Bait Company, Bradley, Illinois; Clearwater, Florida
Date: c. 1957
Length: 4"
Notes: The lip on this floating lure could be inverted to give either a diving or surface action.
Value: $5.00 or less

Sassy Susie
Lakeside Lure Company, Dallas, Texas
Date: c. 1948
Length: 2½"
Notes: The deep running Sassy Susie features an unusual diving lip and body configuration.
Value: $10.00 – 15.00

Swiv-A-Lure
LaMothe-Stokes, Detroit, Michigan
Date: c. 1949
Length: 3¼", 3⅛"
Notes: Made first of wood (L) and then plastic (R), the Swiv-A-Lure was a complicated wiggling lure design.
Value: $35.00 – 45.00

Land-Em Lure
Land-Em Lure Co., Emmetsburg, Iowa
Date: c. 1938
Length: 3⅝"
Notes: This plastic lure has very sharp, quick, and strong spring hooks. The wise collector keeps the hooks tied in place with string.
Value: $60.00 – 65.00

Weedsplitter
Larson Bait Co., Aitkin, Minnesota
Date: c. 1940
Length: 3"
Notes: This Babe Oreno type lure used an unusual weedless hook design.
Value: $10.00 – 15.00

Weed Splitter Spoon
Larson Bait Co., Aitkin, Minnesota
Date: c. 1940
Length: 3¾"
Notes: This Daredevle "look-alike" has two weedless hooks (belly hook not visible in photo).
Value: $10.00 – 15.00

Lazy Ike
Kautzky Lazy Ike Co., Fort Dodge, Iowa
Date: c. 1938
Length: 4½", 3⅜"
Notes: These lures show the fat, humpy body shape that brought success to the company. Later models would have a painted, flush metal reinforced lip.
Value: $5.00 or less

Deep Ike
Kautzky Lazy Ike Co., Fort Dodge, Iowa
Date: c. 1955
Length: 2½"
Notes: A 3½" size of the Deep Ike was also made.
Value: $5.00 or less

Flex Ike
Kautzky Lazy Ike Co., Fort Dodge, Iowa
Date: c. 1955
Length: 3"
Notes: A jointed body gave an exaggerated wobble to this lure.
Value: $5.00 or less

Top Ike
Kautzky Lazy Ike Co., Fort Dodge, Iowa
Date: c. 1953
Length: 3½"
Notes: This lure was designed to break the surface on retrieve. A 3" size was also produced.
Value: $5.00 or less

Chug Ike
Kautzky Lazy Ike Co., Fort Dodge, Iowa
Date: c. 1950
Length: 2¾"
Notes: The Chug Ike was a streamlined plastic surface "Plunker."
Value: $5.00 or less

Sail Shark
Kautzky Lazy Ike Co., Fort Dodge, Iowa
Date: c. 1960
Length: 1⅜"
Notes: The Sail Shark was called the Shark Ike when it was first marketed.
Value: $5.00 – 10.00

Skitter Ike
Kautzky Lazy Ike Co., Fort Dodge, Iowa
Date: c. 1960
Length: 3"
Notes: This lure was designed to vibrate and break the surface when retrieved quickly.
Value: $5.00 – 10.00

Natural Ike
Kautzky Lazy Ike Co., Fort Dodge, Iowa
Date: c. 1975
Length: 2⅞"
Note: The realistically finished Natural Ike was on the cutting edge of realistically painted crankbaits.
Value: $5.00 – 10.00

Water Ranger
E.H. LeBlanc, Opelousas, Louisiana
Date: c. 1940
Length: 5" overall
Notes: Designed to be fished deep or shallow, the Water Ranger features a well-tied and attractive hook dressing.
Value: $5.00 – 10.00

Chase-A-Bug
Leon Tackle Co., Detroit, Michigan
Date: c. 1956
Length: 3"
Notes: When retrieved, the Chase-A-Bug's propeller turns an inner mechanism which causes the mouth to open and close as if in pursuit of an insect.
Value: $30.00 – 35.00

Kentucky Leader
Lex Baits, Louisville, Kentucky
Date: c. 1955
Length: 2½"
Notes: When retrieved rapidly, this handpainted lure would have a vibrating action.
Value: $10.00 – 15.00

Fisherman's Friend
Liar's Brand
Date: c. 1947
Length: 3¾"
Notes: This unusual glass liquor bottle is a great novelty collectible.
Value: $45.00 – 50.00

Whamee
Lipman Lures, Inc., St. Louis, Missouri
Date: c. 1950
Length: 1¼" diameter body
Notes: Looking like a large eyeball, this spoon-type lure makes a great addition to a novelty collection.
Value: $10.00 – 15.00

Lippy's Big Eye (Baby Special)
Lipman Lures, Inc., St. Louis, Missouri
Date: c. 1950
Length: ½" diameter head
Notes: Simple but stylish, this weight-forward lure features rubber tails.
Value: $5.00 – 10.00

Hungry Jack
Lloyd and Co., Chicago, Illinois
Date: c. 1939
Length: 4½"
Notes: The Hungry Jack has all the eye appeal a collector could want. Glass eyes, fish-eating-fish design, great color, and rarity make this a highly prized collectible.
Value: $300.00+

"Musky" Electrolure
Lloyd and Co., Chicago, Illinois
Date: c. 1939
Length: 4⅝"
Notes: This is the early version of the lighted Electrolure before Lloyd and Co. sold out to Paul Bunyan.
Value: $50.00 – 55.00

Bodi-Action Wobbler
Lloyd and Co., Chicago, Illinois
Date: c. 1939
Length: 3⅛"
Notes: This unusual revolving lure featured spiral fins and a wiggling lip.
Value: $50.00 – 55.00

Lil' Huey
Loomco Products, Transfer, Pennsylvania
Date: c. 1985
Length: 3¼"
Notes: Lil' Huey's big selling point was different colored interchangeable body inserts.
Value: $5.00 – 10.00

Siren Life Action Fishing Lure
Los Angeles, California
Date: c. 1947
Length: 2¼"
Notes: The example shown is missing the rubber "ribbon" between the head and tail. The ribbon would ripple attractively on retrieve.
Value: $15.00 – 20.00

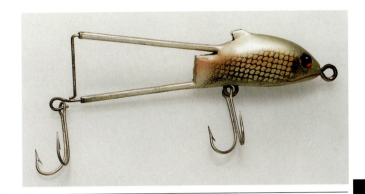

Lovelace Breathing Minnow
Lovelace Mfg. Co., San Antonio, Texas
Date: c. 1938
Length: 3½" overall
Notes: Water flowing through a hole in the head of this lure would fill the cloth tail section, giving a natural look and feel.
Value: $45.00 – 50.00

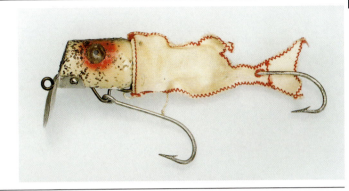

Dubl-Pop
Lucky Day Bait Company, Long Lake, Minnesota
Date: c. 1953
Length: 2¾", 1¾"
Notes: This surface lure features two popping cups.
Value: $10.00 – 15.00

Go-Getter
Lucky Day Bait Company, Long Lake, Minnesota
Date: c. 1953
Length: 3⅝"
Notes: This is a diving version of the Dubl-Pop.
Value: $10.00 – 15.00

Show-Off
Lucky Day Bait Company, Long Lake, Minnesota
Date: c. 1953
Length: 2¾"
Notes: This lure is a floater diver.
Value: $10.00 – 15.00

Holey Cow
Lures and Stuff, Fridley, Minnesota
Date: c. 1994
Length: 3"
Notes: The package for this lure states: "Made in America by Americans from parts made in countries with strange sounding names that you have to get shots to go to."
Value: $5.00 – 10.00

The Flying Pig
Lures and Stuff, Fridley, Minnesota
Date: c. 1993
Length: 2¾"
Notes: Called Sven & Ole's Miracle Lutefisk Lure VII. "Will it catch Lutefisk? Ya, Sure, When Pigs Fly!"
Value: $5.00 – 10.00

Original Polish Bass Plug
Lures and Stuff, Fridley, Minnesota
Date: c. 1993
Length: 1½"
Notes: "If it catches a fish, it's a miracle!"
Value: $5.00 – 10.00

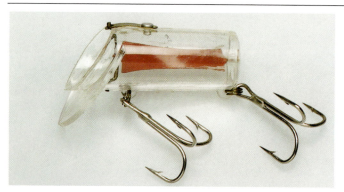

Pluger Joe
Lynx Mfg. Co., Phoenix, Arizona
Date: c. 1960
Length: 2½"
Notes: The colored strip inside this hollow lure is designed to spin when drawn through the water.
Value: $10.00 – 15.00

M.O.S. Combination Bait
M.O.S. Bait Co., Argo, Illinois
Date: c. 1955
Length: 3⅝"
Notes: By twisting the spring-loaded head 180°, this lure could be adjusted for surface or sub-surface fishing.
Value: $30.00 – 35.00

Minno-Bug
Mack's Tackle Workshop, San Antonio, Texas
Date: c. 1946
Length: ¾" body
Notes: The early Minno-Bug featured a more rounded body than the example shown.
Value: $10.00 – 15.00

The Wedge
Philip F. Maguire, Providence, Rhode Island
Date: c. 1946
Length: 2¼"
Notes: The unusually shaped wedge is made of wood and features a metal line tie hinged at the body.
Value: $35.00 – 40.00

Fliko
Makall Corp., Detroit, Michigan
Date: c. 1957
Length: 3⅞" overall
Notes: An internal water driven "screw" mechanism causes Fliko's tail to move back and forth.
Value: $15.00 – 20.00

Series K-10 Waddle Bug
Makinen Tackle Co., Kaleva, Michigan
Date: c. 1947
Length: 2¾"
Notes: This lure was first made of wood (as shown), then made of Tenite plastic in eight colors.
Value: $20.00 – 25.00

Makilure; Junior Makilure
Makinen Tackle Co., Kaleva, Michigan
Date: c. 1947
Length: 3½"; 2⅝"
Notes: This "Bass Oreno" style floater/diver was also made in a musky size.
Value: $15.00 – 20.00

Series L-10 Merry-Widow
Makinen Tackle Co., Kaleva, Michigan
Date: c. 1947
Length: 3¾"
Notes: Made first of wood and later of plastic, this lure features an unusual joint design.
Value: $15.00 – 20.00

Series P-10 Holi-Comet
Makinen Tackle Co., Kaleva, Michigan
Date: c. 1947
Length: 4"
Notes: Originally made of wood and then made of Tenite plastic in eight colors, the Holi-Comet featured a hole through the head.
Value: $15.00 – 20.00

Wonderlure – Series 0-10
Makinen Tackle Co., Kaleva, Michigan
Date: c. 1947
Length: 2½"
Notes: Made of Tenite plastic in eight colors, this lure has spinners imitating pectoral fins.
Value: $15.00 – 20.00

Spin Wonderlure
Makinen Tackle Co., Kaleva, Michigan
Date: c. 1947
Length: 1¾"
Notes: This is the spinning size Wonderlure.
Value: $15.00 – 20.00

Mann's Big Bad Leroy Brown
Mann's Bait Co., Eufaula, Alabama
Date: c. 1983
Length: 2¾"
Notes: This lure was named in honor of Big Bad Leroy Brown, a large bass in the aquarium at Tom Mann's Bait Co. The name was also the title of a popular Jim Croce song.
Value: $5.00 – 10.00

Frog Mann
Mann's Bait Co., Eufaula, Alabama
Date: c. 1984
Length: 3"
Notes: Frog Mann is a stylized frog surface lure.
Value: $5.00 – 10.00

Mann's Hardworm
Mann's Bait Co., Eufaula, Alabama
Date: c. 1984
Length: 5¼"
Notes: The Hardworm looks like a worm but is a hard plastic crankbait with a flipping tail.
Value: $5.00 – 10.00

Tail Chaser
Mann's Bait Co., Eufaula, Alabama
Date: c. 1999
Length: 4"
Notes: This recent lure is a topwater "walking" lure.
Value: $5.00 or less

Dale Earnhardt 200 MPH Crankbait
Mann's Bait Co., Eufaula, Alabama
Date: c. 1997
Length: 3"
Notes: This novel lure was part of NASCAR's 50-year anniversary, and as it turned out, a great souvenir of a great racer, Dale Earnhardt.
Value: $15.00 – 20.00

Manning's Tasty Shrimp Lure Bait
Man's Shrimp Lure Co., New Orleans, Louisiana
Date: c. 1954
Length: 3¾"
Notes: This realistic looking shrimp features monofilament legs/antennae and a screw-apart body which allows real shrimp to be inserted for fish-attracting scent.
Value: $25.00 – 30.00

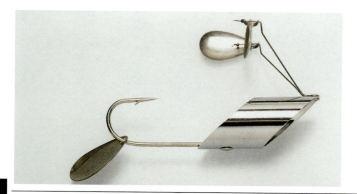

Tubulure
The Manucraft Company, Evergreen Park, Illinois
Date: c. 1958
Length: 1⅞" body
Notes: The plated tube body on this twin-spinnered lure gave it a gliding action.
Value: $5.00 or less

Catwisker
Marathon Bait Company, Wausau, Wisconsin
Date: c. 1950
Length: 4¼" overall
Notes: This attractive lure features a dual offset blade and bucktail tied weedguards from whence the lure got its name.
Value: $10.00 – 15.00

Medium Rattle Spoon
Marathon Bait Company, Wausau, Wisconsin
Date: c. 1965
Length: 2¾"
Notes: This standard style of spoon featured two dangling willow leaf spinners for legs.
Value: $5.00 – 10.00

Martin's Lizzard
Jack Martin, Drumright, Oklahoma
Date: c. 1955
Length: 3"
Notes: Martin's Lizzard was a very popular deep diving lure in its day. Pristine examples are very rare.
Value: $25.00 – 30.00

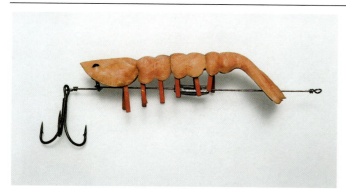

The Martin Shrimp
Martin Bait Co., Amarillo, Texas
Date: c. 1950
Length: 4⅜"
Notes: The segmented sections of this lure move along a shaft which allows a variety of natural shrimp actions.
Value: $25.00 – 30.00

Vee Bug
Martz Tackle Company, Detroit, Michigan
Date: c. 1950
Length: 3⅝"
Notes: The Vee Bug is a floater/diver which was made first in wood and later in plastic.
Value: $10.00 – 15.00

Pop X
Megabass, General Baits, Inc., Japan
Date: c. 1999
Length: 2½"
Notes: This recent floater from Cabella's features flow-thru gills and realistic finish.
Value: $5.00 or less

Mercury Minnow
The Mercoy Tackle Co., Grosse Point, Michigan
Date: c. 1947
Length: 3⅞"
Notes: This plastic "flatfish" type lure has mercury within the body to produce a variety of balance-related actions and sound.
Value: $10.00 – 15.00

Scatback
Mermade Bait Co., Cleveland, Ohio
Date: c. 1948
Length: 2⅝"
Notes: The Scatback is a plastic surface lure with a "walking" plate at the rear. Note the tail hook attachment designed to allow the lure to move freely, independent of the hook.
Value: $15.00 – 20.00

Glitter Glitter
Metro Specialty, Kansas City, Missouri
Date: c. 1976
Length: 2⅜"
Notes: Moving metal flakes floating in an oil-filled cavity gave this lure the appearance of scales on a small fish.
Value: $10.00 – 15.00

Flipper Fish (wooden)
Michigan Tackle Company, Detroit, Michigan
Date: c. 1948
Length: 3½"
Notes: Commonly found made of plastic, this early flipper fish is made of wood.
Value: $30.00 – 35.00

Flipper Fish
Michigan Tackle Co., Detroit, Michigan
Date: c. 1952
Length: 4¼", 1½"
Notes: Shown are the plastic versions of the casting and flyrod size Flipper Fish.
Value: $15.00 – 20.00

Beetle Bug
Millsite, Howell, Michigan
Date: c. 1938
Length: 1" body
Notes: This attractive beetle was an early lure for Millsite who bought the rights to produce it from the Lur-All Co. in 1937.
Value: $20.00 – 25.00

Beetle Bug with Lip
Millsite, Howell, Michigan
Date: c. 1938
Length: 1" body
Notes: The addition of a swimming lip to the Beetle Bug created another lure for Millsite. Beetle type lures are very collectible.
Value: $20.00 – 25.00

Rattle Bug
Millsite, Howell, Michigan
Date: c. 1940
Length: 1¾"
Notes: This great little beetle had a built-in rattle and was made in six colors.
Value: $10.00 – 15.00

Paddle Plug
Millsite, Howell, Michigan
Date: c. 1940
Length: 1¾"
Notes: This is a surface version of the Rattle Bug and features a flat Jitterbug style lip.
Value: $10.00 – 15.00

Daily Double
Millsite, Howell, Michigan
Date: c. 1940
Length: 3⅜"
Notes: This lure featured a line tie at each end, providing two different actions and two different depths.
Value: $10.00 – 15.00

Spin-E-Bee
Millsite, Howell, Michigan
Date: c. 1947
Length: 1½"
Notes: The Spin-E-Bee is a spinning size version of the Millsite 2¾" Bassur.
Value: $5.00 or less

"No-Lip Wig-Wag"
Millsite, Howell, Michigan
Date: c. 1948
Length: 2⅜"
Notes: The authors have not seen this lipless lure catalogued by Millsite, but the lure's characteristics suggest it was made by them. The Wig-Wag had a metal diving lip.
Value: $10.00 – 15.00

Little Mo
Miracle Lure, Inc., Largo, Florida
Date: c. 1956
Length: 2⅞"
Notes: The plastic Little Mo was manufactured in several sizes, using the 1915 Heddon #1600 design.
Value: $10.00 – 15.00

The Mitey Atom
Mitey Atom Tackle Co., Dallas, Texas
Date: c. 1947
Length: 2⅜"
Notes: The wooden Mitey Atom was a Bomber type deep runner shown here in crab finish.
Value: $15.00 – 20.00

Motorola's Flashing LED Fishing Lure
Motorola Semiconductor Products, Inc., Phoenix, Arizona
Date: c. 1985
Length: 4¼"
Notes: The "flashiest lure in the fishing world" from one of America's foremost electronics companies.
Value: $20.00 – 25.00

Crazy Legs
Mueller-Perry Company, St. Louis, Missouri
Date: c. 1975
Length: 2⅝"
Notes: Water turning the tail prop on this lure causes the legs to "dance" when retrieved.
Value: $15.00 – 20.00

Crazy Legs
Mueller-Perry Company, St. Louis, Missouri
Date: c. 1975
Length: 2"
Notes: This is the small version of the Crazy Legs.
Value: $15.00 – 20.00

Multi-Lure
Multi-Lure Co., New Castle, Pennsylvania
Date: c. 1972
Length: 2⅝"
Notes: This lure could easily be changed from surface action to diving by simply reversing the plastic lip.
Value: $10.00 – 15.00

Spin Tail Shad
D.C. Murphy, Lexington, Kentucky
Date: c. 1947
Length: 2"
Notes: This was an early attempt by D.C. Murphy at designing a shad type lure for casting to jumping schools of bass.
Value: $40.00 – 50.00

Murph's Irish Shad
D.C. Murphy, Lexington, Kentucky
Date: c. 1949 – 1952
Length: 2½", 2¾"
Notes: The Irish Shad was a "vibrating" lure featuring a flat back surface.
Value: $20.00 – 25.00

Murph's Fly Size Irish Shad
D.C. Murphy, Lexington, Kentucky
Date: c. 1952
Length: 1¼"
Notes: Shown next to a 2¾" Irish Shad for scale, the flyrod size appears tiny. Ultralight spinning tackle would have made the little lure swim easier than a flyrod would.
Date: $45.00 – 50.00

Murph's Topwater Irish Shad
D.C. Murphy, Lexington, Kentucky
Date: c. 1952
Length: 2¾"
Notes: Made of red cedar, this top water lure was made both with and without a spinnered tail.
Value: $45.00 – 50.00

Murph's "New" Irish Shad; Pregnant Shad
D.C. Murphy, Lexington, Kentucky
Date: c. 1952 – 1953
Length: 2¼", 2¾"; 2⅝"
Notes: The "new" Irish Shad had a narrow rounded back surface. The Pregnant Shad was deeper than the standard version.
Value: $45.00 – 50.00

Mubago Irish Shad
Mubago Bait Co., Lexington, Kentucky
Date: c. 1952 – 1954
Length: 2½"
Notes: This is the plastic version of the Irish Shad, shown in the successful red & yellow "Wolf Creek" color.
Value: $15.00 – 20.00

Mubago Irish Shad
Mubago Bait Co., Lexington, Kentucky
Date: c. 1952 – 1954
Length: 2½"
Notes: Painted in natural trout patterns as an experiment to attract Great Lakes fish, these lures were not offered for sale.
Value: $45.00 – 50.00

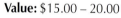

"Mike, The Fisherman's Lure"
My Fair Lady Products, Modesto, California
Date: c. 1960
Length: 3⅛"
Notes: A plastic door in "Mike's" side allowed cheese, fish guts, etc., to be inserted as a fish attractor. Water flowing through the vents dispersed the scent.
Value: $15.00 – 20.00

Old Timer Nipple-Dipper
Nation-Wide Sportsman, Inc., Jackson Center, Ohio
Date: c. 1959
Length: 2"
Notes: This surface "dappling" lure is copied from the Moonlight Fish Nipple of 1911.
Value: $10.00 – 15.00

Strikee Minnow
Naturalure Bait Co., Pasadena, California
Date: c. 1950
Length: 3", 1¼"
Notes: This highly detailed minnow features sharkskin fins which soften and flex naturally when wet.
Value: $25.00 – 30.00

Tropical Floater
Naturalure Bait Co., Pasadena, California
Date: c. 1950
Length: 4"
Notes: This floater features unique propellers and sharkskin fins. Since the sharkskin wrinkles as it dries, collectors have learned to wet the misshapen fins and press them between pieces of folded cardboard to flatten them.
Value: $25.00 – 30.00

Strikie Frog
Naturalure Bait Co., Pasadena, California
Date: c. 1950
Length: 1½"
Notes: The Strikie Frog is rarer than the minnows and features sharkskin legs.
Value: $25.00 – 30.00

Neon Mickey
Neon Mickey Bait Company, Oregon
Date: c. 1955
Length: 4"
Notes: Neon Mickey was designed to light up with movement due to a reaction between the mercury and neon gas sealed inside.
Value: $20.00 – 25.00

Nichols Shrimp
Nichols Lure Co., Corpus Christi, Texas
Date: c. 1938
Length: 3⅝"
Notes: This plastic lure was handmade by Fred Nichols. In 1946 Fred Nichols sold his company which, under the new ownership, became Nichols Lure Co. Inc.
Value: $65.00 – 80.00

Plastic Shrimp Lure
Nichols Lure Co./Nichols Lure Co. Inc., Corpus Christi, Texas
Date: c. 1947
Length: 3¼"
Notes: This version of the Nichols Shrimp was produced after Fred Nichols sold the original company in 1946.
Value: $20.00 – 25.00

Diving Zinger

Nichols Lure Co., Corpus Christi, Texas

Date: c. 1942

Length: 3¼"

Notes: The Diving Zinger is a wood lure designed in the style of the Rush Tango of 1916.

Date: $35.00 – 40.00

Jumbo Killer

Nichols Lure Co./Nichols Lure Co., Inc., Corpus Christi, Texas

Date: c. 1947

Length: 3¾"

Notes: Some confusion exists concerning the Nichols/Pico relationship. In 1948 the Nichols Lure Co. Inc. was sold to Pico (Padre Island Co., San Antonio, Texas). The new company basically produced the same lures but stamped the lure name on the belly. The Nichols lures are not stamped.

Value: $30.00 – 40.00

Junior Killer

Nichols Lure Co./Nichols Lure Co., Inc., Corpus Christi, Texas

Date: c. 1947

Length: 2⅞"

Notes: This is the small version of the Jumbo Killer.

Value: $30.00 – 35.00

Wizzen Killer

Nichols Lure Co./Nichols Lure Co. Inc., Corpus Christi, Texas

Date: c. 1947

Length: 3¾"

Notes: This Nichols Lure is a CCBCO Darter look-alike.

Value: $30.00 – 35.00

Corpus Pet

Nichols Lure Co./Nichols Lure Co. Inc., Corpus Christi, Texas

Date: c. 1947

Length: 2⅜"

Notes: This lure is reminiscent of the Heddon Wood River Runt design of 1935.

Value: $25.00 – 30.00

Mystic Minnow
Nickel Tackle Co., Jacksonville, Florida
Date: c.1950
Length: 3"
Notes: The Mystic Minnow has interchangeable heads and colored body inserts, providing a wide variety of options in a single lure.
Value: $25.00 – 30.00

Nimtz Bait – Twin Spin
Nimtz Bros., Benton Harbor, Michigan
Date: c. 1947
Length: 1¾" body
Notes: This attractive Twin Spinner features mother-of-pearl spinner blades.
Value: $10.00 – 15.00

The Fluke
Norkin Laboratories, Kansas City, Missouri
Date: c. 1959
Length: 1⅜"
Notes: This small buggy looking lure is one of those lures that looks homemade but isn't.
Value: $10.00 – 15.00

Gurgling Joe
North American Specialties, Wayne, Michigan
Date: c. 1940
Length: 2⅞"
Notes: Well made of solid plastic, Gurgling Joe featured a "Jitterbug" style lip and came packaged in a round cardboard tube.
Value: $25.00 – 30.00

Porky Weedless Minnow
Northern Tackle Co., Trevor, Wisconsin
Date: c. 1958
Length: 1¾" body
Notes: The bucktail trailers give this weedless spoon a froggy profile.
Value: $5.00 or less

Curv-A-Lure
Northwood Tackle Co., Royal Oak, Michigan
Date: c. 1951
Length: 3"
Note: This "Flatfish" type lure is shaped in a leftward curve.
Value: $5.00 or less

Sam-Bo
Novelty Lure Co., Lincoln, Nebraska
Date: c. 1952
Length: 2⅞"
Notes: A novelty lure, Sam-Bo is naked when the barrel is lifted.
Value: $25.00 – 30.00

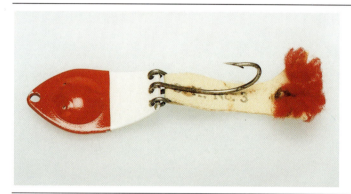

Blackjack Shamyhook
O.K. Bait Co., Chicago, Illinois
Date: c. 1935
Length: 1¾" body
Notes: This neat little spoon was patented by G.T. Buddle, Chicago, Illinois, in 1931, but it is believed that production began in the mid-1930s.
Value: $10.00 – 15.00

Unner-Flash
O.M. Bait Co., Hazel Park, Michigan
Date: c. 1955
Length: 2"
Notes: This nicely crafted lure gets its name from the placement of the spinner under the chin.
Value: $10.00 – 15.00

Wee Pee
"Dar-Gee" Lures, Wagga Wagga, Australia
Date: c. 1997
Length: 2⅜"
Notes: The Wee Pee is a deep running Australian Crank Bait.
Value: $5.00 or less

Glitter Bug
O'Gene Co., Texas
Date: c. 1944
Length: 2"
Notes: The Glitter Bug is a heavy little underwater lure with eccentric props.
Value: $30.00 – 35.00

Weedwing
Johnny O'Neil
Date: c. 1968
Length: 2", 1¾" body
Notes: Designed for fishing in weeds, the Weedwing bears a resemblance to the Johnson Silver Minnow.
Value: $5.00 or less

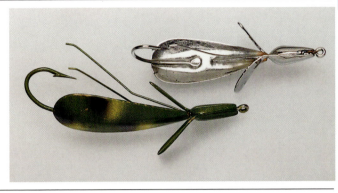

Bottom Scratcher
Orchard Industries, Inc., Detroit, Michigan
Date: c. 1950
Length: 2⅜"
Notes: Probably the most common of the Orchard Industries lures, the Bottom Scratcher came in a very collectible variety of colors.
Value: $25.00 – 30.00

Kick-N-Kackle
Orchard Industries, Inc., Detroit, Michigan
Date: c. 1950
Length: 2½"
Notes: This unusual looking top water features side hooks and a pronounced popping head.
Value: $30.00 – 35.00

Slippery Slim
Orchard Industries, Inc., Detroit, Michigan
Date: c. 1950
Length: 2⅜"
Notes: Slippery Slim is the most difficult of the Orchard Industries lures to find. Note the unusual angled body joint.
Value: $40.00 – 50.00

Woodchopper
Ozark Mountain Lures, Carthage, Missouri
Date: c. 1985
Length: 3", 4", 2¼"
Notes: The Woodchoppers were highly crafted products from Dan and Phil Wyatt.
Value: $5.00 – 10.00

Big Game Woodchopper
Ozark Mountain Lures, Carthage, Missouri
Date: c. 1985
Length: 6⅝"
Notes: This is the largest production lure in the Woodchopper line.
Value: $10.00 – 15.00

Woodwalker
Ozark Mountain Lures, Carthage, Missouri
Date: c. 1985
Length: 4½", 3⅛"
Notes: Well-known Ozarks bass fisherman Charlie Campbell worked with the Woodchopper to develop this "dog walking" topwater lure. Experimental models were tested in the old Drury University swimming pool. The top example is signed.
Value: $15.00 – 20.00

Woodpopper
Ozark Mountain Lures, Carthage, Missouri
Date: c. 1985
Length: 3"
Notes: The Woodpopper was a productive topwater lure with a Woodchopper spinner at the tail. Note the unusual spinner design.
Value: $5.00 – 10.00

Pop-Eye
Ozark Mountain Lures, Carthage, Missouri
Date: c. 1985
Length: 2¼"
Notes: This is the smallest and lightest lure in the Woodchopper line.
Value: $5.00 or less

Experimental Big Game Woodchopper

Ozark Mountain Lures, Carthage, Missouri
Date: c. 1985
Length: 6"
Notes: This large lure was produced during the developmental stage and was custom painted for the authors.
Value: $25.00 – 30.00

Experimental Woodwalker

Ozark Mountain Lures, Carthage, Missouri
Date: c. 1985
Length: 4¼"
Notes: Salvaged from the factory, this lure was an experiment to test the effectiveness of a spinner and weight attached at the nose of a Woodwalker.
Value: $25.00 – 30.00

Experimental Jointed Woodchopper

Ozark Mountain Lures, Carthage, Missouri
Date: c. 1985
Length: 4⅛"
Notes: This experimental bait combined components to produce a jointed surface lure.
Value: $25.00 – 30.00

Famous Red Wing Black Bird

P & V Bait Co., Joliet, Illinois
Date: c. 1960s
Length: 4"
Notes: This large plastic musky bait was also made in a smaller bass size.
Value: $30.00 – 35.00

Mega Bait Yabby

Pace Products Inc., Japan
Date: c. 2000
Length: 2⅜" body
Notes: Although a new lure, this little crawfish lure has a lot of eye appeal.
Value: $5.00 or less

Whirl-A-Way
Pachner and Koehler, Inc., Momence, Illinois
Date: c. 1935
Length: 2⅞"
Notes: Designed to spin violently on retrieve, the plastic Whirl-A-Way had a heavy lead keel to prevent line twist.
Value: $20.00 – 25.00

Bright Eyes
Pachner and Koehler, Inc., Momence, Illinois
Date: c. 1946
Length: 2¾"
Notes: The forward-looking eyes lend a "buggy" quality to this attractive lure. Bright Eyes was made in a variety of colors and makes an attractive display.
Value: $10.00 – 15.00

Amazin' Maizie
Pachner and Koehler, Inc., Momence, Illinois
Date: c. 1946
Length: 2¼"
Notes: The Amazin' Maizie is a diving lure which features an unusual braced diving lip.
Value: $10.00 – 15.00

Spinning Minnie
Pachner and Koehler, Inc., Momence, Illinois
Date: c. 1946
Length: 2¾", 1"
Notes: Shown here in both casting and flyrod size, Spinning Minnie had a rotating body within a wire frame similar to the Bite 'Em bait of 1920.
Value: $10.00 – 15.00

Softy the Wonder Crab
Pachner and Koehler, Inc., Momence, Illinois
Date: c. 1946
Length: 2¼"
Notes: P & K also made two other soft baits: Spotty the Wonder Frog and the P & K Mouse.
Value: $10.00 – 15.00

MISCELLANEOUS LURES

The Baitcasting Feather Minnow
E.H. Peckinpaugh, Chattanooga, Tennessee
Date: c. 1925 – 1950
Length: ¾" head
Notes: This popular lure "carried over" into the 1940s and 1950s. Tied in a variety of patterns, the "Pecks" make a great color display.
Value: $5.00 or less

Streamlined Minnow
Joe E. Pepper Bait Co., Rome, New York
Date: c. 1939
Length: 1½"
Notes: Pepper was making lures in the 1890s and continued in business until 1961. The example shown has a metal body.
Value: $30.00 – 35.00

Red Devil Spinner
Joe E. Pepper Bait Co., Rome, New York
Date: c. 1940
Length: 3¾" shaft
Notes: The attractive Red Devil Spinner features graduated red glass beads on the wire shaft.
Value: $30.00 – 35.00

Pop Eye Wobbler
Joe Pepper Bait Co., Rome, New York
Date: c. 1939
Length: 2¼"
Notes: The Pop Eye Wobbler was also made out of pearl shell.
Value: $5.00 – 10.00

Crippled Killer #1000
Phillips Fly & Tackle Co., Alexandria, Pennsylvania
Date: c. 1950
Length: 2¾"
Notes: This popular surface lure is still being made today.
Value: $5.00 or less

Crippled Killer #300
Phillips Fly & Tackle Co., Alexandria, Pennsylvania
Date: c. 1950
Length: 2"
Notes: This is the small version of the Crippled Killer.
Value: $5.00 or less

Midget Killer #900
Phillips Fly & Tackle Co., Alexandria, Pennsylvania
Date: c. 1950
Length: 1⅜"
Notes: This good-looking little bait is a great "color set" collectible.
Value: $5.00 or less

Fat Boy #1400
Phillips Fly & Tackle Co., Alexandria, Pennsylvania
Date: c. 1950
Length: 1⅜"
Notes: The Fat Boy is a #900 Midget Killer with a feather instead of a treble hook and spinner at the tail.
Value: $5.00 or less

Phillips "Flatside Underwater"
Phillips Fly & Tackle Co., Alexandria, Pennsylvania
Date: c. 1950
Length: 1¾"
Notes: This solid plastic underwater lure uses the standard Phillips prop.
Value: $5.00 or less

"Unknown Spin Phillips"
Phillips Fly & Tackle Co., Alexandria, Pennsylvania
Date: c. 1950
Length: ¾"
Notes: This conical spinning lure was made in two weights.
Value: $5.00 or less

Spin Popper #500
Phillips Fly & Tackle Co., Alexandria, Pennsylvania
Date: c. 1950
Length: 1⅜"
Notes: A 2" size of the Spin Popper was also produced.
Value: $5.00 or less

"Unknown Phillips"
Phillips Fly & Tackle Co., Alexandria, Pennsylvania
Date: c. 1950
Length: 1⅜"
Notes: This lure appears to be a Spin Popper body reversed on the hook.
Value: $5.00 or less

Rainbow Runner
Phillips Fly & Tackle Co., Alexandria, Pennsylvania
Date: c. 1960
Length: 2⅜"
Notes: The Rainbow Runner is an asymmetrically-shaped minnow imitation.
Value: $5.00 or less

Water-Whacker
Piro Realistic-Bait Company, Mangham, Louisiana
Date: c. 1954
Length: 3½"
Notes: By passing the line through the screw eye in the lower lip and attaching it to screw eyes in both the lower and upper lips, the mouth on this lure could be made to snap and bite as it opened and closed.
Value: $30.00 – 35.00

Live Action Minnow
Pit-Kan Bait Co., Pittsburgh, Kansas
Date: c. 1949
Length: 2⅝"
Notes: This is a wood lure with a hole through the body to create a fish-attracting action.
Value: $15.00 – 20.00

Yellow Duckling
Plantico and Son, Stevens Point, Wisconsin
Date: c. 1940
Length: 2¼"
Notes: This lure features a bulbous wood body, plastic diving lip, side hooks, and feather wings. . . a lot of eye appeal.
Value: $20.00 – 25.00

Loco-Motion
Poe's Lure Co., Modesto, California
Date: c. 1960
Length: 2¼"
Notes: Usually found with a belly treble hook instead of fixed side hooks, the Loco-Motion features a spinner in the belly.
Value: $15.00 – 20.00

Poe's RC1
Poe's Lure Co., Modesto, California
Date: c. 1988
Length: 2½"
Notes: This wooden lure is still a competitor in the crankbait market.
Value: $5.00 or less

Poe's Super Cedar Series 300
Poe's Lure Co., Modesto, California
Date: c. 1988
Length: 2¼"
Notes: This deep diver is still popular with bass fishermen.
Value: $5.00 or less

Hot Shot (wood), Hot Shot (flysize)
Eddie Pope & Co., Altadena, California
Date: c. 1950
Length: 2⅜", 1¼"
Notes: The wooden Hot Shot is the early version. The flysize Hot Shot is often collected in color sets.
Value: $25.00 – 30.00; $10.00 – 15.00

Hot Shot
Eddie Pope & Co., Altadena, California
Date: c. 1954
Length: 3¾"
Note: The plastic Hot Shot was a deep diver made in a variety of color patterns.
Value: $5.00 or less

Sea Hawk
Porter Bait Co., Daytona Beach, Florida
Date: c. 1940
Length: 2¾"
Notes: The Sea Hawk is a saltwater bait with attractive paint and a stylized fish shape.
Value: $10.00 – 15.00

Cedar Stump, wood
M.W. Powell, Lexington, Kentucky
Date: c. 1953
Length: 2⅝"
Notes: The Cedar Stump was a competitor of the Mubago Irish Shad in the hot new vibrating lure market.
Value: $15.00 – 20.00

Cedar Stump, plastic
M.W. Powell, Lexington, Kentucky
Date: c. 1954
Length: 2¼"
Notes: This is the more recent plastic version of the Cedar Stump.
Value: $10.00 – 15.00

Powerpak Frog
Powerpak Lures, Inc., Dallas, Texas
Date: c. 1994
Length: 3⅛" overall
Notes: One of the most collectible lures of the 1990s, this frog has a spring-loaded kicking mechanism which is activated by pulling the line tie string out a couple of inches.
Value: $15.00 – 20.00

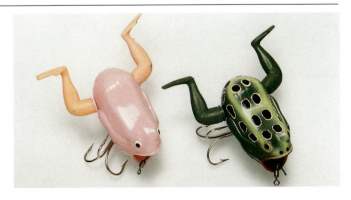

Powerpak Minnow
Powerpak Lures, Inc., Dallas, Texas
Date: c. 1994
Length: 3¾" overall
Notes: The tail on this lure moves rapidly back and forth when the line tie is pulled out.
Value: $15.00 – 20.00

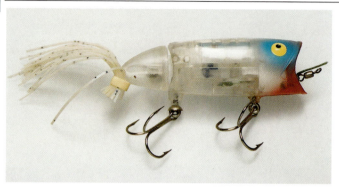

Powerpak Skirted Floater
Powerpak Lures, Inc., Dallas, Texas
Date: c. 1994
Length: 3"
Notes: This lure shakes its "hula skirt" when the line tie is pulled out and released.
Value: $15.00 – 20.00

Rainbow Wiggler
V.O. Pritchard, Springfield, Missouri
Date: c. 1949
Length: 2¾"
Notes: This bait is interestingly constructed of two pieces of Lucite plastic laminated with color in between. An example has been seen with two names stamped on the belly: Pritchard-Anderson.
Value: $20.00 – 25.00

Cyclone Spinner
Puls & Wencka Bait Co., Milwaukee, Wisconsin
Date: c. 1956
Length: 4½"
Notes: Certainly one of the most action-packed topwater lures of all time, the complex Cyclone Spinner was promoted by 1950s basketball star Don Kojis.
Value: $55.00 – 60.00

Pul-V-Riser
Lynn E. Pulver, Swea City, Iowa
Date: c. 1953
Length: 2⅞"
Notes: This lure cleverly uses the maker's last name in the name of the lure, describing the fish catching effectiveness of the lure.
Value: $5.00 – 10.00

Original Floating Rapala

Rapala, Finland

Date: c. 1936 – present

Length: 4", 3"

Notes: The first Rapalas were handmade by Lauri Rapala of pine bark covered with foil. It was thought that the earliest imported balsa Rapalas had stars embossed in the metallic foil. The "diamond" embossed foil shown at bottom likely pre-dates the stars.

Value: $10.00 – 15.00

Original Floating Rapala

Rapala, Finland

Date: c. 1965

Length: 4⅝", 6¼"

Notes: These foil-covered balsa lures represent the "$100.00/day rental" era when demand outweighed supply and can be identified by the "Original Rapala" stamping in black on the diving lip and the word "Finland" stamped on the belly. Early Rapalas featured a white "tape" strip on the belly instead of paint.

Value: $5.00 – 10.00

J-7 Jointed Floating Rapala

Rapala, Finland

Date: c. 1970

Length: 2⅝"

Notes: Like many companies, Rapala found success in a jointed version of their famous lure.

Value: $5.00 or less

Countdown Rapala; Shallow Fat Rap – 3

Rapala, Finland

Date: c. 1970

Length: 3⅜"; 1⅜"

Notes: The Countdown series was designed to sink at a predictable rate to allow fishermen to fish at a particular depth.

Value: $5.00 or less

Magnum Floating Rapala

Rapala, Finland

Date: c. 1970

Length: 6⅞"

Notes: The Magnum size appeared in the 1970 catalog and perhaps earlier. The version shown is a later version with a painted belly.

Value: $5.00 – 10.00

CD-13 Floating Magnum Rapala; CD-18 Sinking Magnum Rapala
Rapala, Finland
Date: c. 1968
Length: 5"; 6⅝"
Notes: This large metal-lipped bait was designed for large game fish.
Value: $5.00 – 10.00

90-7 Deep Diving Rapala; 90 Deep Diving Rapala
Rapala, Finland
Date: c. 1974
Length: 2⁹⁄₁₆"; 3¼"
Notes: The metal lip on these lures is stamped with name and model.
Value: $5.00 or less

FR-7 Fat Rap; FR-5 Fat Rap
Rapala, Finland
Date: c. 1978
Length: 2¾"; 2"
Notes: The Fat Rap Series is still a popular bass lure.
Value: $5.00 or less

Shad Rap Deep Runner-5; Shad Rap Shallow-5
Rapala, Finland
Date: c. 1983
Length: 2⅛"; 2¼"
Notes: The flattened Shad Rap is the first deviation by Rapala from their lures with a round or oval cross section.
Value: $5.00 or less

Pilkki
Rapala, Finland
Date: c. 1985
Length: 2¼"
Notes: This is a solid metal lure designed for ice fishing.
Value: $5.00 or less

Rattl'n Rapala
Rapala, Finland
Date: c. 1991
Length: 2⅞"
Notes: Derivative of Murph's 1950 Irish Shad, this vibrating lure is made of molded plastic with BBs inside 2 interior chambers.
Value: $5.00 or less

Skitter Pop
Rapala, Finland (made in Ireland)
Date: c. 1999
Length: 2¾"
Notes: Rapala's first all-topwater balsa wood lure. Modern Rapalas are made in Ireland.
Value: $5.00 or less

Ray-Lure Plug
Ray-Lure Tackle Co., Dallas, Texas
Date: c. 1954
Length: 2⅞"
Notes: The Ray-Lure Plug is a twisted piece of plastic which spins on a shaft.
Value: $5.00 or less

F-100 Rebel Minnow; Rebel Jointed Minnow; J-49 Rebel Deep Runner; F-49 Rebel Minnow
Plastics Research & Development Corp., Ft. Smith, Arkansas
Date: c. 1969
Length: 3½"; 4½"; 2½"; 1½"
Notes: Rebel was quick to answer the challenge brought by the Rapala of Finland and still successfully competes in today's market.
Value: $5.00 or less

Rebel Humpback
Plastics Research & Development Corp., Ft. Smith, Arkansas
Date: c. 1967
Length: 1¾"
Notes: The Humpback was a short, stubby version of the Rebel Minnow.
Value: $5.00 or less

Rebel Humpy
Plastics Research & Development Corp., Ft. Smith, Arkansas
Date: c. 1970
Length: 1¾"
Notes: This lure answered the demand for a deep running version of the Humpback.
Value: $5.00 or less

Rebel Little Suspend R; Rebel Deep Teeny R
Plastics Research & Development Corp., Ft. Smith, Arkansas
Date: c. 1975
Length: 2"; 1⅝"
Notes: Commonly classified as "alphabet" lures, the "R" Series shared the spotlight with "As," "Bs," "Ns," and "Os" by other manufacturers.
Value: $5.00 or less

Rebel Popper
Plastics Research & Development Corp., Ft. Smith, Arkansas
Date: c. 1969
Length: 3¾"
Notes: This lure uses the traditional design of the CCBCO Plunker of 1927.
Value: $5.00 or less

Rebel Racket Shad
Plastics Research & Development Corp., Ft. Smith, Arkansas
Date: c. 1982
Length: 2⅞"
Notes: The Racket Shad contains BBs which rattle on retrieve. This and several other modern vibrating lures use the 1950 design of Murph's Irish Shad.
Value: $5.00 or less

Rebel Deepwater Crawfish; Rebel Wee Crawfish Floater
Plastics Research & Development Corp., Ft. Smith, Arkansas
Date: c. 1983
Length: 2"
Notes: These "craws" look similar to Bagley's Small Fry Crawfish but are made of plastic.
Value: $5.00 or less

Natural Bream

Plastics Research & Development Corp., Ft. Smith, Arkansas
Date: c. 1985
Length: 2½"
Notes: Rebel also made a natural crappie and was an early manufacturer of "natural finish" lures. The "baitfish" Baby Bream was new in 1979.
Value: $5.00 or less

Rebel Helgrammite; Rebel Teeny Wee Crawfish Floater; Rebel Crickhopper; Rebel Teeny Wee Frog

Plastics Research & Development Corp., Ft. Smith, Arkansas
Date: c. 1985 – 1989
Length: 1¾"; 1½"; 1½"; 1½"
Notes: These readily available ultralight spinning lures are great modern collectibles.
Value: $5.00 or less

Bumble Bug; Creek Creature

Plastics Research & Development Corp., Ft. Smith, Arkansas
Dates: c. 2000; c. 1989
Length: 1⅜"; 1½"
Notes: Like the previous four lures, these lures are made in various colors and are great collectibles.
Value: $5.00 or less

Buzz Tail Frog

Plastics Research & Development Corp., Ft. Smith, Arkansas
Date: c. 1982
Length: 3"
Notes: Frequently misidentified as a rare pre-1900 unknown lure, the plastic Buzz Tail Frog was commonly available in the 1980s.
Value: $5.00 or less

Slick Nike

Reeal Lures, Inc., Three Rivers, Massachusetts
Date: c. 1955
Length: 4⅜"
Notes: Bearing a strong resemblance to the much older Keeling Bearcat of 1920, the box top for the Slick Nike refers to it as a famous Floyd Roman bait.
Value: $15.00 – 20.00

Scooter
Reef Runner Tackle Co., Port Clinton, Ohio
Date: c. 1995
Length: 2⅛"
Notes: This recent lure was made in a variety of beautiful colors and features hooks with barbs on the outside of the points.
Value: $5.00 or less

Crankin Guido Frog
Renosky Lures, Indiana, Pennsylvania
Date: c. 1996
Length: 2⅝"
Notes: This new lure features a jointed head and flashing feet.
Value: $5.00 or less

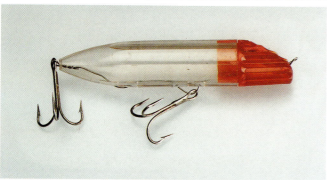

Vita-Lure
Rice Engineering Co. Inc., Detroit, Michigan
Date: c. 1946
Length: 4"
Notes: The Vita-Lure had four interchangeable heads, each a different color.
Value: $10.00 – 15.00

Musky Jinx; Surfcaster; Jinx
Rinehart Tackle Co., Marietta, Ohio
Date: c. 1940
Length: 4¾"; 4¾"; 2¼"
Notes: These plastic lures were offered in numerous beautiful colors and make an eye-catching color display.
Value: $15.00 – 20.00

Musky Buzer; Buzer
Rinehart Tackle Co., Marietta, Ohio
Date: c. 1948
Length: 4¾"; 2¼"
Notes: These lures use the same bodies as the Jinx and Surfcaster but have spinners instead of a diving lip.
Value: $20.00 – 25.00

Chief
Rinehart Tackle Co., Marietta, Ohio
Date: c. 1948
Length: 2⅜"
Notes: The Chief was a River Runt competitor. Note the protruding eyes which are unique among lures of this type.
Value: $15.00 – 20.00

Mud Puppy; River Pup
C.C. Roberts, Mosinee, Wisconsin
Date: c. 1947
Length: 6⅞"; 4½"
Notes: Shown here with painted eyes, the early version of the famous Mud Puppy featured glass eyes.
Value: $25.00 – 30.00

Fincheroo
Robfin, Scottsdale, Arizona
Date: c. 1972
Length: 3¼"
Notes: The plastic Fincheroo is easy to identify by the large hole through the body.
Value: $10.00 – 15.00

Jackrabbit Crankbait (unmarked)
Solly "Jackrabbit", Robicheaux, Louisiana
Date: c. 1970
Length: 3"
Notes: The mad rush toward balsa crankbaits during the late 1960s and early 1970s brought many imitations of the Tennessee Shad, Big O, and Bagley Balsa B's. The Jackrabbit Baits were all hand crafted and enjoyed a popular reputation among fishermen as fish catchers.
Value: $45.00 – 60.00

Jackrabbit Crankbait (marked)
Solly "Jackrabbit", Robicheaux, Louisiana
Date: c. 1972
Length: 3", 2½", 1⅝"
Notes: The later versions of the Jackrabbit Crankbait featured high quality paint jobs and a logo of a bunny stenciled under the diving lip. All Jackrabbit baits are extremely rare.
Value: $45.00 – 60.00

Roller Flasher
Roller Flasher Co., Detroit, Michigan
Date: c. 1949
Length: 2½"
Notes: This lure features a belly strip covered with polished metal.
Value: $30.00 – 40.00

Tumblebug
Ross Bait Co., Akron, Ohio
Date: c. 1947
Length: 3¼"
Notes: The flat-bodied Tumble Bug features a single hook and two weedguards.
Value: $10.00 – 15.00

Russelure Casting Plug
Russelure Mfg. Co., Inc., Los Angeles, California
Date: c. 1949
Length: 2⅛"
Notes: This version of the Russelure features interchangeable anodized aluminum sleeves.
Value: $5.00 – 10.00

Muskie-Head
A. Saarimaa Tackle Co., Lansing, Ontario, Canada
Date: c. 1952
Length: 3"
Notes: This is a spoon-type lure with a wood back for flotation.
Value: $15.00 – 20.00

Bullhead
Salmo, Poland
Date: c. 2000
Length: 2¼"
Notes: This is a new lure purchased from Cabella's who stock a variety of unusual lure designs.
Value: $5.00 or less

Turbulent Surface Lure
O.C. Schaefer, Racine, Wisconsin
Date: c. 1940
Length: 3"
Notes: This festive-looking paint job is typical of Turbulent lures. Several sizes and shapes were made.
Value: $45.00 – 50.00

Charley's Silver Frog
Charles Schilpp, Cleveland, Ohio
Date: c. 1935
Length: 1½" body
Notes: Schlipp worked as a lure designer for Al Foss and stayed on when True Temper purchased the company in 1929. He began his own company, Mill Run Products, after leaving True Temper and made this frog and several other lures.
Value: $45.00 – 50.00

Charley's Crawfish Crawler
Charles Schilpp, Cleveland, Ohio
Date: c. 1935
Length: 1⅝" body
Notes: Like Charley's Silver Frog, this lure bears a strong resemblance to the Al Foss and True Temper lure designs.
Value: $45.00 – 50.00

Scooterpooper
Scooterpooper Sales, Inc., Columbia, South Carolina
Date: c. 1948
Length: 1½" body
Notes: This is a hollow metal surface lure. The example shown has likely had the original treble hooks replaced by a fisherman.
Value: $30.00 – 35.00

Flathead
E.V. Selby and Co., Illinois
Date: c. 1948
Length: 2⅞"
Notes: Inexpensively made, the smiling Flathead was made in several colors.
Value: $5.00 – 10.00

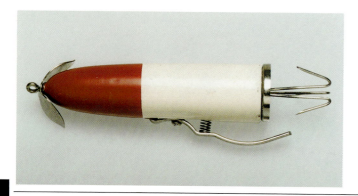

Weed King
Sevdy Automotive Enterprises, Worthington, Minnesota
Date: c. 1950
Length: 3¾"
Notes: By pressing the barbless hooks into the lure body, this lure could be "cocked" and ready to release the hooks into a fish's mouth when struck.
Value: $45.00 – 50.00

Six's Special
Charles M. Six Company, Carthage, Missouri
Date: c. 1950
Length: 2¼"
Notes: The Six's Special was a major competitor of the Clark Water Scout and a great fish catcher as well.
Value: $20.00 – 25.00

"Shurebite Minnow Bait"
Shure-Bite Artificial Bait Co., Ohio
Date: c. 1938
Length: 3⅜" overall
Notes: Featuring a metal head with adjustable fins and a flexible rubber tail, this little bait was designed to wiggle on retrieve.
Value: $35.00 – 40.00

Shure-Bite Frog
Shure-Bite, Inc., Bronson, Michigan
Date: c. 1948
Length: 2¾" body
Notes: This good-looking plastic frog was first made of wood with a sponge rubber belly.
Value: $20.00 – 25.00

Allpur Grand Master
Silver Baits Inc., Rochester, New York
Date: c. 1954
Length: 3¼"
Notes: The name "Allpur" is a shortened version of "all purpose" and describes the manufacturer's intent for this interchangeable lure.
Value: $15.00 – 20.00

Sampson Lure
Smith Advertising Co., Ohio
Date: c. 1954
Length: 2"
Notes: This lure's unusual design makes it quite collectible.
Value: $10.00 – 15.00

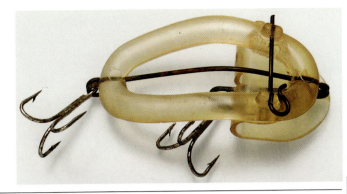

Myopic Minnow
Ed Smith-Kono Mfg. Co., Charleston, South Carolina
Date: c. 1952
Length: 3¼"
Notes: These handmade wooden lures wore black glasses. The standard color is white; yellow is quite rare.
Value: $50.00 – 55.00

Crawpappy
Smith and Yelton Co., Kansas City, Missouri
Date: c. 1951
Length: 2⅞"
Notes: This attractive wood crawfish is sought after by collectors of both crawfish and Missouri lures.
Value: $45.00 – 50.00

The Burrellure
Smithcraft Products Co., Kenvil, New Jersey
Date: c. 1947
Length: 3½"
Notes: This lure was made in several sizes and also in a jointed feather streamer fly using a small version of this unique wiggling lip.
Value: $20.00 – 25.00

Top-N-Bottom
Smithwick Lures, Shreveport, Louisiana
Date: c. 1946
Length: 2⅞"
Notes: This was the first Smithwick lure produced.
Value: $40.00 – 50.00

Gandy Dancer
Smithwick Lures, Shreveport, Louisiana
Date: c. 1946
Length: 3"
Notes: This lure sported cut-down Eger props.
Value: $40.00 – 50.00

Twister
Smithwick Lures, Shreveport, Louisiana
Date: c. 1946
Length: 2½"
Notes: The Twister featured a slanted head and a diving lip.
Value: $40.00 – 50.00

Buck-N-Bawl
Smithwick Lures, Shreveport, Louisiana
Date: c. 1946
Length: 3"
Notes: This is the first model, also called Hick-N-Haul.
Value: $35.00 – 40.00

Snapper
Smithwick Lures, Shreveport, Louisiana
Date: c. 1946
Length: 2¾"
Notes: This lure is very rare.
Value: $40.00 – 50.00

Stud Duck
Smithwick Lures, Shreveport, Louisiana
Date: c. 1946
Length: 3"
Notes: The name "Stud Duck" was used again for a completely different lure in 1975.
Value: $40.00 – 50.00

Devil's Horse
Smithwick Lures, Shreveport, Louisiana
Date: c. 1945 or 1946
Length: 3¾"
Notes: This was the very first hand-carved Devil's Horse and was carved by Bob Embrey for Jack Smithwick.
Value: $55.00 – 60.00

F-200 Devil's Horse; F-300 Devil's Horse
Jack Smithwick & Son Mfg., Smithwick Lures, Inc., Shreveport, Louisiana
Date: c. 1947
Length: 4⅛"; 4"
Notes: The top lure is the earlier of the two Devil's Horse lures shown.
Value: $5.00 – 10.00

King Snipe
Smithwick Lures, Shreveport, Louisiana
Date: c. 1946
Length: 2⅞"
Notes: This is a small version of the famous Devil's Horse.
Value: $15.00 – 20.00

Musky Devil's Horse
Smithwick Lures, Shreveport, Louisiana
Date: c. 1950
Length: 6½"
Notes: The largest Devil's Horse.
Value: $25.00 – 30.00

Slo-Sinking Devil's Horse
Smithwick Lures, Shreveport, Louisiana
Date: c. 1948
Length: 3⅞"
Notes: This lure has extra large props and heavier hardware.
Value: $10.00 – 15.00

B-900 Devil's Horse Ma Scooter
Smithwick Lures, Shreveport, Louisiana
Date: c. 1970
Length: 3¾"
Notes: Note the flat belly on this floating lure.
Value: $5.00 – 10.00

Scooter
Smithwick Lures, Shreveport, Louisiana
Date: c. 1948
Length: 2"
Notes: This is a small fat version of the Devil's Horse Ma Scooter.
Value: $10.00 – 15.00

Racehorse
Smithwick Lures, Shreveport, Louisiana
Date: c. 1948
Length: 2"
Notes: This is a small light version of the famous Devil's Horse.
Value: $10.00 – 15.00

Jack Sprat
Smithwick Lures, Shreveport, Louisiana
Date: c. 1948 – 1950
Length: 1¾"
Notes: This is the smallest of the Devil's Horse variations.
Value: $25.00 – 30.00

Devil's Horse Fly
Smithwick Lures, Shreveport, Louisiana
Date: c. 1946
Length: 1¾"
Notes: This is a single propeller version of the Jack Sprat.
Value: $20.00 – 25.00

Devil's Horse, weedless
Smithwick Lures, Shreveport, Louisiana
Date: c. 1946
Length: 4"
Notes: This fixed single hook Devil's Horse is very rare.
Value: $35.00 – 40.00

Baby War Horse
Smithwick Lures, Shreveport, Louisiana
Date: c. 1948
Length: 2¼"
Notes: This lure was often called the Carrot Top.
Value: $10.00 – 15.00

Salt Horse
Smithwick Lures, Shreveport, Louisiana
Date: c. 1950
Length: 6⅜"
Value: $40.00 – 50.00

Largest War Horse
Smithwick Lures, Shreveport, Louisiana
Date: c. 1950
Length: 6"
Notes: This lure is either salt water or musky size.
Value: $50.00 – 60.00

My Pet
Smithwick Lures, Shreveport, Louisiana
Date: c. 1946
Length: 2⅜"
Notes: This topwater lure has a notched forehead.
Value: $35.00 – 40.00

Tootsie Bug
Smithwick Lures, Shreveport, Louisiana
Date: c. 1946
Length: 1¾"
Notes: This lure has a "Woods" type lip.
Value: $15.00 – 20.00

Walking Scorpion
Smithwick Lures, Shreveport, Louisiana
Date: c. 1946
Length: 6" overall
Notes: This lure came with a bucktail and a rubber skirt tail.
Value: $30.00 – 35.00

Devil's Horse Rooter
Smithwick Lures, Shreveport, Louisiana
Date: c. 1946
Length: 3¼"
Notes: This was first of nine diving models of the Devil's Horse.
Value: $10.00 – 15.00

Devil's Horse Rooter, later model
Smithwick Lures, Shreveport, Louisiana
Date: c. 1950
Length: 2⅜"
Notes: This lure was also called "Snakehead."
Value: $10.00 – 15.00

Devil's Horse Rooter, later model
Smithwick Lures, Shreveport, Louisiana
Date: c. 1952
Length: 3"
Notes: Note the fat body profile of this version of the Rooter.
Value: $10.00 – 15.00

Devil's Horse Rooter, later model
Smithwick Lures, Shreveport, Louisiana
Date: c. 1952
Length: 2½"
Notes: Note the "neck" of this version of the Rooter.
Value: $10.00 – 15.00

A-700 Devil's Horse Rooter, Jr.
Smithwick Lures, Shreveport, Louisiana
Date: c. 1970
Length: 1¾"
Notes: This small version of the Rooter features a foil finish and a balance weight under the chin.
Value: $10.00 – 15.00

Blinker
Smithwick Lures, Shreveport, Louisiana
Date: c. 1975
Length: 2¾"
Notes: This lure is battery operated with flashing eyes.
Value: $10.00 – 15.00

Bo-Jack
Smithwick Lures, Shreveport, Louisiana
Date: c. 1979
Length: 2¾"
Notes: This lure was named after son Bo. There was also a flat balsa wood model.
Value: $10.00 – 15.00

Stud Duck
Smithwick Lures, Shreveport, Louisiana
Date: c. 1975
Length: 4¼"
Notes: This is the second version of the Stud Duck.
Value: $10.00 – 15.00

RB-1200 Rattlin' Rogue; RA-1200, Rattlin' Rogue; SRB-1200 Spoonbill Deep Diving Rogue
Smithwick Lures, Shreveport, Louisiana
Date: c. 1975 – present
Length: 4½"; 3½"; 4½"
Notes: This lure was popular with bass fishermen and featured a rattle inside.
Value: $5.00 or less

Highroller
Smithwick Lures, Shreveport, Louisiana
Date: c. 1975
Length: 4¼"
Notes: This lure has a "metallized" finish.
Value: $5.00 – 10.00

"Scalloped Wiggler"
Southern Artificial Bait Co., St. Louis, Missouri
Date: c. 1950
Length: 3½"
Notes: The real name of this unusual bait with "scalloped" or indented sides is unknown, thus the use of quotation marks.
Value: $25.00 – 30.00

"Flat Top Wiggler"
Southern Artificial Bait Co., St. Louis, Missouri
Date: c. 1950
Length: 2"
Notes: The real name of this little flat top lure is unknown, thus the use of quotation marks.

Spiral-Lure
Spiral Tackle Co., Detroit, Michigan
Date: c. 1952
Length: 3⅛"
Notes: Similar in design to the P & K Spinning Minnie, the Spiral-Lure is made of wood.
Value: $30.00 – 35.00

Judas (frog)
Sporting Industries, Chicago, Illinois
Date: c. 1947
Length: 3⅝"
Notes: "The Fish Betrayer Supreme," Judas is a plastic frog lure with a diving lip.
Value: $25.00 – 30.00

Shimmy Shiner
Sportland Mfg. Co. Inc., Oklahoma City, Oklahoma
Date: c. 1956
Length: 3⅜"
Notes: The unusual four-section body has tricked a few collectors into thinking this lure was made by the Haas Tackle Co. in the 1935 – 1940 era.
Value: $15.00 – 20.00

Shurbite She-Devil
The Sportsman's Co., Chicago, Illinois
Date: c. 1949
Length: 3⅞"
Notes: The two-tone plastic lure was made with different colors on each side.
Value: $10.00 – 15.00

Lucid-Lure
Sportsman's Specialties Co., Grand Rapids, Michigan
Date: c. 1958
Length: 4⅜"
Notes: This is a plastic "live minnow tube" lure.
Value: $10.00 – 15.00

Twin Min
Staley Johnson Mfg. Co., Fort Wayne, Indiana
Date: c. 1947
Length: 2¾" overall
Notes: This attractive lure was designed to give the impression of two minnows swimming side by side.
Value: $25.00 – 30.00

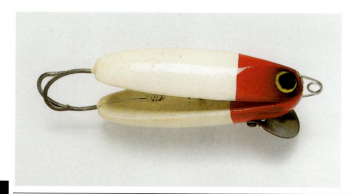

Johnson Weedo
St. Croix Lures, Park Falls, Wisconsin
Date: c. 1948
Length: 3"
Notes: The Weedo features a diving lip and weedless "scissor action" hooks.
Value: $30.00 – 35.00

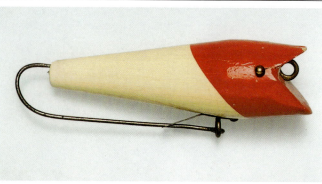

Johnson Darto
St. Croix Lures, Park Falls, Wisconsin
Date: c. 1947
Length: 3¼"
Notes: The Darto features a spring-loaded hook designed to release when struck by a fish; the eyes are brass tacks.
Value: $30.00 – 35.00

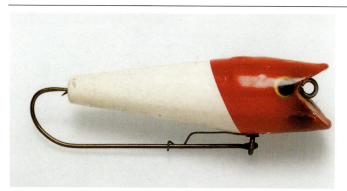

Johnson Darto
St. Croix Lures, Park Falls, Wisconsin
Date: c. 1948
Length: 3⅜"
Notes: This late version of the Darto features painted eyes.
Value: $20.00 – 25.00

St. Croix Snipe
St. Croix Lures, Park Falls, Minnesota
Date: c. 1956
Length: 2¾"
Notes: The Snipe features an unusual metal flasher attached to the rear hook.
Value: $15.00 – 20.00

Steel's Wigglefrog
Frank Steel, Inc., Chicago, Illinois
Date: c. 1949
Length: 2⅛"
Notes: This rubber frog features a clear plastic diving lip and hinged legs (the fuzzy "nylon" feet are missing on this example).
Value: $30.00 – 35.00

Rogers Dragon Fly
Stevens Agencies, Toronto, Canada
Date: c. 1960
Length: 2⅞"
Notes: The tail propeller turns a shaft which causes the wings on this neat wood lure to move.
Value: $30.00 – 40.00

Crippled Mouse
Elman "Bud" Stewart, Fenton, Michigan
Date: 1940s
Length: 2¾"
Notes: Bud Stewart's lures are highly imaginative hand craved representations of fish, frogs, mice, ducks, etc. This Mouse features an asymmetrical body and Bud's unique paint finish.
Value: $50.00 – 55.00

Crippled Minnow
Elman "Bud" Stewart, Fenton, Michigan
Date: c. 1955
Length: 2¾"
Notes: Typically asymmetrical in shape, this Crippled Minnow features a protruding pectoral fin.
Value: $45.00 – 60.00

Crippled Wiggler
Elman "Bud" Stewart, Fenton, Michigan
Date: c. 1970
Length: 2¾"
Notes: Bud Stewart's lures often feature cuts and indentations to suggest injury. This Wiggler has a tail prop and a cut on the belly side.
Value: $45.00 – 60.00

"One-eyed Minnow"
Elman "Bud" Stewart, Fenton, Michigan
Date: c. 1968
Length: 2¾"
Notes: Attributed to Bud Stewart, this fish-shaped lure has so many "cuts" that it was difficult to determine which view best depicted the lure.
Value: $45.00 – 60.00

Crawdad
Elman "Bud" Stewart, Fenton, Michigan
Date: c. 1970
Length: 2"
Notes: This is a clever plastic Crawdad from Bud Stewart's production period.
Value: $15.00 – 20.00

"Interchangeable Bait"
Stone's Baits, Dolgeville, New York
Date: c. 1940
Length: 3"
Notes: This unusual lure features a spring-loaded stainless steel frame which allows quick replacement of bodies.
Value: $40.00 – 50.00

ThinFin
Storm Mfg. Co., Norman, Oklahoma
Date: c. 1967
Length: 2⅞", 2⅜"
Notes: When the ThinFin was introduced, it was the closest artificial lure on the market to a live shad.
Value: $5.00 or less

ThinFin Shiner
Storm Mfg. Co., Norman, Oklahoma
Date: c. 1967
Length: 3¼", 2⅜"
Notes: This is the slim version of the ThinFin.
Value: $5.00 or less

Wiggle Wart; Wee Wart; Pee Wee Wart
Storm Mfg. Co., Norman, Oklahoma
Date: c. 1972
Length: 1¼"; 1½"; 2"
Notes: A fantastic fish catcher, the Wiggle Wart was, and is, an extremely popular lure with bass fishermen.
Value: $5.00 or less

Hot 'n Tot
Storm Mfg. Co., Norman, Oklahoma
Date: c. 1972
Length: 2"
Notes: This deep diver was made in several sizes and colors.
Value: $5.00 or less

Bug Plug
Storm Mfg. Co., Norman, Oklahoma
Date: c. 1981
Length: 2"
Notes: The Bug Plug is one of the most attractive "beetles" in recent years, suggesting its future collectibility.
Value: $5.00 or less

Deep Jr. Thunderstick (Desert Camo, Patriot)
Storm Mfg. Co., Norman, Oklahoma
Date: c. 1988
Length: 3⅜"
Notes: Painted in patriotic colors after the Gulf War, this deep runner is shown here in Desert Camo and Patriot.
Value: $5.00 or less

Glop!
Storm Manufacturing Co., Norman, Oklahoma
Date: c. 1960
Length: 2"
Notes: The unusual Glop! might be considered a feeding fish or frog.
Value: $5.00 – 10.00

Virgin Mermaid
Stream-Eze, Inc., South Bend, Indiana
Date: c. 1957
Length: 3⅞"
Notes: The Virgin Mermaid was made in a variety of styles and hair colors. This bait is very popular with collectors of novelty lures.
Value: $20.00 – 25.00

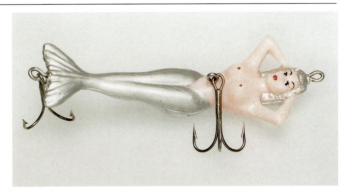

Chubby Minnow
Streamline Products, Inc., Meadows, Illinois
Date: c. 1946
Length: 3¼"
Notes: This wood lure is similar to the L & S Bassmaster design.
Value: $40.00 – 55.00

"Sugarwood Crank Bait"
Sugarwood Lures, Coweta, Oklahoma
Date: c. 1978
Length: 3"
Notes: This was another entry into the 1970s crankbait race.
Value: $10.00 – 15.00

Quicksilver Bait
Sunco
Date: c. 1948
Length: 3¾"
Notes: This lure uses mercury within a clear chamber to move and flash attractively.
Value: $20.00 – 25.00

"Sidehook Diver"
Sunco
Date: c. 1950
Length: 3⅜"
Notes: This unusual deep diver features side hooks and is catalogued here because of its similarity to the previous bait.
Value: $15.00 – 20.00

Cree Duck
Bill Szabo, Oregon, Ohio
Date: c. 1950
Length: 2¼"
Notes: These popular Cree Duck is made of plastic with spinner blades imitating swimming feet.
Value: $20.00 – 25.00

Jitter Spoon
10,000 Lakes, Minnesota
Date: c. 1948
Length: 2¾"
Notes: The Jitter Spoon features a bucktail/feather hook dressing and a "coil spring" weedguard.
Value: $5.00 or less

Thoren Minnow Chaser
A.H. Thoren, Chicago, Illinois
Date: c. 1940
Length: 5½"
Notes: This lure mimics a small fish chasing a minnow.
Value: $200.00 – 250.00

Gizmo
Tom Bait Co., Mattoon, Illinois
Date: c. 1948
Length: 3⅝"
Notes: Gizmo must have a wild surface action with a jointed, spinnered body and a lipped, popping head.
Value: $10.00 – 15.00

Surface Doodler
Trenton Manufacturing Co., Trenton, Ohio
Date: c. 1946
Length: 2⅝"
Notes: The Surface Doodler has a "Jitterbug" type surface action, caused by the large aluminum "ears."
Value: $25.00 – 30.00

Mad Mouse
Trenton Manufacturing Co., Trenton, Ohio
Date: c. 1947
Length: 1¾"
Notes: The eyes of the Mad Mouse are the painted screws that secure the diving lip.
Value: $25.00 – 35.00

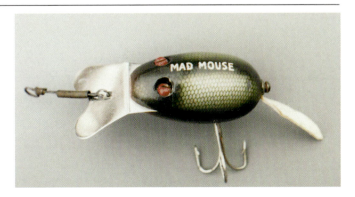

Spin Diver
Trenton Manufacturing Co., Trenton, Ohio
Date: c. 1946
Length: 3"
Note: This lure was designed to dive, wiggle, and shake. Note the unbalanced tail spinner.
Value: $30.00 – 35.00

Tail-Spin
Trenton Manufacturing Co., Trenton, Ohio
Date: c. 1949
Length: 4⅝"
Notes: The floating Tail Spin featured one or two unbalanced spinners.
Value: $30.00 – 35.00

Wham! Doodler
Trenton Manufacturing Co., Trenton, Ohio
Date: c. 1946 – 1948
Length: 2⅞"
Notes: The Wham Doodler was Trenton's entry into the metal spoon market.
Value: $10.00 – 15.00

Gentleman Jim
Troll-Rite Co., Chicago, Illinois
Date: c. 1947
Length: 3⅞"
Notes: This lure gets its action from the curved horizontal tail.
Value: $5.00 – 10.00

Stormy Petral Frog
Tropical Bait Co., Indianapolis, Indiana
Date: c. 1946
Length: 1⅜" diameter
Notes: This floating frog bears a strong resemblance to Pac-Man in the video game. Popping action is enhanced by the hollowed mouth.
Value: $30.00 – 35.00

Tru-Shad; Deep Tru-Shad; Topwater Tru-Shad; Midgit Tru-Shad
Tru-Shad Mfg. Co., Monroe, Louisiana
Date: c. 1965
Length: clockwise from upper left: 2¼"; 2⅜"; 2¼"; 1¾"
Notes: This terrific vibrating lure eventually ended up in the Arbogast catalog, after the purchase of the True-Shad Mfg. Co.
Value: $5.00 or less

Oriental Wiggler
True Temper Products, Geneva, Ohio
Date: c. 1940
Length: 1⅞"
Notes: This painted eye version of the Oriental Wiggler was the last model made.
Value: $5.00 – 10.00

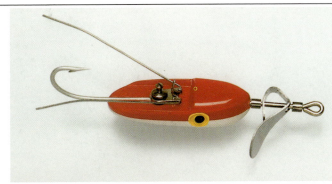

Bass Pop/Wood Frog
True Temper Products, Geneva, Ohio
Date: c. 1941
Length: 1⅛" frog body
Notes: Collectors frequently find Bass Pop lures, but the glass-eyed wood frog is a rare treasure which is highly prized by those who own them.
Value: $5.00 or less/$60.00 – 90.00

Speed Shad
True Temper Products, Geneva, Ohio
Date: c. 1940
Length: 2¼"
Notes: The Speed Shad was one of True Temper's most popular baits and makes a great color collection. Note the wire weed deflector on the lip.
Value: $10.00 – 15.00

Crippled Shad
True Temper Products, Geneva, Ohio
Date: c. 1940
Length: 2⅞"
Notes: This unique side-swimming variation of the Speed Shad featured an unusual wire weed deflector on the lip.
Value: $10.00 – 15.00

Di-Dipper
Tulsa Fishing Tackle Co., Tulsa, Oklahoma
Date: c. 1945 – 1956
Length: 2¼", 2⅜"
Notes: The four lures pictured represent the evolution of the Di-Dipper from 1945 (L) to 1956 (R).
Value: $20.00 – 25.00

7-11
Tulsa Fishing Tackle Co. Tulsa, Oklahoma
Date: c. 1945 – 1956
Length: 3¾"
Notes: This Lucky 13 look-alike features beautiful paint and pressed eyes.
Value: $20.00 – 25.00

Bee Popper; Ba-Bee Popper
Tulsa Fishing Tackle Co., Tulsa, Oklahoma
Date: 1945 – 1956
Length: 2⅞"; 1⅞"
Notes: These little floating divers are rare and beautiful.
Value: $20.00 – 25.00

Bee; Stunter
Tulsa Fishing Tackle Co., Tulsa, Oklahoma
Date: c. 1945 – 1956
Length: 1¾"; 2⅛"
Notes: Collectors frequently find Stunters, but the feather tail Bee is a welcome and rare acquisition.
Value: $15.00 – 20.00

Water Wiggler; Bizzy-Bee
Tulsa Fishing Tackle Co., Tulsa, Oklahoma
Date: c. 1945 – 1956
Length: 2½"; 1½"
Notes: Both of these examples are relatively rare collectibles.
Value: $15.00 – 20.00

Spinnabee
Tulsa Fishing Tackle Co., Tulsa, Oklahoma
Date: c. 1945 – 1956
Length: ⅞" body
Notes: The rare Spinnabee was designed for spin fishing.
Value: $15.00 – 20.00

Doodlebug
Twin-City Bait Co., Marinette, Wisconson
Date: c. 1937
Length: 1½"
Notes: This simple little spoon came cleverly packaged in a plastic tube with the line- tie of the lure attached to the metal screw-off lid.
Value: $5.00 – 10.00

Slim Sweeney's Twinminnow
Twinminnow Bait Company, Fresno, California
Date: c. 1939
Length: 3½"
Notes: The double line tie gave this lure two actions: surface and underwater, thus the name Twinminnow.
Value: $20.00 – 30.00

"Aluminum Frog"
Unknown maker
Date: c. 1950
Length: 3"
Notes: Made of hollow stamped aluminum with a spray-painted finish, this is the only example of this lure the authors have seen.
Value: $35.00 – 40.00

Bassanova
Unknown maker
Date: c. 1960
Length: 1⅞" body
Notes: The Bassanova is a plunking frog type surface lure with hair legs.
Value: $15.00 – 20.00

"Black Twinspinner"
Unknown Missouri maker
Date: c. 1970
Length: ⅝" body
Notes: This example has a free-moving bucktail hook attached to a lead body.
Value: $5.00 or less

Carpenter's Triple Depth Lure
Unknown maker
Date: c. 1955
Length: 2⅝"
Notes: Interchangeable bodies for the metal harness plus a pocket in the belly for lead weights gave this lure a variety of options.
Value: $30.00 – 35.00

Cobra
Unknown maker
Date: c. 1979
Length: 2⅝"
Notes: This lure is a "two way" bait in the style of the Millsite Daily Double, a shallow or deep action may be used depending on which end the line is tied.
Value: $5.00 – 10.00

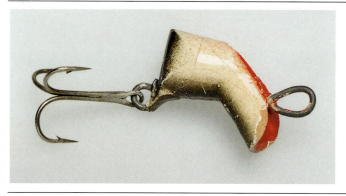

"Cut Plug"
Unknown maker
Date: c. 1940
Length: 1½"
Notes: At first glance this unusual lure appears to be the front portion of a jointed lure but on closer examination is indeed a complete wood lure.
Value: $15.00 – 20.00

Deluxe Red Head
Unknown maker
Date: c. 1958
Length: 3⅜"
Notes: "The all rubber minnow for better luck in fishing."
Value: $10.00 – 15.00

Do-All Trojan
Unknown maker
Date: c. 1958
Length: 3"
Notes: With six possible line tie options, this grooved face wobbler offered a variety of action-producing options.
Value: $15.00 – 20.00

The Dolly Rotator
Unknown maker
Date: c. 1964
Length: 3⅞"
Notes: The grooved head causes this bait to wobble while the spiral tail section rotates.
Value: $15.00 – 20.00

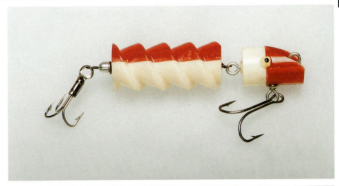

"Ear of Corn"
Unknown maker
Date: c. 1970
Length: 3¼"
Notes: This novelty lure is made of molded plastic.
Value: $15.00 – 20.00

Ecksi-Lure
Unknown maker
Date: c. 1968
Length: 4⅛"
Notes: Two hidden hooks pop out of the body when the line tie is pulled.
Value: $10.00 – 15.00

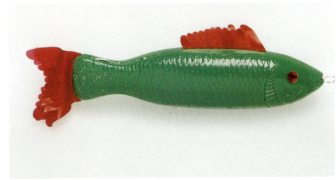

"Feather Minnow"
Unknown maker
Date: c. 1953
Length: 3¼"
Notes: This rare and unusual lure has a jointed rubber body with feathers glued to the surface.
Value: $30.00 – 35.00

"Frog Wiggler"
Unknown maker
Date: c. 1948
Length: 2¾"
Notes: This little lure features an exceptional hand-painted frog finish.
Value: $25.00 – 30.00

"Black & Yellow Wiggler"
Unknown maker
Date: c. 1948
Length: 2⅜"
Notes: Created by the same maker as the previous lure, this lipped version also features hand-painted details.
Value: $25.00 – 30.00

"Small Craw"
Unknown maker
Date: c. 1948
Length: 2¼"
Notes: By the same maker as the previous two lures, this little craw features attractive natural paint and bead eyes.
Value: $25.00 – 30.00

"Horse Fly-Surface"
Unknown maker
Date: c. 1938
Length: 1⅞" body
Notes: This rare wood-bodied lure was designed to have a surface "buzzing" action.
Value: $40.00 – 50.00

June Fly; Horse Fly
Unknown maker
Date: c. 1938
Length: 1½"; 2¼"
Notes: These lures are underwater versions of the Horse Fly.
Value: $20.00 – 25.00

"Jointed Minnow"
Unknown maker
Date: c. 1950
Length: 3⅞"
Notes: Featuring glass eyes, carved gills, and attractive paint, this jointed wooden lure is an excellent collectible.
Value: $20.00 – 30.00

"Kitchen Sink"
Unknown maker
Date: c. 1965
Length: 3"
Notes: Several companies made a Kitchen Sink lure, and this is one of the better looking versions: "I threw everything at them but the kitchen sink."
Value: $5.00 – 10.00

Lake Wappapello Special
Unknown maker
Date: c. 1972
Length: 1¾" spinner
Notes: This handmade buzz bait was created for fishing on southeast Missouri's Lake Wappapello.
Value: $5.00 – 10.00

"Lighted Lure"
Unknown maker
Date: c. 1975
Length: 3⅝"
Notes: This interesting plastic "diamond"-eyed lure features a light bulb at the tail.
Value: $20.00 – 25.00

"Longhorn Surface Bait"
Unknown maker
Date: c. 1955
Length: 2½"
Notes: On retrieve, this lure likely had a rocking, side-to-side motion similar to a Jitterbug or Crazy Crawler.
Value: $25.00 – 30.00

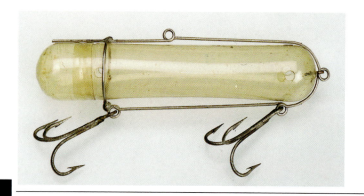

"Minnow Tube"
Unknown maker
Date: c. 1939
Length: 3¾"
Notes: Made of thin plastic with a wire frame, this tube has a screw-off cap to allow a live minnow to be placed inside.
Value: $15.00 – 20.00

"Mr. Frog"
Unknown maker
Date: c. 1950
Length: 3¾"
Notes: This great lure has tremendous eye appeal; nothing else is known about it.
Value: $30.00 – 35.00

Palsa Minnow
Unknown maker, Finland
Date: c. 1970
Length: 3½", 4¼", 7"
Notes: The Palsa was a balsa wood Rapala look-alike from Finland.
Value: $5.00 – 10.00

Pocono Hair Frog
Unknown maker, Mt. Wolf area, Pocono Mountains, Pennysylvania
Date: c. 1952
Length: 1¾"
Notes: A simple popper, this frog gets its action from the hair legs.
Value: $5.00 – 10.00

Presto Motor-Lure
Unknown maker
Date: c. 1960
Length: 5½"
Notes: This self-propelled lure can be set to run in a specified direction by adjusting the plastic rudder.
Value: $35.00 – 40.00

Radford Metal Minnow
Unknown maker
Date: c. 1946
Length: 3⅜"
Notes: While unpainted versions of this aluminum lure are often found, this painted example with inset "jewels" is indeed rare.
Value: $10.00 – 15.00

Rat Bait
Unknown maker
Date: c. 1964
Length: 5¼"
Notes: This unusual rat features a wood body covered with real animal hair.
Value: $40.00 – 50.00

"Red Fish"
Unknown maker
Date: c. 1956
Length: 2¼"
Notes: This interesting lure features an unusual two-piece plastic body sandwiching a soft plastic tail. Except for the hooks, the hardware is unplated brass.
Value: $25.00 – 30.00

Redtop Beer bait
Unknown maker
Date: c. 1950
Length: 1¾"
Notes: This little toughie is a promotional novelty item with an opener for a diving lip.
Value: $35.00 – 40.00

"Ribbed Bigmouth"
Unknown maker
Date: c. 1950
Length: 2⅛"
Notes: This little unidentified lure has a lot of eye appeal.
Value: $25.00 – 30.00

"Rocket Lure"
Unknown maker, Livonia, Michigan
Date: c. 1960
Length: 3"
Notes: This handsome rubber lure features five fins and twin single hooks.
Value: $30.00 – 35.00

"Rubber Worm"
Unknown maker
Date: c. 1940
Length: 4¾" overall
Notes: Attaching line to the eyes of both sets of hooks would make this hollow rubber worm dangle realistically.
Value: $5.00 – 10.00

Single-Spin
Unknown Missouri maker
Date: c. 1965
Length: 2" shaft
Notes: This unusual design featured an offset weight to prevent line twist.
Value: $5.00 or less

"Speckled Minnow Lure"
Unknown maker
Date: c. 1950
Length: 2⅜"
Note: This attractive lure features festive paint and five lead weights positioned through the body.
Value: $10.00 – 15.00

"Spin Diver Cigar Bait"
Unknown maker
Date: c. 1960
Length: 3¾"
Notes: This wiggling diver features a tail spinner and optional line tie. . . now if only fish smoked cigars.
Value: $25.00 – 30.00

Spinno Minnow
Uniline Mfg. Corp., Dallas, Texas
Date: c. 1947
Length: 2¾"
Notes: This plastic wiggling bait features an unusual "spinner" in the body reminiscent of the 1913 Immel Chippewa bait.
Value: $25.00 – 35.00

"Spin/Wiggle Minnow"
Unknown maker
Date: c. 1950
Length: 3⅞"
Notes: This rare unidentified plastic bait has an unusual combination of features: metal spinner, hole in mouth exiting under each plastic fin, ball-bearing mounted spinning tail with a clip-on hook mount, beautiful paint, and gloss eyes.
Value: $50.00 – 60.00

Split Fish
Unknown maker, Ohio
Date: c. 1951
Length: 2¾"
Notes: Despite its name, the plastic Split Fish seems to have a frog-like profile.
Value: $10.00 – 15.00

Ideel Fish Lure
Ideel Fish Lures, Chicago, Illinois
Date: c. 1954
Length: 3"
Notes: Basically a "springhook," this lure has a wooden body and is designed to swim with a lazy wobble.
Value: $25.00 – 30.00

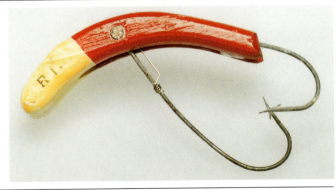

"Winged Flatfish"
Unknown maker
Date: c. 1941
Length: 4¼"
Notes: Dated 1941, this lure features a Flatfish design with cloth fins.
Value: $15.00 – 20.00

Wise Old Owl
Unknown maker
Date: c. 1960
Length: 2¼"
Notes: Made of solid plastic, the Wise Old Owl is definitely unusual.
Value: $20.00 – 30.00

Trav-L-Plug
Upstate Enterprises, Post Falls, Idaho
Date: c. 1979
Length: 3⅝"
Notes: The Trav-L-Plug is designed to glide on retrieve.
Value: $10.00 – 15.00

Viking Frog
Viking Bait & Novelty Co., St. Paul, Minnesota
Date: c. 1936
Length: 2" body
Notes: This is a rare and desirable frog which features hinged hind legs. The front legs are basically a loose hook on a screw.
Value: $250.00+

Depth Seeker; Little Lightning
Viking Lures, Inc., Scottsdale, Arizona
Date: c. 1983
Length: 2⅜"; 2½"
Notes: Made of bulletproof Lexan, these unusual electronic lures were the first battery-powered lures that shut themselves off without removing the batteries. The company was unable to keep up with the demands from fishermen and subsequently shut down — business failure due to success.
Value: $5.00 – 10.00

Finney Ferret
Vogels of California, Artesia, California
Date: c. 1960
Length: 4"
Notes: This "bent" plastic lure features fins, unusual line tie placement, and a tail prop.
Value: $10.00 – 15.00

Cisco Kid #300
Wallsten Tackle Co., Chicago, Illinois
Date: c. 1950
Length: 3⅞"
Notes: Early Cisco Kid lures featured small, painted eyes. All Ciscos were plastic with metal lips, and the divers usually had a wire "leader" line tie.
Value: $5.00 – 10.00

Spinning Cisco Kid #200
Wallsten Tackle Co., Chicago, Illinois
Date: c. 1955
Length: 2¼"
Notes: This is the small version of the previous lure.
Value: $5.00 – 10.00

"Jeweled Cisco Kid"
Wallsten Tackle Co., Chicago, Illinois
Date: c. 1950
Length: 2⅛"
Notes: Basically a #200 size, this correct lure has pink "rhinestone" eyes and nine white "rhinestones" on each side.
Value: $20.00 – 25.00

Musky Cisco Kid
Wallsten Tackle Co., Chicago, Illinois
Date: c. 1965
Length: 6¼"
Note: This is a late vintage diver and features large painted eyes and transparent plastic body with reflective insert.
Value: $5.00 – 10.00

Injured Cisco
Wallsten Tackle Co., Chicago, Illinois
Date: c. 1950
Length: 3¼"
Notes: The spinnered Injured Cisco was a surface lure designed to float on its side.
Value: $5.00 – 10.00

Topper
Wallsten Tackle Co., Chicago, Illinois
Date: c. 1955
Length: 4"
Notes: The Topper is a buoyant surface bait designed for big fish.
Value: $10.00 – 15.00

Topper – "Flaptail"
Wallsten Tackle Co., Chicago, Illinois
Date: c. 1955
Length: 4"
Notes: Using the same body as the regular Topper, this lure features a floppy tail spinner similar to that on Heddon's Flaptail. The variety of models and colors make Cisco Kid a very collectible company.
Value: $10.00 – 15.00

Skip-N-Cisco
Wallsten Tackle Co., Chicago, Illinois
Date: c. 1965
Length: 2¼"
Notes: The Skip-N-Cisco was a great surface lure when fished over schools of white and black bass feeding on shad.
Value: $5.00 or less

Fly-Plug
Tom Ware Fishing Tackle Company, Sedalia, Missouri
Date: c. 1959
Length: 1⅞" metal body
Notes: This neat little plug features a cork body on a curved metal plate and a dressed trailing hook.
Value: $10.00 – 15.00

Doc's Duck
Watson's Wrats
Date: c. 1999
Length: 4½"
Notes: Available from Cabella's, this lure is made to represent a duckling in the water.
Value: $30.00 – 35.00

Micro Mini Wrat
Watson's Wrats
Date: c. 1999
Length: 4½"
Notes: Made of fur, this is a small bass size Wrat.
Value: $30.00 – 35.00

Big Ears Wrat
Watson's Wrats
Date: c. 1999
Length: 7"
Notes: This lure represents a small swimming muskrat on retrieve.
Value: $30.00 – 35.00

Twirling Twirp
Watt Tackle Company, Detroit, Michigan
Date: c. 1947
Length: 3"
Notes: This attractive revolving lure features three fixed single hooks and a tail treble.
Value: $35.00 – 40.00

Weezel Sparrow
The Weezel Bait Co., Cincinnati, Ohio
Date: c. 1948
Length: 3¼"
Notes: The feathered Sparrow is an attractive spinnered floater.
Value: $20.00 – 25.00

The Weezel
The Weezel Bait Co., Cincinnati, Ohio
Date: c. 1937
Length: 5" overall
Notes: This spinner could be fished as shown or with the optional lip provided on the card.
Value: $5.00 – 10.00

Baby Weezel Feather Minnow
The Weezel Bait Co., Cincinnati, Ohio
Date: c. 1940
Length: 1¼" spinner shaft
Notes: This is the flyrod sized Weezel packaged in a neat kit.
Value: $5.00 – 10.00

Rex Spoon
Weezel Bait Co., Cincinnati, Ohio
Date: c. 1940
Length: 2⅛"
Notes: The Rex Spoon could be fished in the ordinary manner or as a surface-skittering lure in mossy cover.
Value: $5.00 or less

Flipper
Erwin Weller Co., Sioux City, Iowa
Date: c. 1968
Length: 4" overall
Notes: The Flipper is a Lazy Ike style design with "rhinestone" eyes and a rubber tail. Weller also made several classic wooden lures in the 1930s. See *Fishing Lure Collectibles Volume 1*.
Value: $10.00 – 15.00

Whirling Dervish
Whirling Dervish Bait Co., Oklahoma City, Oklahoma
Date: c. 1952
Length: 1⅞"
Notes: This lure was designed to spin and skitter across the surface.
Value: $10.00 – 15.00

Whopper-Stopper #200 (wood)
Whopper-Stopper Inc., Sherman, Texas
Date: c. late 1940s
Length: 2⅜"
Notes: The first Whopper-Stoppers were made of wood. Early examples are difficult to find and are very desirable.
Value: $20.00 – 25.00

Whopper-Stopper #100; Whopper Stopper #300; Whopper-Stopper #600 (flyrod-size)
Whopper-Stopper Inc., Sherman, Texas
Date: c. mid-1950s
Length: 2¾"; 2"; 1¼"
Notes: Plastic Whopper-Stoppers feature attractive paint patterns and make a beautiful display.
Value: $10.00 – 15.00 (flyrod lure); $5.00 or less (other 2 lures)

BB Series Whopper-Stopper, jointed

#100 BB; #300BB
Whopper-Stopper Inc., Sherman, Texas
Date: c. mid-1950s
Length: 3"; 2¾"
Notes: The "BB" stands for "broken back."
Value: $10.00 – 15.00

Hellbender Family
Whopper-Stopper Inc., Sherman, Texas
Date: c. early 1950s
Length: 3" (top left); 2⅛" (bottom left); 2⅝" (top right); 3½" (bottom right)
Note: The Hellbender is a deep diving lure which was used to probe the depths of impoundments.
Value: $5.00 – 10.00

Stumper (wood); Stumper (plastic)
Whopper-Stopper Inc., Sherman, Texas
Date: c. late1940s – mid-1950s
Length: 2³⁄₁₆" (top, wood); 2⅛" (bottom, plastic)
Notes: Like most Whopper-Stoppers, the Stumper makes a great color set display.
Value: $15.00 – 20.00 (wood); $5.00 or less (plastic)

Whopper-Stopper Minnow #500; Whopper-Stopper Baby Minnow #500
Whopper-Stopper Inc., Sherman, Texas
Date: mid-1950s
Length: 2¾"; 1⅝"
Notes: This lure design was highly influenced by Bomber Bait Company's Bomberette.
Value: $10.00 – 15.00

Hellraiser

Whopper-Stopper, Inc. Sherman, Texas
Date: mid-1960s
Length: 2⅞"
Notes: Produced both with and without a tailspinner, the Hellraiser was a popular topwater lure.
Value: $5.00 – 10.00

Topper; Fly Boogie

Whopper-Stopper Inc., Sherman, Texas
Date: c. late 1960s
Length: 1¾" (left), 1¾" (middle); 1³⁄₁₆" (right)
Notes: These fish-shaped floaters make an attractive color set display.
Value: $10.00 – 15.00

Whopper-Stopper Lizard

Whopper Stopper, Inc., Sherman, Texas
Date: c. 1950s
Length: 4½" (top), 3¼" (bottom)
Notes: This Lizard has protruding eyes and the tail hook near the center of the tail section. Whopper-Stopper is clearly marked on the lip.
Value: $10.00 – 15.00

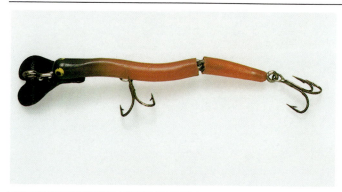

Whopper-Stopper Lizard

Whopper-Stopper, Inc., Sherman, Texas
Date: 1950s
Length: 3⁵⁄₁₆"
Notes: Thin, with painted eyes and the rear treble hook at the end of the tail, this version of the Lizard is quite different from the previous version. Whopper-Stopper is printed on the lip.
Value: $10.00 – 15.00

Rippin Rattler

Whopper-Stopper Inc., Sherman, Texas
Date: c. 1987
Length: 3"
Note: This is a recent lure which uses the old idea of replaceable inserts of different colors to change the appearance of the lure.
Value: $5.00 or less

Fuzzy Bug
Willey-J-Bait Co., Springfield, Missouri
Date: c. 1955
Length: 1⅛" body
Notes: The Fuzzy Bug was a very early Missouri spinner bait.
Value: $5.00 or less

Kast-A-Mino
Willinger Products Co., Minneapolis, Minnesota
Date: c. 1939
Length: 3¾"
Notes: This plastic lure was made to hold a live minnow.
Value: $30.00 – 35.00

Fantail Wizard
Wizard Lure Mfg. Co., Gambier, Ohio
Date: c. 1948
Length: 2¾"
Notes: Similar to the "Split Fish," this lure has a divided or frog-like body.
Value: $10.00 – 15.00

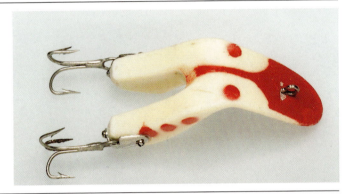

The Bug-R-Bird
Wonder State Products Co., Helena, Arkansas
Date: c. 1948
Length: 2⅜"
Notes: This lure was produced for one year before the company closed down. A few attempts at producing a plastic version never made it into production.
Value: $40.00 – 50.00

Crab Crawler
Ed Wood Bait Co., Wayne, Michigan
Date: c. 1940
Length: 2"
Notes: This is a cast metal bait with painted eyes.
Value: $20.00 – 25.00

Dipsy Doodle #400; Dipsy Doodle #500
Wood Manufacturing Co., Eldorado, Arkansas
Date: c. 1946 – 1950
Length: 1¾"; 2"
Notes: In 1940 Conrad Wood was making two lures, the #100 Crippled Shad and the #200 Speedy Shad in his Eldorado, Arkansas shop. He sold his business that same year to American Fork & Hoe Co., in Geneva, Ohio, makers of True Temper Baits (see True Temper, Speed Shad & Crippled Shad, pg. 257). In 1946 Wood Mfg. Co. was formed and began producing the Dipsy Doodle.
Value: $15.00 – 20.00

Doodler #1200; Doodler #600
Wood Manufacturing Co., Eldorado, Arkansas
Date: c. 1946 – 1948
Length: 4"; 3¼"
Notes: Conrad Wood formed a partnership with J.B. Wood (not related) in the spring of 1946, the Wood Mfg. Co. in Eldorado, Arkansas. The #1200 Doodler and #600 Doodler followed closely on the success of the earlier Dipsy Doodle. Wooden Doodlers are rare.
Value: $30.00 – 35.00; $25.00 – 30.00

Arkansas Wiggler #900
Wood Manufacturing Co., Eldorado, Arkansas
Date: c. 1947 – 1948
Length: 2½"
Notes: This lure was stamped from a single sheet of metal and was only produced for one year. Conrad Wood was a master lure designer.
Value: $25.00 – 30.00

Jointed Spot Tail Minnow #1300
Wood Manufacturing Co., Eldorado, Arkansas
Date: c. 1947
Length: 3¼"
Notes: The Jointed Spot Tail Minnow was a very realistic lure for its time and featured masterful paint work.
Value: $15.00 – 20.00

Spot Tail #700
Wood Manufacturing Co., Eldorado, Arkansas
Date: c. 1947
Length: 2"
Notes: This is a small, unjointed version of the previous bait.
Value: $15.00 – 20.00

Deep-R-Doodle #1000; Deep-R-Doodle #800; Deep-R-Doodle #300
Wood Manufacturing Co., Eldorado, Arkansas
Date: c. 1948 – 1953
Length: 3"; 2¼"; 1⅜"
Notes: Similar in looks to the early "Flat Face" Dipsy Doodle, this is a deep diving lure. The small 1⅜" lure was the first size produced.
Value: $15.00 – 20.00

Spot Tail Minnow #1100; Spot Tail Minnow #2000
Wood Manufacturing Co., Eldorado, Arkansas
Date: c. 1948 – 1950
Length: 2⅞"
Notes: These lures are variations on the same body style: a floater/diver and a floater.
Value: $15.00 – 20.00

Dipsy Doodle #1500; Dipsy Doodle #1400
Wood Manufacturing Co., Eldorado, Arkansas
Date: c. 1950
Length: 2¼"; 1¾"
Notes: These Dipsy Doodles are molded in two pieces and painted from the inside before assembly. The Sardine color shown was available only on Dipsy Doodles.
Value: $15.00 – 20.00

Doodler #1700; Doodler #1600
Wood Manufacturing Co., Eldorado, Arkansas
Date: c. 1950
Length: 4"; 3¼"
Notes: This is the most recent version of the Doodler and is made of plastic. According to an interview with a factory employee, the pearl paint was made from powdered oyster shell.
Value: $20.00 – 25.00

Dipsy Doodle #1800
Wood Manufacturing Co., Eldorado, Arkansas
Date: c. 1952
Length: 1¾"
Notes: This spinnered lure appears to be the same body as the #1400 Dipsy Doodle. Note: Conrad Wood was a fishing buddy of Pop Adam who made the Roto-Fli.
Value: $15.00 – 20.00

Poppa-Doodle #3100
Wood Mfg. Co., Conway, Arkansas
Date: c. 1960
Length: 3⅝"
Notes: By September 1958, the Wood Mfg. Co. had been sold and moved to Conway, Arkansas, and Conrad Wood was manufacturing a little lure he designed and developed for Heddon: The Sonic, and later, the Fidget Series.
Value: $10.00 – 15.00

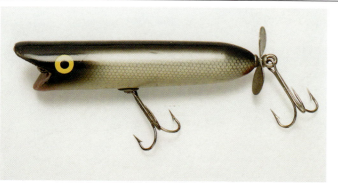

Big Poppa
Wood Mfg. Co., Conway, Arkansas
Date: c. 1962
Length: 4"
Notes: The Big Poppa is rarer than the similar but thinner Poppa Doodle.
Value: $20.00 – 25.00

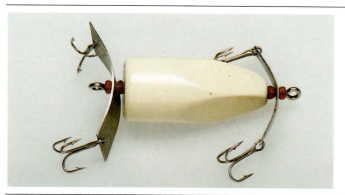

Whir-Li-Gig
Woods and Waters Co., Vicksburg, Michigan
Date: c. 1947
Length: 2¼"
Notes: With two large spinners, the Whir-Li-Gig must have been a terrible line twister.
Value: $35.00 – 40.00

Worden's Bass Creeper
Worden Floating Spinner Co., Granger, Washington
Date: c. 1941
Length: 1⅜" blade
Notes: Although the box for this bait listed no company name or address it is suspected that the lure was indeed made by this Washington company who also made the "Bonefish" under the name of Yakima Bait Co.
Value: $15.00 – 20.00

Big Hawk; Hawk
Wright & McGill Company, Denver, Colorado
Date: c. 1948
Length: 1¾"; 2½"
Notes: The Hawk lures are very collectible and nicely made.
Value: $15.00 – 20.00

Miracle Minnow #305; #601; #304
Wright & McGill Co., Denver, Colorado
Date: c. 1948
Length: 3"; 1¾; 3½"
Notes: This series of lures features Wright & McGill's attractive eyes and a gently curved profile.
Value: $10.00 – 15.00

Miracle Minnow #471W
Wright & McGill Co., Denver, Colorado
Date: c. 1949
Length: 1¾"
Notes: This version of the Miracle Minnow had a metal tail cap and belly strip.
Value: $10.00 – 15.00

Jointed Miracle Minnow #472-J
Wright & McGill Co., Denver, Colorado
Date: c. 1950
Length: 2⅜"
Notes: Available in a variety of colors, this lure features a jointed body.
Value: $5.00 – 10.00

Eagle Claw Hijacker
Wright & McGill Co., Denver, Colorado
Date: c. 1948
Length: 3⅜"
Notes: Made in 12 assorted colors, the Hijacker is shown here with a plastic lip.
Value: $15.00 – 20.00

Bug-A-Boo #303 Series; #600 Series
Wright & McGill Co., Denver, Colorado
Date: c. 1950
Length: 2⅜"; 1¾"
Notes: The fat Bug-A-Boo Series are floating lures designed to dive and run shallow on retrieve. These lures, like many Wright & McGill lures, were made with both metal and plastic lips.
Value: $10.00 – 15.00

Dixie Dandy No. 600
Wright & McGill Co., Denver, Colorado
Date: c. 1950
Length: 1¾"
Notes: This is basically a spinnered Bug-A-Boo without the lip.
Value: $25.00 – 30.00

Rustler
Wright & McGill Co., Denver, Colorado
Date: c. 1950
Length: 2¼", 2"
Notes: Similar to the standard Babe Oreno design, the plastic Rustler featured a tail spinner.
Value: $10.00 – 15.00

Flasher Minnow
Wright & McGill Co., Denver, Colorado
Date: c. 1950
Length: 2½"
Notes: This was Wright & McGill's entry into the spoon market.
Value: $5.00 – 10.00

Red Hot
Wright & McGill Co., Denver, Colorado
Date: c. 1960
Length: 1¼" blade
Notes: The Red Hot has a "diamond band" which rotates and flashes on retrieve.
Value: $5.00 or less

Bass Nabber
Wright & McGill Co., Denver, Colorado
Date: c. 1940
Length: 2¾"
Notes: This wood lure features hair legs and glass eyes.
Value: $60.00 – 65.00

Ol' Skipper Lucky Tail Wobbler, chubby
Wynne Precision Co., Griffin, Georgia
Date: 1946 – 1953
Length: 2¼"
Notes: This lure was made in a variety of beautiful colors and makes a great color collection.
Value: $15.00 – 20.00

Ol' Skipper Lucky Tail Jointed Wobbler
Wynne Precision Co., Griffin, Georgia
Date: c. 1946 – 1953
Length: 3⅝"
Notes: This is a larger jointed version of the previous lure.
Value: $15.00 – 20.00

Ol' Skipper Lucky Bug Plug
Wynne Precision Co., Griffin, Georgia
Date: c. 1946 – 1953
Length: 2⅜"
Notes: The Lucky Bug Plug features a sponge foam body and rubber legs with a split leather tail.
Value: $15.00 – 20.00

Big-O
Fred Young, Oak Ridge, Tennessee
Date: c. 1967
Length: 3½"
Notes: Big-O is stamped on the back of the circuit board lip of this lure. Big-O lures were made of balsa wood.
Value: $125.00 – 150.00

Mr. Fred
Fred Young, Oak Ridge, Tennessee
Date: c. 1968
Length: 2¾"
Note: This early version has "FCY" written on the back of the lip; Fred Young's initials. Later lures were stamped "Mr. Fred."
Value: $125.00 – 150.00

Topwater Bait
Fred Young, Oak Ridge, Tennessee
Date: c. 1968
Length: 3⅛"
Notes: Only a few Topwater baits were made, thus they are quite rare.
Value: $125.00 – 150.00

Little Fred
Fred Young, Oak Ridge, Tennessee
Date: c. 1970
Length: 3"
Notes: This early flat-sided bait has Big-O handwritten on the lip and Fred Young's signature on the side. Later versions were stamped Little Fred.
Value: $125.00 – 150.00

Small Big-O
Fred Young, Oak Ridge, Tennessee
Date: c. 1972
Length: 3"
Notes: Another version of the signed Big-O.
Value: $125.00 – 150.00

Big-O
Fred Young, Oak Ridge, Tennessee
Date: c. 1974
Length: 3"
Notes: All original Big-O lures have square diving lips made of circuit board. A number visible beneath the lip was required by the IRS after Fred Young sold the rights to the Big-O to Cotton Cordell. Apparently the number allowed the IRS to monitor sales. The commemorative Big-O was modeled after this bait.
Value: $125.00

Big-O Rattler
Fred Young, Oak Ridge, Tennessee
Date: c. 1972
Length: 3¼"
Notes: A red "R" is stamped above the Big-O name on the back of the lip on this lure. A "rattle" chamber is built into this lure.
Value: $125.00

Boiling Big Y
Young Lures, Inc., Piedmont, South Carolina
Date: c. 1979
Length: 2¼"
Notes: When a special tablet is inserted in the slotted back, this lure is ready to boil and bubble on retrieve.
Value: $5.00 – 10.00

Oh Bug Floating Lure
Yo-Zuri Co. Ltd., Japan
Date: c. 1999
Length: 2½"
Notes: This is a new lure but interestingly features old-style feather wings and a lot of hand-painted line detail on the body.
Value: $5.00 or less

Zink Screwtail
Zink Artificial Bait Co., Dixon, Illinois
Date: c. 1946
Length: 2½"
Notes: Weedless with a wiggling action, the Screwtail featured a rotating section.
Value: $25.00 – 30.00

Zoli
Zoli, Inc., Perth Amboy, New Jersey
Date: c. 1955
Length: 4½"
Notes: This lure features a plug in the back which can be removed to add water and affect the lure's action. The hooks could be removed by pulling up on the red knobs.
Value: $10.00 – 15.00

Whip Tail Sucker
Ed Zumski, Schiller Park, Illinois
Date: c. 1947
Length: 10" overall
Notes: This is a handmade musky lure featuring carved gills, glass eyes, and a rubber tail.
Value: $40.00 – 50.00

An enjoyable and affordable way to

get started in the lure collecting hobby

is to select a few inexpensive lures

that have eye appeal and collect those

lures in colors. Color sets of nearly

any lure can be very attractive when

arranged in a display case. When a

wise initial selection has been made,

the beginning collector will grow in

experience, make new collector

friends, and gain an affordable

understanding of the hobby.

Spinning Lures

The fundamentals of spinning, or at least spin-cast reels, are based in the nineteenth century. A reel designed by Peter Malloch laid the groundwork, and a later design by Alfred Illingworth in the early twentieth century looks strikingly similar to the spinning reels of the twenty-first century. However, the big breakthrough in spin-fishing occurred after World War II when Dupont introduced nylon monofilament at approximately the same time fiberglass rods replaced their bamboo and metal forerunners. To these developments add the wildly popular reel made in France by Mitchell, and we have the emergence of modern spinning.

Lure manufacturers in the post-war era were quick to address these new developments. Molded plastic lures offered toughness, lighter weight, and color-fast alternatives to the wooden plugs that preceded them. Suddenly a new generation of fishermen could cast farther — often with the same accuracy — and reach areas previously inaccessible to the old timers with fly and bait cast rigs. A genuine revolution was underway.

With the dawn of a new millennium, a new breed of fishing lure collector looks to the recent past and finds beauty, ingenuity of design, a wide array of colors, and thankfully, affordable alternatives to classic wooden baits. Their interest is not limited to plastic; balsa lures and lightweight metal lures have captured the fancy of collectors as well. For some, collecting spinning lures is a sentimental journey to the memories of their youth. For others it is the simple expedient of getting more bang for the buck as they sidestep the stampede of mainstream collecting.

Gary Smith
Woodstock, Georgia

"Salmon Egg Lure"
The Actual Lure Inc., New York, New York
Date: c. 1960
Length: 1⅜" body
Notes: The "eyes" in this lure appear to be actual fish eggs blackened by time and preserved in soft plastic. The Actual Lure Co. also encased minnows, shrimp, grasshoppers, and crickets in plastic.
Value: $5.00 or less

Aerospin Spinner Troller
Aerospin
Date: c. 1954
Length: 5¼" overall
Notes: This attractive lure features glass beads and copper/nickel spinners.
Value: $10.00 – 15.00

Preska Perche #500
Airex Co., Bache Brown, New York, New York
Date: c. 1941
Length: 2½" overall
Notes: While in France in 1935, Bache Brown witnessed fishermen using spinning tackle. An avid fisherman himself, Brown returned to America and began the Airex Co. In 1941, Bache Brown introduced spinning via Airex to America. The first lure looked similar to the examples shown but with a single hook and no wool.

Brown Godart #504
Airex Co., Bache Brown, New York, New York
Date: c. 1941
Length: 1" blade
Notes: Three variations of the Brown Godart are shown here for comparison. At least 37 variations of this lure are known to have been made.
Value: $5.00 – 10.00

Preska Wobbler
Airex Co., Bache Brown, New York, New York
Date: c. 1948
Length: 1" body
Notes: This early Airex lure is unmarked. It and the following three lures were found on cards taken from the William Mills Co. basement in the 1960s. Similar to the Vogue, this version has a wool fiber "patch" near the line tie.
Value: $15.00 – 20.00

Terrible

Airex Co., Bache Brown, New York, New York
Date: c. 1948
Length: 1⁵⁄₁₆" blade
Notes: In 1948 the Lionel Corp. became the owner of Airex.
Lionel continued producing Airex lures and added some new
models of their own.
Value: $10.00 – 15.00

Frisker

Airex Co., Bache Brown, New York, New York
Date: c. 1948
Length: 3¼" overall
Notes: This rubber-skirted lure has a "june bug" type spinner
blade.
Value: $10.00 – 15.00

Spinnaire #508

Airex Co., Bache Brown, New York, New York
Date: c. 1948
Length: ¾" body
Notes: Early Airex lures like this example used glass beads instead
of plastic.
Value: $10.00 – 15.00

Unidentified Airex Lures

Airex Co., Bache Brown, New York, New York
Date: c. 1941
Length: ⁷⁄₈" body
Notes: Resembling the Brown Godart, these lures feature attrac-
tively detailed bodies. Although blades are marked and the spinner
clevis matches the previous lure, some questions remain regarding
the authenticity of these lures as Airex products.
Value: $15.00 – 20.00

Ablette #505

Airex Corp., a division of the Lionel Co., New York, New York
Date: c. 1948
Length: 1⁵⁄₈" body
Notes: This lure features a stylized fish-shaped body. In 1948 the
Lionel Corp. became the owner of Airex and continued producing
Airex spinning tackle.
Value: $5.00 – 10.00

Vogue #502
Airex Corp., a division of the Lionel Co., New York, New York
Date: c. 1948
Length: ¾" body
Notes: The Vogue is similar in design to the Preska Wobbler.
Value: $5.00 – 10.00

Pixie #570
Airex Corp., a division of the Lionel Co., New York, New York
Date: c. 1950
Length: 2¾"
Notes: Two slightly different Pixies are shown. The top version has the pectoral fins replaced with a metal weight and uses a plastic lip instead of a metal lip as in the bottom version.
Value: $15.00 – 20.00

One-eyed Wobbler #510
Airex Corp., a division of the Lionel Co., New York, New York
Date: c. 1950
Length: 1⅜"
Notes: The One-eyed Wobbler has no identifying markings. This is a cast brass spoon with a scale pattern finish and a fluorescent bead on the short wire leaderr.
Value: $5.00 – 10.00

Popit #550
Airex Corp., a division of the Lionel Co., New York, New York
Date: c. 1950
Length: 2"
Notes: This plastic lure features a conical tail cap and an aluminum mounting harness for hook attachment.
Value: $10.00 – 15.00

Merry Widow #516; Gold Digger #512
Airex Corp., a division of the Lionel Co., New York, New York
Date: c. 1951; 1952
Length: 1½" blade; ¾" blade
Notes: These spinners both use similar body shapes.
Value: $5.00 – 10.00

Devil Dog #573

Airex Corp., a division of the Lionel Co., New York, New York
Date: c. 1952
Length: 2"
Notes: The Devil Dog featured a plastic body molded over a wire frame. The body could be bent in slightly different shapes to create new actions.
Value: $5.00 – 10.00

Wild Cat #513

Airex Corp., a division of the Lionel Co., New York, New York
Date: c. 1952
Length: ⅜" body
Notes: The little Wild Cat often had different colored plastic spinners.
Value: $5.00 – 10.00

Twin Spinner Devon #515

Airex Corp., a division of the Lionel Co., New York, New York
Date: c. 1952
Length: 1¼"
Note: The Twin Spinner Devon (top) is very similar to the unidentified lure below it shown for comparison.
Value: $5.00 – 10.00

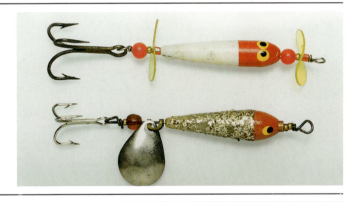

"Brown Godart Type;" Godie #524

Airex Corp., a division of the Lionel Co., New York, New York
Date: c. 1954
Length: 1" blade; 2¼" shaft
Notes: The Godie (bottom) features a plastic spiral rotating body.
Value: $5.00 – 10.00

Buggie #546

Airex Corp., a division of the Lionel Co., New York, New York
Date: c. 1954
Length: 1⅝"
Notes: This is a plastic spinning size lure based on the traditional flyrod popper design.
Value: $10.00 – 15.00

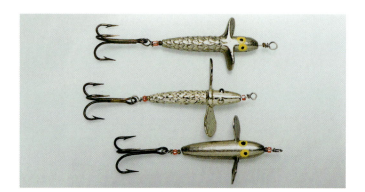

Devon-Aire #525
Airex Corp., a division of the Lionel Co., New York, New York
Date: c. 1954
Length: 1½", 1⅜", 1¼"
Notes: Shown are three variations of this solid metal Devon.
Value: $5.00 – 10.00

Crosstail #526
Airex Corp., a division of the Lionel Co., New York, New York
Date: c. 1954
Length: 1⅞"
Notes: The Crosstail has a heavy metal body with a thick, smooth paint finish. The tail is positioned at 90° to the body.
Value: $5.00 – 10.00

Rani
Airex Corp., a division of the Lionel Co., New York, New York
Date: c. 1958
Length: 1¾" blade, 1¼" blade
Notes: Often sold in boxed kits, these spinners feature a design reminiscent of the Abu Reflex Spinner.
Value: $5.00 – 10.00

Guppy
Allcock, Laight & Westwood Co., Ltd., Canada
Date: c. 1950
Length: 2"
Notes: The Guppy is a small plastic spinning plug weighted to sink.
Value: $15.00 – 20.00

Al-Lure-O
Al-Lure-O Baits, Brainard, Minnesota
Date: c. 1957
Length: 1⅝"
Notes: This lure features a soft foam body to protect the hooks from hang-ups.
Value: $10.00 – 15.00

Al's Goldfish; Al's Hellegrammite
Al's Goldfish
Date: c. 1949
Length: 2"; 1¾"
Notes: These spoons were highly touted by Gadabout Gaddis on his popular television show.
Value: $5.00 or less

Arjon Bassy
Arjon, Sweden
Date: c. 1948
Length: 2⅜"
Notes: The Bassy has a plastic body molded over a metal core.
Value: $5.00 – 10.00

Rogen Popular
Arjon, Sweden
Date: c. 1948
Length: 1⅜" blade
Notes: This attractive spinner features a smiling face "keel" design.
Value: $10.00 – 15.00

Cha Cha
Arnold Tackle Corp., Paw Paw, Michigan
Date: c. 1950
Length: ⅞" body
Notes: The Cha Cha must have had an action that imitated the popular dance, thus the name.
Value: $5.00 – 10.00

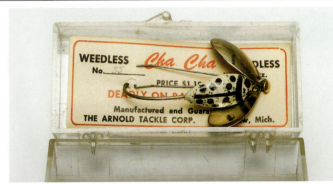

Jet Lure
Arrez, Switzerland
Date: c. 1947
Length: 2¾"
Notes: This lure features a complicated metal stamping design which is completely open except where the body sections touch.
Value: $5.00 – 10.00

SPINNING LURES

Kala
Arrowhead Lures, Virginia, Minnesota
Date: c. 1970
Length: 2⅞", 2⅛"
Note: This lure has a clear plastic body with a metallic foil insert and side fins.
Value: $5.00 – 10.00

"Beacon Pike"
Beacon
Date: c. 1963
Length: 2¼"
Notes: The Beacon lures imitate fish, eels, and minnows.
Value: $5.00 – 10.00

"Beacon Perch"
Beacon
Date: c. 1963
Length: 2⅝"
Notes: This nice perch features a thin, reverse wiggling lip beneath the chin.
Value: $5.00 – 10.00

"Beacon Chub"
Beacon
Date: c. 1963
Length: 2⅛"
Notes: The Beacon Chub features good fin detail.
Value: $5.00 – 10.00

"Beacon Yellow Perch"
Beacon
Date: c. 1963
Length: 1¼"
Notes: This example shows the molded wire-thru construction common to Beacon lures.
Value: $5.00 – 10.00

"Beacon Cutie Pie"
Beacon
Date: c. 1963
Length: 1"
Notes: This tiny bait features a front propeller and a stabilizing fin.
Value: $5.00 – 10.00

"Beacon Sunfish"
Beacon
Date: c. 1963
Length: 1¹⁄₁₆", 1¹⁄₁₆"
Notes: These little Sunfish demonstrate the use of a flat, wiggling plate and a nose prop, two different actions using the same body design.
Value: $5.00 – 10.00

"Beacon Swimming Eel"
Beacon
Date: c. 1963
Length: 2⅛"
Notes: This eel is one of the most attractive lures in the Beacon line. Body detail and paint finish are exemplary.
Value: $15.00 – 20.00

Spin-O-Pop
Bradley Bait Co.
Date: c. 1965
Length: 1½"
Notes: This small spinning popper has the maker's decal inside the popping mouth.
Value: $10.00 – 15.00

Devon Spinners (West Germany)
D.A.M., Germany
Date: c. 1950
Length: 1¼", 1½"
Notes: The devon body shape began in England in the 1800s. The D.A.M. examples shown accurately duplicate those early English lures.
Value: $10.00 – 15.00

Record Spinner (West Germany)
D.A.M., Germany
Date: c. 1950
Length: ⅞" blade
Notes: An old company, D.A.M. made an attractive line of glass-eyed and painted eye wooden lures. The spinner shown is silver plated.
Value: $5.00 or less

Record Spinner
D.A.M., Germany
Date: c. 1960
Length: 1¼" blade
Notes: This spinner was introduced to compete with the French Mepps Spinner.
Value: $5.00 or less

Turbler (West Germany)
D.A.M., Germany
Date: c. 1960
Length: 2½", 1¾", 1⅛"
Notes: The handsomely painted Turbler is a bubble-producing variation on the old Devon design.
Value: $10.00 – 15.00

Wiggle Wonder
Dayton Bait Company, Dayton, Ohio
Date: c. 1949
Length: 2¼"
Notes: This little River Runt type lure is cheaply made of molded plastic.
Value: $5.00 – 10.00

Doty Raider
D.B. Doty Inc., Columbia, Missouri
Date: c. 1951
Length: 1¼" blade
Notes: The Doty Raider remained in production until 1980.
Value: $5.00 or less

Limpy; Spin Devon; Flappy; Double Bubbler; Shaker
John C. Herschel, New York, New York
Date: c. 1950
Length: 1⅝"; 1⅞"; 2"; 1⅞"; 1⅞"
Notes: John C. Herschel made an attractive line of jewelry quality spinning lures.
Value: $10.00 – 15.00

Edwards Spinnaren
Edwards, Sweden
Date: c. 1960
Length: 1½" blade
Notes: This handsome lure features a fish-shaped plastic head and a scale textured blade.
Value: $10.00 – 15.00

Fish-N-Fool
Falls Bait Co., Chippewa Falls, Wisconsin
Date: c. 1950
Length: 1⅞"
Notes: This is a Jitterbug type surface lure which was made in at least two sizes. Handsomely painted, the Fish-N-Fool had a chamois trailer.
Value: $15.00 – 20.00

"Falls Minnow"
Falls Bait Company, Chippewa Falls, Wisconsin
Date: c. 1950
Length: 1½" overall
Notes: This lure simply says "Falls Bait" on the front of the lip and features pressed eyes and nylon back dressing.
Value: $10.00 – 15.00

Big Inch; Inch Minnow
Falls Bait Co., Chippewa Falls, Wisconsin
Date: c. 1960
Length: 1⁷⁄₁₆"; 1"
Notes: Made recently by several other companies, the Inch Minnows were originated by the Falls Bait Co. Painted in a variety of colors, these little spinning baits make a great color display.
Value: $5.00 – 10.00

"Fingerling Shiner"
Felmlee Enterprises, Louistown, Pennsylvania
Date: c. 1958
Length: 3⅞"
Notes: This realistic plastic shiner features attractive paint work and an off-balance spinner at the nose. Felmlee probably also made the smaller Beacon lures shown earlier in this chapter.
Value: $10.00 – 15.00

"Fingerling Minnow"
Felmlee Enterprises, Louistown, Pennsylvania
Date: c. 1958
Length: 2⅝"
Notes: The molded plastic, wire-thru construction is clear in this example.
Value: $10.00 – 15.00

"Spinnered Eel"
Felmlee Enterprises, Louistown, Pennsylvania
Date: c. 1958
Length: 3"
Notes: This very realistic eel features Felmlee's unbalanced spinner and high quality paint.
Value: $10.00 – 15.00

"Fingerling Bull Head"
Felmlee Enterprises, Louistown, Pennsylvania
Date: c. 1958
Length: 2¼"
Notes: This little Bull Head has a nice, stylized catfish profile and features Felmlee's plastic wobbling lip design.
Value: $15.00 – 20.00

"Yellow Perch"
Felmlee Enterprises, Louistown, Pennsylvania
Date: c. 1958
Length: 2½"
Notes: This lure features an unmarked plastic Felmlee lip.
Value: $10.00 – 15.00

Finn-Kala
Finn-Kala, Finland
Date: c. 1960
Length: 2½"
Notes: Originally made by Finn-Kala, this lure was imported to the United States by Nils-Master.
Value: $5.00 – 10.00

Balsa Wobbler with Wings (Finland)
Nils-Master
Date: c. 1960
Length: 3"
Notes: Most likely made by Finn-Kala, this balsa lure featured "pectoral fins" on the side.
Value: $5.00 – 10.00

Balsa Wobbler with Keel (Finland)
Nils-Master
Date: c. 1960
Length: 3"
Notes: A different variation on the previous lure design, this "keeled" Wobbler was probably made by Finn-Kala.
Value: $5.00 – 10.00

Twirlo
Fisher-Motors, Muncie, Indiana
Date: c. 1973
Length: 3" main shaft
Notes: The unusual Twirlo is a surface lure with a hard foam body and an ornate "screw" attached to the prop.
Value: $5.00 – 10.00

Calico Cat; Asspoon
France
Date: c. 1955
Length: 1¼"; 1½"
Notes: The differences in these two lures are merely color, size, and hook dressing. The name difference is puzzling.
Value: $5.00 or less

Regeut
France
Date: c. 1958
Length: 2⅛" body
Notes: Stamped from a flat sheet of copper, this lure has a lead ball at the tail for balance.
Value: $5.00 or less

Lessor
France
Date: c. 1960
Length: 2⅛" blade
Notes: The attractive Lessor has holes in the blade for eyes and a stiff, wired hook.
Value: $5.00 or less

CP Swing
France
Date: c. 1960
Length: 1⅝" blade
Notes: The CP Swing was popular with American fishermen and featured a brass bead body.
Value: $5.00 or less.

Vivif
France
Date: c. 1960
Length: 2¾", 2⅛"
Notes: The unusual Vivif tail design is still in use today to lend action to a variety of soft baits.
Value: $5.00 – 10.00

"Stabil"
France
Date: c. 1952
Length: 2"
Notes: This well-made plastic lure features a cupped face/lip design.
Value: $10.00 – 15.00

Pecos Jointed Top Minnow
France
Date: c. 1952
Length: 2½", 1⅝"
Notes: Featuring jointed bodies and "upright" plastic lips, these minnows were manufactured in several sizes.
Value: $10.00 – 15.00

Pecos Swiveled Devon
France
Date: c. 1952
Length: 1¾"
Notes: The clear plastic "keel" atop the head of this lure was an attempt at eliminating line twist caused by the rotating tail section.
Value: $10.00 – 15.00

Abu Favourite (Sweden)
Charles Garcia & Co., New York, New York
Date: c. 1950
Length: 1¾"
Notes: The Favourite bears a strong resemblance to the Rex Spoon made by the Weezel Bait Co.
Value: $5.00 or less

Record Little-Daffy (Sweden)
Charles Garcia & Co., New York, New York
Date: c. 1950
Length: 1½"
Notes: This little spoon features "fins" and was packaged in a gift pack kit by Garcia.
Value: $5.00 or less

Record Little Ruby (Sweden)
Charles Garcia & Co., New York, New York
Date: c. 1950
Length: 1⅝"
Notes: This spoon has a "corrugated" surface to catch and reflect light.
Value: $5.00 or less

Record Little-Tilly (Sweden)
Charles Garcia & Co., New York, New York
Date: c. 1950
Length: 1¾"
Notes: The fish-shaped Little-Tilly features a painted/polished combination common to early metal spinning lures.
Value: $5.00 or less

Record Little-Glimmy (Sweden)
Charles Garcia & Co., New York, New York
Date: c. 1950
Length: 1¾"
Notes: This spoon uses the basic Daredevl design.
Value: $5.00 or less

Voblex 10 (France)
Charles Garcia & Co., Inc., New York, New York
Date: c. 1950
Length: 1" blade
Note: The molded rubber head of the Voblex features attractive paint which in combination with a unique spinner blade shape creates an unusual lure design.
Value: $5.00 or less

Lurex (France)
Charles Garcia & Co., Inc., New York, New York
Date: c. 1950
Length: 1" blade
Note: This lure featured a "shaftless" spinner blade mounted to a Swivel.
Value: $5.00 or less

Veltic (France)
Charles Garcia & Co., Inc., New York, New York
Date: c. 1950
Length: 1⅛" blade
Notes: Part of the same kit as the previous seven lures, the Veltic featured an attractively painted spinner blade design.
Value: $5.00 or less

Eelet (France)
Charles Garcia & Co., Inc., New York, New York
Date: c. 1950
Length: 3¾", 4¾"
Notes: The popular Eelet had a terrific natural-looking action in the water.
Value: $5.00 – 10.00

Abu Virveln (Sweden)
Charles Garcia & Co., Inc., New York, New York
Date: c. 1955
Length: ⅞" body
Notes: This unique spinner features a flat, spiral metal band which spins around the body.
Value: $5.00 or less

Abu Reflex (Sweden)
Charles Garcia & Co., Inc., New York, New York
Date: c. 1955
Length: 9/16" body (top), 1 1/16" body (bottom)
Notes: Made in a variety of sizes, the Abu Reflex was Garcia's best seller. This design is still popular today.
Value: $5.00 or less

Abu Reflex (Sweden)
Charles Garcia & Co., Inc., New York, New York
Date: c. 1955
Length: 1¼" body
Notes: This is an unusual tandem version of the previous lure.
Value: $5.00 or less

Mitchell Spinner (France)
Charles Garcia & Co., Inc., New York, New York
Date: c. 1955
Length: 2⅜" overall
Notes: Garcia's connection with the famous Mitchell spinning reels continued with this lure.
Value: $5.00 or less

Abu Svangsta Spinner (Sweden)
Charles Garcia & Co., Inc., New York, New York
Date: c. 1955
Length: 1⅛"
Notes: This lure with its louvered blade uses a fish-shaped hook hanger designed to allow the hook to ride off-balance and minimize line twist. The Abu Reflex also used this hanger.
Value: $5.00 or less

Abu Hi-Fi (Sweden)
Charles Garcia & Co., Inc., New York, New York
Date: c. 1955
Length: ¾", 1³⁄₁₆"
Notes: This lure body design is an attempt to control line twist. Note the louvers in the blade.
Value: $5.00 or less

Plucky, Medium (France)
Charles Garcia & Co., Inc., New York, New York
Date: c. 1957
Length: 2⅝"
Notes: The Plucky is a hollow rubber lure with a molded lip, unlike the similar Airex Pixie which has an inserted lip.
Value: $10.00 – 15.00

Abu Luster (Sweden)
Charles Garcia & Co., Inc., New York, New York
Date: c. 1960
Length: 2⅜"
Note: The Abu Luster features a clear plastic body molded over a reflective metal core.
Value: $10.00 – 15.00

Abu Hi-Lo (Sweden)
Charles Garcia & Co., Inc., New York, New York
Date: c. 1960
Length: 3⅛"
Notes: Similar to Heddon's River Runt design, the Hi-Lo featured an adjustable lip which offered several depth options.
Value: $10.00 – 15.00

Finlandia Wobbler (Finland)
Charles Garcia & Co., Inc., New York, New York
Date: c. 1964
Length: 4⅜", 10"
Notes: The Finlandia bears an eerie resemblance to the Rapala including the star pattern foil. The Finlandia was never able to capture Rapala's market.
Value: $5.00 – 10.00

Flopy (France)
Charles Garcia & Co., Inc., New York, New York
Date: c. 1965
Length: 2½"
Notes: This hollow rubber lure was molded around a metal armature and featured an adjustable lip. A 3½" version called the Lippy Lure was also made.
Value: $5.00 – 10.00

Abu Killer (Sweden)
Charles Garcia & Co., Inc., New York, New York
Date: c. 1975
Length: 4⅞", 4"
Notes: This lure is made of hard plastic with an integral molded lip.
Value: $5.00 or less

Blinkin' Beauty
Glo-Lure Company, Chicago, Illinois
Date: c. 1944
Length: 1¾" body
Notes: The Blinkin' Beauty features a luminous body and a transparent red plastic "blade." When retrieved, the rotating blade appears to "blink" as the blade passes across the luminous body.
Value: $5.00 or less

Hall Lure
William C. Hall, Wheeling, West Virginia
Date: c. 1952
Length: 2"
Notes: This handmade wood lure was made in a flyrod size with no eyes (shown) and a casting size with eyes.
Value: $10.00 – 15.00

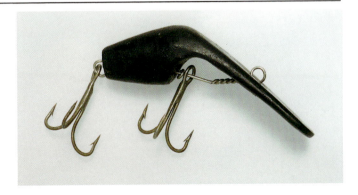

Bottom Dollar
J.J. Hildebrandt & Co., Indiana
Date: c. 1939
Length: 1¼" diameter
Note: The Bottom Dollar is perhaps Hildebrandt's most unusual and attractive metal lure. Hildebrandt was an early maker of metal lures. See Hildebrandt, *Fishing Lure Collectibles Volume 1*.
Value: $35.00 – 40.00

Shady Lady
J.J. Hildebrandt & Co., Indiana
Date: c. 1950
Length: 1⅜" blade
Notes: The wide, slightly concave head caused the Shady Lady to dart and glide on retrieve.
Value: $5.00 – 10.00

Flicker Spoon
J.J. Hildebrandt & Co., Indiana
Date: c. 1960
Length: 1⅝"
Notes: This spoon was available with a weedless attachment and also with a plated line tie weight.
Value: $5.00 or less

Flicker Spin; Beetle
J.J. Hildebrandt & Co., Indiana
Date: c. 1960
Length: 1⅛" blade; 1⅜" body
Notes: The Flicker Spin and Beetle both have small marked "fin" blades.
Value: $5.00 or less

Wig Wag
J.J. Hildebrandt & Co., Indiana
Date: c. 1965
Length: 1¼" blade
Notes: This casting lure had a weighted body and an "upright" lip design.
Value: $5.00 or less

"Tandem Spinner"
J.J. Hildebrandt & Co., Indiana
Date: c. 1965
Length: 2" shaft, 1⅞" shaft
Note: Shown are two examples of the "Tandem Spinner," each using different body components.
Value: $5.00 or less

"Spinner"
J.J. Hildebrandt & Co., Indiana
Date: c. 1965
Length: 1" blade
Notes: This is a single spinner version of the previous lure.
Value: $5.00 or less

Screw-Ball
Hills Bait Co., Detroit, Michigan
Date: c. 1959
Length: 2¼"
Notes: This is a floating lure which uses the early Decker design (see *Fishing Lure Collectibles Volume 1*).
Value: $10.00 – 15.00

Glitterfish
Hobbs Bros., Jewetts Associates, Santa Maria, California
Date: 1950
Length: 3", 1¾"
Notes: The Glitterfish was made in a variety of attractive colors and shapes (see the Show and Tell chapter of this book).
Value: $10.00 – 15.00

Hornet
Hornet, Inc., Elyria, Ohio
Date: c. 1949
Length: 5¼" overall
Notes: The Hornet was made in several sizes and featured a clever body stamped from a single piece of metal.
Value: $5.00 or less

Rangley Minnow
Horrocks-Ibbotson, Utica, New York
Date: c. 1952
Length: 1¾"
Notes: This lure is a "Lazy Ike" type design with a thin tail spinner and thru-wire construction.
Value: $5.00 or less

Hootenanny
Horrocks-Ibbotson Co., Utica, New York
Date: c. 1960
Length: 1¾" shaft
Notes: The Hootenanny blister package states: "Fine fishing tackle since 1812." This is a desirable and attractive spinning lure.
Value: $5.00 – 10.00

Jeff's Real Eel
Jeffers Mfg. Co., Fresno, California
Date: c. 1955
Length: 4"
Notes: Jeffers used a soft foam for their lure bodies and also made a Master Minnow lure similar in design to the Real Eel.
Value: $5.00 or less

Strike Star
Keel Guard Lures Inc., Mansfield, Ohio
Date: c. 1964
Length: 2⅞", 2¼" main shaft
Notes: These lures have perhaps the most intricate weedless attachment of all spinning lures.
Value: $5.00 or less

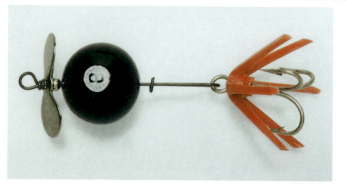

"8" Ball
Kiva Products, Inc., U.S.A.
Date: c. 1960
Length: ⅝" diameter
Notes: This novelty lures uses a plastic weedguard.
Value: $5.00 – 10.00

Larue Frog
Larue Baits, Illinois
Date: c. 1946
Length: 1½" body
Notes: This neat little metal frog has been found both with and without a forward shaft holding two spinners. A nickel plated version is also commonly found.
Value: $20.00 – 30.00

Lemax "Devon"
Lemax, Switzerland
Date: c. 1940
Length: shaft: 1¼", 1⅝", 1½", 2"
Notes: Perhaps the most elaborate and attractive spinning lures ever made, the Lemax lures featured mother-of-pearl, abalone, copper, and brass riveted together to create flash and action. Charles F. Orvis Co. imported these lures to America.
Value: $20.00 – 30.00

Lemax "Pin Devon"
Lemax, Switzerland
Date: c. 1940
Length: shaft: 1½"
Notes: The revolving head on this lure locks into a pin in the body, providing two actions. On fast retrieve, the head and body spin together; when allowed to sink, the head slides away from the body and spins alone.
Value: $20.00 – 30.00

Lemax "Knife Handle"
Lemax, Switzerland
Date: c. 1940
Length: 2¼"
Notes: At a glance this lure might appear to be made from the handle of a pocket knife or small tool, but a closer look reveals a clever twisted "blade" designed to cause the lure to spin on retrieve.
Value: $20.00 – 30.00

Lemax Spoon
Lemax, Switzerland
Date: c. 1940
Length: 1½"
Notes: This beautiful lure has a pearl overlay riveted to a hammered brass spoon. A 1⅞" size was also made.
Value: $15.00 – 20.00

Lemax Devon
Lemax, Switzerland
Date: c. 1950
Length: shaft: 1½", 2¼"
Notes: This is the later version of the Lemax Devon. Note the absence of mother-of-pearl which was replaced by painted aluminum.
Value: $10.00 – 15.00

Lemax "Ringed Devon"
Lemax, Switzerland
Date: c. 1950
Length: 1⅜" shaft
Notes: Made of a heavy metal similar to lead, this lure is similar in design to the Lemax "Pin Devon" but without the pin lock and mother-of-pearl.
Value: $10.00 – 15.00

Lemax "Scaled Spoon"
Lemax, Switzerland
Date: c. 1950
Length: 1⅞"
Notes: Made of copper with a silverplated concave side, this lure features the typical plastic Lemax tail.
Value: $10.00 – 15.00

Le Tourby
Le Tourbillon, France
Date: c. 1948
Length: 3"
Notes: Lead weights could be added or removed via a slot in the mouth of this flexible rubber lure, providing a variety of depths and actions.
Value: $10.00 – 20.00

Hinky-Dink
Libby Mfg. Co., Glendale, California
Date: c. 1950
Length: 2⅜"
Notes: The Hinky-Dink is cleverly stamped from one piece of metal.
Value: $5.00 or less

Pole Kat
Lisk Fly Mfg. Co., Greensboro, North Carolina
Date: c. 1967
Length: 1⅛" body
Notes: The Pole Kat has a lead body which is triangular in cross section.
Value: $5.00 – 10.00

Valse (France)
Marathon Bait Co., Wausau, Wisconsin
Date: c. 1960
Length: 1¼" blade
Notes: The interesting spinner features a flat keel strip attached to the shaft which shifts by gravity to offset line twist.
Value: $5.00 or less

Aglia (early); Aglia (black); Aglia Long; Elix Mepps (France)
Imported to America by Sheldon's, Inc., Antigo, Wisconsin
Date: c. 1946 – 1960
Length: blades: 1¼"; 1¼"; 1⁹⁄₁₆"; ⅞"
Notes: When Sheldon's imported the Mepps to America, a new era in spinning began. The silverplated blades and attractive design caught both fish and fishermen.
Value: $5.00 or less

Supper Mepps
Mepps, France
Sheldon's, Inc., Antigo, Wisconsin
Date: c. 1950
Length: 1¼" blade
Notes: This appears to be an early design from the Mepps line. Note the unusual spinner shape.
Value: $5.00 or less

Lusox
Mepps, France
Sheldon's, Inc., Antigo, Wisconsin
Date: 1960
Length: ⅞" blade
Notes: This weight-forward spinner was produced in several sizes.
Value: $5.00 or less

Comet; Tandem Minno Spin
Mepps, France
Sheldon's, Inc., Antigo, Wisconsin
Date: c. 1978
Length: 2½" (Minno Spin)
Note: By adding a realistic soft plastic minnow to the already successful Mepps design, a deadly new lure was born.
Value: $5.00 or less

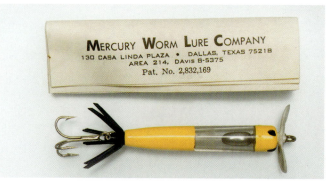

Mercury Worm
Mercury Worm Lure Co., Dallas, Texas
Date: c. 1965
Length: 2¼"
Notes: This lure features the movement and flash of mercury to attract fish.
Value: $10.00 – 15.00

Top Kick
Miller Lures, Kansas City, Missouri
Date: c. 1965
Length: 2½"
Notes: This animated lure featured a rotating head and jointed body. A 3⅜" model was also made.
Value: $10.00 – 15.00

The Boss #835; Double Trouble #862; Destroyer #833; Eelie #849
Ocean City Mfg. Co., Philadelphia, Pennsylvania
Date: c. 1955
Length: 1³⁄₁₆"; 1½"; 1½"; 1½"
Notes: In addition to lures, Ocean City also made reels.
Value: $5.00 or less

Luxor Cyclor
Pezon & Michel, France
Date: c. 1941
Length: 1½" blade
Notes: This French design has a straight wire hook connection, lead body, and unusual blade shape.
Value: $5.00 – 10.00

Psycho Lure Hot Dog
Psycho Lures, Tarzana, California
Date: c. 1967
Length: 3" shaft
Notes: The Psycho lure series are among the most interesting novelty baits made. The fish appeal of malts and hot dogs is questionable at best.
Value: $10.00 – 15.00

Psycho Lure Hamburger
Psycho Lures, Tarzana, California
Date: c. 1967
Length: 3" shaft
Notes: Psycho lures appear to be made for fishermen rather than fish but make great collectibles.
Value: $10.00 – 15.00

Psycho Lure Martini
Psycho Lures, Tarzana, California
Date: c. 1967
Length: 3" shaft
Notes: Perhaps a lure for the end of a long, unsuccessful day's fishing.
Value: $10.00 – 15.00

The Demon Fish Getter Vibrating Minnow;
The Demon Fish Getter Vibrating Bucktail Minnow
Republic Tackle Co., Republic, Washington
Date: c. 1955
Length: 2½", 2⅛
Notes: This little spinning bait might be referred to as the Chippewa Bait of the plastic era (see Immell Chippewa Bait, *Fishing Lure Collectibles Volume 1*).
Value: $15.00 – 20.00

Mirrored Trout Spoon
Roy Self, Montana
Date: c. 1960
Length: 1¾"
Note: This interesting spoon features thin "mirror silver" flakes placed into the wet red paint. Note the rubber stamping for Jack's Tavern & Sport Shop on the card.
Value: $5.00 – 10.00

Mirrored Silver Side Long Wobbler
Roy Self, Montana
Date: c. 1960
Length: 1¾"
Notes: This is the long version of the previous lure.
Value: $5.00 – 10.00

Wob-L-Rite
Seneca Tackle Co., Providence, Rhode Island
Date: c. 1946
Length: 1⅜"
Notes: Claimed by its designer, C.V. Clark, to be the first spinning lure made in America, the Wob-L-Rite quickly became popular as a prolific fish catcher.
Value: $5.00 or less

Little Cleo
Seneca Tackle Co., Providence, Rhode Island
Date: c. 1946
Length: 1½"
Notes: Designed by C.V. Clark, the Little Cleo remains a popular spoon today.
Value: $5.00 or less

Spin Flipper
Spavin Lurey Tackle Co., Rochester, Michigan
Date: c. 1965
Length: 2½" shaft
Notes: The Spin Flipper features a colorful transparent plastic blade and "pearl" beads.
Value: $5.00 or less

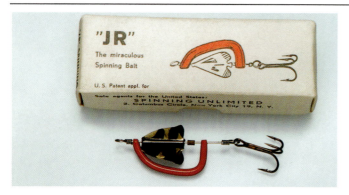

"JR" Spinning Bait (Sweden)
Spinning Unlimited, New York, New York
Date: c. 1958
Length: ¾" blade
Notes: The "JR" features an arrowhead-style blade and a wire loop keel to counter line twist.
Value: $5.00 or less

Bete/Lil' Swede
Sweden/Weber Tackle Co., Stevens Point, Wisconsin
Date: c. 1954
Length: 1¾" body
Notes: Although the blade is marked Bete on this nice-looking bait, Weber also marketed it as the Lil' Swede.
Value: $10.00 – 15.00

Monti
Switzerland
Date: c. 1955
Length: 3⅛" overall
Notes: Monti lures are often painted with red and black linear patterns. Note the combination of a front propeller and a rear Indiana-style spinner.
Value: $5.00 or less

Monti "Spinner"
Switzerland
Date: c. 1955
Length: 1⅞" blade
Notes: This spinner features a brass beaded body.
Value: $5.00 or less

Monti "Arrowhead"
Switzerland
Date: c. 1955
Length: 1⅜"
Notes: This attractive design features brass beads for the body and an arrowhead blade shape.
Value: $5.00 or less

Midjet
Tackle Industries, Shreveport, Louisiana
Date: c. 1968
Length: 1⅜"
Notes: This little plastic topwater lure was a popular fish catcher on streams and ponds.
Value: $5.00 – 10.00

Doctor Spoon
10,000 Lakes Co., St. Paul, Minnesota
Date: c. 1965
Length: 1⅞"
Notes: The Doctor Spoon was designed by Charlie Stapf who formed the Prescott Spinner Co. in Prescott, Minnesota, in 1919. The company was sold to the Fred Arbogast Co. in 1971. The Doctor Spoon is still popular today.
Value: $5.00 or less

Arrow Spoon; Copper Spoon; Spinner; Buoyant; Small Spoon (clockwise from top right)
Thomas, Europe
Date: c. 1950
Length: 1⅜"; 1⅝"; 1⅝" blade; 1½"; 1⅛"
Notes: Not much is known about the Thomas Company. The lures are highly crafted and appear to be European.
Value: $5.00 or less

Doofer
Uncle Hub's Enterprises, Ft. Lauderdale, Florida
Date: c. 1946
Length: 1½"
Notes: This is the smaller of the two sizes of the interesting weedless surface Doofer.
Value: $10.00 – 15.00

"Aluminum Rotator"
Unknown maker
Date: c. 1950
Length: 2¼"
Notes: Featuring excellent craftsmanship, this lure remains unidentified.
Value: $10.00 – 15.00

"Silver Spoon"
Unknown maker
Date: c. 1950
Length: 2"
Notes: This unusual design appears to be European in origin.
Value: $5.00 or less

"Revolving Head Spinning Lure"
Unknown maker
Date: c. 1955
Length: 1⅜"
Notes: This little gem has great eye appeal which is often over-looked because of its diminutive size.
Value: $5.00 – 10.00

"Plastic Wobbler"
Unknown maker
Date: c. 1960
Length: 1¼"
Notes: This unknown plastic bait features a dorsal fin, wiggling lip, and flashy spinner.
Value: $5.00 – 10.00

"Plastic Minnow"
Unknown maker
Date: c. 1960
Length: 2"
Notes: This beautiful minnow features a plastic body molded over a brass rod.
Value: $10.00 – 15.00

"Finland Floater"
Unknown maker
Date: c. 1962
Length: 3"
Notes: Featuring a hollow body and a reversed plastic lip, this lure has a lot of eye appeal.
Value: $5.00 – 10.00

Razzle Dazzle
Unknown maker
Date: c. 1962
Length: 1¼" blade
Notes: Similar to the Wright & McGill Red Hot Spinner, this lure features a ring of "rhinestones" which revolves on retrieve.
Value: $5.00 or less

N.L.T. Whirl; N.L.T. Spin
Unknown maker
Date: c. 1965
Length: 1⅝" shaft; 1¼" blade
Notes: The maker of the N.L.T. Whirl and N.L.T. Spin remains unknown at this time. The letters N.L.T. likely refer to the flat keel which allows no line twist.
Value: $5.00 – 10.00

"Pair-O-Dice"
Unknown maker
Date: c. 1965
Length: ½" cubes
Notes: This novelty bait features actual dice to provide fishermen luck.
Value: $5.00 or less

Twilos
Unknown maker, Europe
Date: c. 1950
Length: 3⅜"
Notes: The hollow Twilos features a most unusual lip design and a fake mother-of-pearl body.
Value: $10.00 – 15.00

"Twirling Lure"
Unknown American maker
Date: c. 1970
Length: 2½"
Notes: This wood bodied lure features integral metal "wings" which cause it to spin on retrieve. The paint is extremely thick and shows stress cracks on the "wing" portion.
Value: $5.00 – 10.00

"Hammerhead"
Unknown maker
Date: c. 1963
Length: 1¾", 1½"
Notes: This lure is molded plastic with wire-thru construction. Note the unusual "leader" attachment on the head of the lure.
Value: $5.00 – 10.00

B.S. Hurricane Spinner
Voor
Date: c. 1950
Length: 1½" body
Notes: Resembling the 1920 Bite-Em-Bait, all the information the authors could find is printed on the box.
Value: $10.00 – 15.00

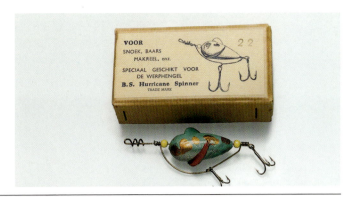

Sting Ray
Wally R Lure Company, Overland, Missouri
Date: c. 1970
Length: 2⅛"
Notes: The unusual Sting Ray has a lot of eye appeal and an interesting hook rigging.
Value: $10.00 – 15.00

Flutter Fin
The Worth Co., Stevens Point, Wisconsin
Date: c. 1962
Length: 1" diameter
Notes: The Flutter Fin was patented in 1962 and was produced into the 1970s.
Value: $10.00 – 15.00

COLLECTING TIPS AND OBSERVATIONS #5

Common Frustrations:

1. Having "first shot" at a lure

means that you probably won't

get the bait; the collector who

has the last shot will!

2. "For Trade Only" usually means

make me an offer I can't refuse.

3. Any lure in the collection of

an advanced collector

is wrongly assumed valuable.

4. If you want it, it must be good

so they will keep it themselves.

5. There always seems to be a collector

"out of state" who will pay more than you.

6. "I didn't call you because I didn't think

you would want to pay that much."

Folk Art Lures

Born of physical need, economic necessity, and inventive curiosity, folk art has transcended its original definition of being the creative efforts of the untrained. The result has been an overwhelming rush by collectors worldwide to acquire folk art of all kinds, from paintings and rustic furniture to curios and fishing lures. Though the supply is rapidly diminishing, collectors seek to use the expressive humanness of folk art to soften the interior lifestyle of the new millennium. Folk art can be narrative, allowing insight into the time of its creation or it can be anonymous, allowing the viewer to imagine and concoct his own story of its creation. In either case, folk art has achieved a level of acceptance by collectors which causes it to be both highly desirable and difficult to find.

Within the fishing lure collecting fraternity, folk art lures have suffered a somewhat controversial and interesting reputation; they seem to be either enjoyed or disregarded as serious collectibles. At the high end, early folk art lures with great eye appeal and craftsmanship, as those shown in *Fishing Lure Collectibles Volume 1*, command a price limited only by one's ability to ask. Conversely, the more recently created folk art lures, such as those in this volume, are often available and affordable. Values simply cannot be placed upon one-of-a-kind lures unless they become available at auction. Even then, values cannot be trusted since the bidding process involves the collector's ego and may bring about a competitive cash flow, stopped only when the losing bidder's funds are exceeded.

Flea markets, antique shows, and fishing lure shows usually have a variety of folk art lures ranging from the most interesting to ordinary junk. The wise collector will study folk art lures, learn to "think down the road," and imagine how he will enjoy a potential purchase over time. While purchases are always more comfortable when the buyer has a degree of knowledge, folk art lures seldom appear in duplicate, suggesting that one should take care passing over a lure they might later wish had been added to their collection.

Dudley Murphy
Springfield, Missouri

"String-Wrapped Tom Thumb"
Anonymous Missouri maker
Date: c. 1937
Length: 2½"
Notes: This lure design is based on the 1920 Tom Thumb made by Keeling. Note the blended paint over the string-wrapped body and the coarse scale effect created by chicken wire.

"Crab"
Anonymous maker
Date: c. 1938
Length: 3"
Notes: Modeled after Heddon's Crab Wiggler, this lure features glass eyes and string appendages.

"Fat Wiggler"
Anonymous maker
Date: c. 1938
Length: 2"
Notes: Borrowing from the CCBCO #800 Deluxe Wag Tail Chub, this fat little lure probably had great action in the water.

"Black Bug"
Anonymous Michigan maker
Date: c. 1939
Length: 3⅝"
Notes: Ten tufts of black bucktail make the legs for this nicely sculpted lure.

"Bream"
Anonymous maker
Date: c. 1940
Length: 2⅜"
Notes: This colorful "Bream" features a weight behind the lip for balance.

"Carrier Spoon"
Anonymous Michigan maker
Date: c. 1940
Length: 2¼"
Notes: Probably cut from an old air conditioner name plate, this spoon is cleverly inventive.

"Pen Cap Lures"
Anonymous maker
Date: c. 1941
Length: 2¼" (left lure)
Notes: These clever lures are great examples of necessity being the mother of invention.

"Punkinseeds"
Anonymous Arizona maker
Date: c. 1942
Length: 1½" (large lure)
Notes: This colorful set of Punkinseeds has a southwest Native American paint quality.

"Beetles"
Anonymous maker
Date: c. 1942
Length: 2", 2½", 2¾"
Notes: These brightly painted festive beetles appear to be designed as surface swimmers.

"O-Bite"
Anonymous maker
Date: c. 1948
Length: 3"
Notes: This lure appears to be an attempt at creating a South Bend Fish-O-Bite. Note the raised "collar" around the tail.

"Vamp"
Anonymous maker
Date: c. 1948
Length: 3½"
Notes: Heddon's Vamp was the likely model for this handcarved creation.

"Duck"
Ken Walkie, Streater, Illinois
Date: c. 1948
Length: 3½"
Notes: This glass-eyed feathered duck uses red spinner blades to imitate feet.

"Jitterbug"
Anonymous maker
Date: c. 1950
Notes: This lure was an interesting attempt at making an Arbogast Jitterbug.

"Hula Popper"
Anonymous maker
Date: c. 1950
Length: 2¾" overall
Notes: This lure is a clever attempt at making an Arbogast Hula Popper.

"Surface Bug"
Anonymous maker
Date: c. 1950
Length: 2⅝" body
Notes: Featuring a complicated aluminum wing inset into the body, this lure was designed to struggle on the surface of the water.

"Leopard"
Anonymous maker
Date: c. 1950
Length: 3"
Notes: Covered with fake leopard fur, this interesting shallow runner has mother-of-pearl button eyes.

"Sparrow"
Anonymous maker
Date: c. 1950
Length: 3¼"
Notes: This wild-looking lure appears to be an attempt at imitating a struggling sparrow.

"Crawdad"
Anonymous maker
Date: c. 1951
Length: 2½"
Notes: With bold paint, bead eyes, and a broad tail, this lure was designed to represent a Crayfish.

"Bomber"
Anonymous Missouri maker
Date: c. 1955
Length: 2½"
Notes: This Bomber look-alike features a brass lip and handmade linetie.

"Bird"
Anonymous Oklahoma maker
Date: c. 1956
Length: 2³⁄₁₆"
Notes: This neat little bird lure was designed to be a floater/diver.

"Surface Scooter"
Anonymous maker
Date: c. 1955
Length: 3½"
Notes: This lure combines design characteristics of several manufacturers: CCBCO Crawdad rubber legs, Scatback tail plate, and a Pflueger Wizard Wiggler back spinner.

"Weedless Surface Bait"
Anonymous Arizona maker
Date: c. 1956
Length: 3⅛"
Notes: This froggy-looking floater provides two clues to its date: Post WWII vintage prop and Band-Aid strips as designs. In 1956 Johnson and Johnson marketed a line of patterned Band-Aids called Stars N Strips. Other than these clues, one might think this is a pre-1940 lure.

"Death Head"
Anonymous Arizona maker
Date: c. 1960
Length: 1¾"
Notes: Made by the same maker as the previous lure, this example also uses a Stars N Strips Band-Aid for colorful design.

"Tulsa Bug"
Anonymous Oklahoma maker
Date: c. 1958
Length: 2⅜"
Notes: This lure appears to be a modification of the Di-Dipper lure by the Tulsa Tackle Company.

"Green Diver"
Anonymous Oklahoma maker
Date: c. 1959
Length: 1½" body
Notes: Mostly diving lip and hooks, this colorful little lure was designed to run deep.

"Clicker"
Leo "Poolie" Sinkovic, Arma, Kansas
Date: c. 1960
Length: 3¼"
Notes: This interesting design features a large fixed prop which turns the shaft against a "gear" inside the body. The resulting sound is similar to a bait casting reel with the click engaged. To control flipping over in the water on retrieve, a large keel and extra flotation corks were added.

"Biter"
Anonymous maker
Date: c. 1960
Length: 4¼"
Notes: This stylish jointed minnow features a toothy spring-loaded lower jaw made to hold a minnow or other live bait as an attractor.

"Wiggling Jig"
Anonymous Oklahoma maker
Date: c. 1960
Length: 1⅝"
Notes: A clever design, this little lure features a lead jig-type head, a wobbling lip, and a buoyant wood body.

"Kansas Folk Lures"
Anonymous Kansas maker
Date: c. 1960
Length: 4¾" (green jointed lure)
Notes: The variety of designs shown here suggests that the maker may have at some time lived near salt water (re: the shrimp lure) as well as in Kansas.

"Frog Floater"
A.C. Hart, Springfield, Missouri
Date: c. 1965
Length: 1¾"
Notes: This interesting little topwater lure was designed to accommodate a piece of split pork rind attached to imitate legs.

"Rapalas"
Anonymous Springfield, Missouri maker
Date: c. 1967
Length: 4¼", 5⅛"
Notes: These lures are the result of a fisherman desiring to fish with a Rapala before Rapalas were readily available.

"Foam Popper"
Anonymous maker
Date: c. 1967
Length: 1¾"
Notes: This topwater popper uses dense foam for the body and squirrel tail hair for the wings.

"Balsa Crankbait"
Anonymous Ohio maker
Date: c. 1974
Length: 3"
Notes: This interesting crankbait represents an individual's attempt to design and fish with a Tennessee Shad/Big-O look-alike.

Contemporary Lures

It is axiomatic for fishing tackle collectors to believe that older is better, and utilitarian objects of past centuries have become the prized possessions of collectors today. Those who believe recently-made lures or spearing decoys have similar value run the risk of apostasy.

There are, however, a growing number of artists and craftsmen who make fishing lures and decoys that meet or exceed the quality of the skilled tackle makers of the past. There is also a growing number of collectors who recognize this artistry and find satisfaction in collecting it. Whether the contemporary creations are made with function in mind — true with at least some lure makers — or designed as artful replications of an earlier tradition, the same talent, creativity, and loving attention to detail are evident in their work. In some instances the artists-craftsmen make every component of the finished product, from glass eyes to hooks. In every case the work exhibits personal expression and exudes individuality. Lures and spearing decoys made by contemporary carvers are at times as sophisticated as the best production pieces of the past or as funky as the homemade pieces of the old cottage industry.

Savvy collectors know that some contemporary pieces will one day command far more than their initial costs. And yet others, devoid of fiscal strategy, find pleasure in owning fishing collectibles that are aesthetically satisfying and a source of contemplative pleasure. Regardless of what motivates the maker or the collector, fishing collectibles made today have already found a niche.

Gary Smith
Woodstock, Georgia

327

Ruby Eye Spinner
Bob Baird, Diamond Baird Lure Co., Salt Lake City, Utah
Date: c. 2000
Length: 2¼" blade
Notes: Bob Baird is internationally renowned for his stained glass restorations. Also a jewelry maker and an avid fisherman, combining the two disciplines when recovering from a back injury was a natural for Bob. He uses precious metals and precious stones in his spinners.
Prices available on request.

Trout Spinner
Bob Baird, Diamond Baird Lure Co., Salt Lake City, Utah
Date: c. 200
Length: 1⅜" blade
Notes: Bob Baird's spinner blades show the evidence of careful hand shaping from sterling silver. He makes the swivels and metal beads by hand, often using 24K gold as a highlight. Blake Peterson ties the attractive patterns on Bob's hand-forged hooks.
Prices available on request.

Flyrod Trout Spinner
Bob Baird, Diamond Baird Lure Co., Salt Lake City, Utah
Date: c. 2000
Length: ⅞" blade
Notes: This small bait features a nicely rounded and hand planished blade pinned to the mount with a 24K gold pin.
Prices available on request.

Midnight Spinner
Bob Baird, Diamond Baird Lure Co., Salt Lake City, Utah
Date: c. 2000
Length: 1⅝" blade
Notes: The blade on this lure is made of silver with a dark patina. Note the 24K gold ball on the shaft.
Prices available on request.

Mother-of-Pearl Spinner
Bob Baird, Diamond Baird Lure Co., Salt Lake City, Utah
Date: c. 2000
Length: 1⅜" blade
Notes: This lure features a wonderfully convoluted mother-of-pearl blade mounted in sterling and pinned with gold. Baird's "shepherd's hook" swivel and shaft design is complimented by Blake Peterson's tasteful hook dressing.
Prices available on request.

Wounded Minnow
Bob Baird, Diamond Baird Lure Co., Salt Lake City, Utah
Date: c. 2000
Length: 2" blade
Notes: While many of Bob Baird's lures are prototypical, it is doubtful that large runs of his fantastic lures will ever be produced because of the time-consuming craftsmanship required. Any collector owning a Baird lure is indeed blessed.
Prices available on request.

Pearl Wounded Minnow
Bob Baird, Diamond Baird Lure Co., Salt Lake City, Utah
Date: c. 2001
Length: 2¾" blade
Notes: Modeled after the previous lure, the Wounded Minnow, this example features an attractive mother-of-pearl body and a "shepherd's hook" at the eye of the bare hook.
Prices available on request.

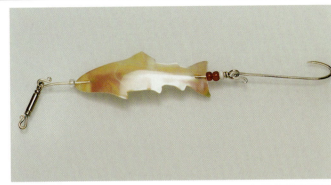

Frog Spinner
Bob Baird, Diamond Baird Lure Co., Salt Lake City, Utah
Date: c. 2001
Length: 2¾" blade
Notes: The Frog Spinner design is similar in concept to the Wounded Minnow but features a frog silhouette with raised eyes. Note the "Diamond Baird" stamp.
Prices available on request.

Floating Frog
Guy Chambers, Ely, Minnesota
Date: c. 1995
Length: 1⅝" body

Bucktail Minnow
Guy Chambers, Ely, Minnesota
Date: c. 1995
Length: 3" body

White Minnow
Guy Chambers, Ely, Minnesota
Date: c. 1995
Length: 2¾"

"Trory Minnow Bait"
Guy Chambers, Ely, Minnesota
Date: c. 1995
Length: 2⅝"

Trolling Spoons
Guy Chambers, Ely, Minnesota
Date: c. 1995
Length: 2⅜", 1½" blades

Sunfish
Carl Christiansen, Newberry, Michigan
Date: c. 1997
Length: 2⅜"
Notes: Carl Christiansen is a prolific carver of ice spearing decoys, lures, tables, benches, signs, and numerous other objects. His fly-rod series of lures are featured in this book. The Sunfish shown features Carl's "trademark" paint style.
Prices available on request.

Pike Minnow
Carl Christiansen, Newberry, Michigan
Date: c. 1998
Length: 2¼"
Notes: This little Pike is designed to float on its side.
Prices available on request.

Brook Trout
Carl Christiansen, Newberry, Michigan
Date: c. 1997
Length: 2½"
Notes: A side floater, this lure exhibits the basic shape and coloration of a brook trout.
Prices available on request.

Brown Trout
Carl Christiansen, Newberry, Michigan
Date: c. 1997
Length: 2 ⅛"
Notes: This little brown trout is designed to float in an upright position.
Prices available on request.

Bullhead
Carl Christiansen, Newberry, Michigan
Date: c. 1997
Length: 2"
Notes: This lure features a typical "catfish" profile and whiskers.
Prices available on request.

Tiger Swallowtail Butterfly
Carl Christiansen, Newberry, Michigan
Date: c. 1998
Length: 2½" wing span
Notes: This colorful design captures the essence of the butterfly it imitates.
Prices available on request.

Blue Moth
Carl Christiansen, Newberry, Michigan
Date: c. 1998
Length: 2¾" wing span
Notes: The intricate line work and red bead eyes give this lure a lot of eye appeal.
Prices available on request.

Sphinx Moth
Carl Christiansen, Newberry, Michigan
Date: c. 1998
Length: 3⅛" wing span
Notes: This attractive moth is painted in natural colors and features bead eyes.
Prices available on request.

Cicada
Carl Christiansen, Newberry, Michigan
Date: c. 1998
Length: 2½"
Notes: Red bead eyes and wire legs are features of this interesting Cicada.
Prices available on request.

Caterpillar on leaf
Carl Christiansen, Newberry, Michigan
Date: c. 1998
Length: 3¼"
Notes: One of Carl's most innovative designs, this caterpillar rides on a leaf floating in the water.
Prices available on request.

Green Bug
Carl Christiansen, Newberry, Michigan
Date: c. 1998
Length: 2"
Notes: This lure was packaged in a three-pack wooden box with two other flyrod lures. Carl's lures are packaged in dovetail wooden boxes.
Prices available on request.

Stickbug
Carl Christiansen, Newberry, Michigan
Date: c. 1998
Length: 2¾"
Notes: This insect features bead eyes, wire legs, and a realistically painted body.
Prices available on request.

Ladybug

Carl Christiansen, Newberry, Michigan
Date: c. 1998
Length: ⅝"
Notes: Christiansen Ladybugs are made in a variety of sizes. The example shown represents the smallest size Carl normally makes.
Prices available on request.

Painted Turtle

Carl Christiansen, Newberry, Michigan
Date: c. 1998
Length: 1¾"
Notes: This attractive little painted turtle expresses Carl's sense of humor with its message painted in red on the shell inviting fish to "eat me."
Prices available on request.

Frog

Carl Christiansen, Newberry, Michigan
Date: c. 1998
Length: 1½"
Notes: This tiny frog features bead eyes and an arched body.
Prices available on request.

Blue Bill

Carl Christiansen, Newberry, Michigan
Date: c. 1998
Length: 2"
Notes: This interesting bird has glass bead eyes and wings. Carl marks his lures with his initials "C.C."
Prices available on request.

Crawfish

Carl Christiansen, Newberry, Michigan
Date: c. 1997
Length: 2"
Note: Sleek and minimal, this crawfish expresses the essential qualities of the crustacean it imitates. Great synergy accompanies the acquisition of Carl Christiansen lures. The larger the display, the more attractive the lures appear.
Prices available on request.

Flyrod Poppers
Sorin Dragoi, Bucharest, Romania
Date: c. 2001
Length: up to ¾" body
Notes: Sorin is an outstanding lure maker whose products are often difficult to find in the United States. These little Poppers are some of Sorin's early work.
Prices available on request.

Winchester 5-Hook Minnow
Rick Edmisten, Phil Beguhl, Santa Barbara, California
Date: c. 2001
Length: 4"
Notes: Rick and Phil purchased the rights to produce Winchester lures from Olin, the parent company. These handsome, well-crafted lures feature silverplated hardware, glass eyes, and paint patterns which differ significantly from the original Winchester lures.
Prices available on request.

"Nymph"
Kelly Galloup, The Troutsman Fly Fishing Shop, Traverse City, Michigan
Date: c. 2000
Length: 1¼"
Notes: The result of a relaxed afternoon at the Troutsman, this beautiful fly features several different kinds of feathers and showcases Kelly's tying mastery.
Prices available on request.

Pike
Bill Grossman, Lower Hudson Valley, New York
Date: c. 1999
Length: 6"
Notes: Bill Grossman's lures are handsomely painted with a special iridescent paint imported from France. Metal components are often salvaged from other lures. This beautiful Pike is typical of Grossman's paint work.
Prices available on request.

Three-Hook Minnow
Bill Grossman, Lower Hudson Valley, New York
Date: c. 1999
Length: 4¾"
Notes: Featuring an incised scale pattern, this lure uses Heddon two-piece hook hangers. Grossman's lures need to be viewed in-hand to appreciate the sense of depth in the paint.
Prices available on request.

Sunfish

Bill Grossman, Lower Hudson Valley, New York
Date: c. 1999
Length: 2 ⅞"
Notes: This attractive Sunfish features incised scales and glass eyes.
Prices available on request.

Crappie

Bill Grossman, Lower Hudson Valley, New York
Date: c. 1999
Length: 3⅝"
Notes: Fitted with Heddon props and hook hardware, this Crappie paint job is simply gorgeous.
Prices available on request.

Pickerel

Bill Grossman, Lower Hudson Valley, New York
Date: c. 1999
Length: 5⅜"
Notes: This slim Pickerel features a realistic profile and is fitted with glass eyes.
Prices available on request.

Frog

Bill Grossman, Lower Hudson Valley, New York
Date: c. 1999
Length: 4⅜"
Notes: A clever design, this Frog features an open leg design to fit the rear hook, making it weedless. The wiggling lip is from a CCBCO lure.
Prices available on request.

Eel

Bill Grossman, Lower Hudson Valley, New York
Date: c. 2001
Length: 8"
Notes: Bill Grossman is an art teacher and a painter who finds self expression in lure making. This unusual Eel reflects Grossman's interesting sense of creativity and design.
Prices available on request.

Flyrod Frogs
Bill Grossman, Lower Hudson Valley, New York
Date: c. 2000
Length: 1", 1¼"
Notes: These simple little frogs feature bead eyes and upturned hooks.
Prices available on request.

Bluejay
Adam Hartmann, Jacksonville, Florida
Date: c. 2001
Length: 5¼"
Notes: This is the first bluejay imitation the authors have ever seen. This lure won second place in the first Carver-Comp competition.
Prices available on request.

June Bug Fly
Adam Hartmann, Jacksonville, Florida
Date: c. 2001
Length: ⅞"
Notes: Adam's little June Bug has the eye appeal factors of diminutive size and large eyes.
Prices available on request.

Dragonfly
Adam Hartmann, Jacksonville, Florida
Date: c. 2001
Length: 3¾"
Notes: This attractive large Dragonfly features realistic paint and veined wings.
Prices available on request.

Blue Bellied Canyon Lizard
Adam Hartmann, Jacksonville, Florida
Date: c. 2001
Length: 4¼"
Notes: True to its name, this unusual lizard has a blue underside.
Prices available on request.

Turtle

Don Hoseney, Washington, Michigan
Date: c. 1987
Length: 2"
Notes: One of the all-time great lure makers, Don Hoseney passed away in 1985. Don's son Ron inherited his dad's sense of design and craftsmanship and carries on the Hoseney tradition. The Turtle shown is an excellent example of Don's work.
Prices available on request.

Turtle

Ron Hoseney, Rapid City, Michigan
Date: c. 2001
Length: 2"
Notes: Very similar to his father's turtle design, Ron Hoseney demonstrates his abilities with his own Turtle.
Prices available on request.

Flyrod Frog

Ron Hoseney, Rapid City, Michigan
Date: c. 2001
Length: 2⅛"
Notes: Ron's Flyrod Frogs are based on his father's designs and provide collectors with an opportunity to own these high quality lures at an affordable price.
Prices available on request.

Flyrod Mouse

Ron Hoseney, Rapid City, Michigan
Date: c. 2001
Length: 1⅝", 1¾"
Notes: All Ron Hoseney lures are packaged in an attractive wood slide-top box. These mice are also available as lapel pins.
Prices available on request.

Frog Ice Spearing Decoy

Ron Hoseney, Rapid City, Michigan
Date: c. 2001
Length: 4"
Notes: This beautiful frog spearing decoy won Hoseney a good bit of attention in 2001 at the National Decoy Carvers Competition in Livonia, Michigan.
Prices available on request.

Brown Trout Ice Spearing Decoy
Ron Hoseney, Rapid City, Michigan
Date: c. 2001
Length: 3"
Notes: This miniature brown trout decoy demonstrates Ron Hoseney's high-quality design and craftsmanship.
Prices available on request.

Chub Minnow
Ron Hoseney, Rapid City, Michigan
Date: c. 2002
Length: 2¾"
Notes: The Chub Minnow is a new-for-2002 design that bears watching. Several variations are planned.
Prices available on request.

Bass: Largemouth; Smallmouth
Ron Hoseney, Rapid City, Michigan
Date: c. 2002
Length: 2¾"
Notes: Designed along the same lines as the Hoseney Chub Minnow, these bass feature realistic paint and small glass eyes.
Prices available on request.

The Pomme De Terre
Lanier Feemster, Little Sac Tackle, Springfield, Missouri
Date: c. 1998
Length: 4⅜"
Notes: Following the traditions of the major companies in the early twentieth century, Lanier Feemster makes all of his components except screw eyes, hooks, and glass eyes. Note his distinctive spinner design.
Prices available on request.

The Niangua Minnow
Little Sac Tackle, Springfield, Missouri
Date: c. 2001
Length: 3⅜"
Notes: Like the five-hook Pomme de Terre, the three-hook Niangua Minnow features special spinners and beautiful paint. The "scramble" finish shown was new in 2000. Wood boxes are available for Little Sac baits.
Prices available on request.

The Little Osage
Little Sac Tackle, Springfield, Missouri
Date: c. 2001
Length: 1⅞"
Notes: This little bait is an early attempt at using a bucktail-dressed tail hook.
Prices available on request.

Smilie
Little Sac Tackle, Springfield, Missouri
Date: c. 1997
Length: 4¼"
Notes: Lanier named this lure because of the smiling expression. Made concurrently with the Gasconade River Minnow, Smilie uses only one propeller.
Prices available on request.

The Gasconade River Minnow
Little Sac Tackle, Springfield, Missouri
Date: c. 2000
Length: 4¼"
Notes: The beautiful paint on this surface lure gives it instant eye appeal.
Prices available on request.

Walkie-Popper
Little Sac Tackle, Springfield, Missouri
Date: c. 2001
Length: 4"
Notes: This angled, flat-faced surface popper features glass eyes.
Prices available on request.

One Killer Minnow
Little Sac Tackle, Springfield, Missouri
Date: c. 2001
Length: 6"
Notes: The giant of the Little Sac line. The One Killer Minnow was made in very limited quantities.
Prices available on request.

Walking Stick
Little Sac Tackle, Springfield, Missouri
Date: c. 2001
Length: 4¾"
Notes: Designed as a Zara Spook type surface lure, the Walking Stick features glass eyes and beautiful paint.
Prices available on request.

Catch and Keep, Toad/Hopper
David Martin, Sparks, Nevada
Date: c. 2001
Length: 1⅝" frog body
Notes: This amazingly realistic fly is a testimonial to David's prowess tying ultra realistic flies and establishes a new benchmark for others to strive for.
Prices available on request.

Catch and Keep, Poison Arrow Frog/Damselfly
David Martin, Sparks, Nevada
Date: c. 2001
Length: 1⅛" frog body
Notes: This exotic South American frog is captured here enjoying a damselfly snack.
Prices available on request.

Catch & Keep, Tree Frog/Damselfly
David Martin, Sparks, Nevada
Date: c. 2001
Length: 1½"
Note: This hungry little tree frog certainly appears to be enjoying his freshly-caught damselfly meal. David is the undisputed king of realistic fly tying.
Prices available on request.

Catch & Keep, Dragonfly/Mayfly
David Martin, Sparks, Nevada
Date: c. 2001
Length: 3¾"
Notes: This large dragonfly has just captured a mayfly.
Prices available on request.

Katydid
David Martin, Sparks, Nevada
Date: c. 2000
Length: 2¼" body
Notes: This particular fly is the very first version of this pattern and was tied while an actual katydid (Katy) was perched beside the tying vise.
Prices available on request.

Crawfish
David Martin, Sparks, Nevada
Date: c. 2000
Length: 1½"
Notes: This ultra realistic crawfish appears ready and able to move.
Prices available on request.

Frog
David Martin, Sparks, Nevada
Date: c. 2000
Length: 1¾"
Notes: A noted wildlife sculptor, David Martin sought to tie flies that could be fished with. David calls this little lure a "fishing frog."
Prices available on request.

Beetle
David Martin, Sparks, Nevada
Date: c. 2000
Length: ⅞"
Notes: This is a generic Martin fishing beetle.
Prices available on request.

Grasshopper
David Martin, Sparks, Nevada
Date: c. 200
Length: 1⅝"
Notes: David often teaches others how to tie his popular grasshopper at fly tying workshops.
Prices available on request.

Bumblebee
David Martin, Sparks, Nevada
Date: c. 2000
Length: 1"
Notes: Martin's Western Bumblebee has all the elements of eye appeal, making it highly collectible.
Prices available on request.

Wasp
David Martin, Sparks, Nevada
Date: c. 2000
Length: 1 1⁄16"
Notes: This ultra realistic wasp, whether displayed alone or in a group of Martin flies, appears to be a real insect.
Prices available on request.

Honey Bee
David Martin, Sparks, Nevada
Date: c. 2000
Length: ½"
Notes: The highly detailed honey bee even has pollen sacks on its hind legs.
Prices available on request.

Carpenter Ant
David Martin, Sparks, Nevada
Date: c. 2000
Length: ½"
Notes: David claims that this little ant is deadly for Trukee River trout.
Prices available on request.

Red Skimmer
David Martin, Sparks, Nevada
Date: c. 2000
Length: 1¼"
Notes: This beautiful dragonfly features David's own handmade wings. Only God makes them better!
Prices available on request.

Damselfly
David Martin, Sparks, Nevada
Date: c. 2000
Length: 1⅛"
Notes: This is what the damselfly looks like before David's frogs catch them.
Prices available on request.

Cricket
David Martin, Sparks, Nevada
Date: c. 2000
Length: 1"
Notes: The old timers used to say "a cricket on the hearth brings good luck." So does a cricket in the lure collection.
Prices available on request.

Mayfly, Hexagenia
David Martin, Sparks, Nevada
Date: c. 2000
Length: 1⅜" body
Notes: The "Hex" hatch in northern Michigan is legendary, resulting in the largest mayflies in the world. David's Hex is a perfect representation.
Prices available on request.

Golden Stonefly
David Martin, Sparks, Nevada
Date: c. 2000
Length: 1⅛"
Notes: If viewed side by side, one would have difficulty distinguishing a David Martin Stonefly from the real thing.
Prices available on request.

Black Scorpion
David Martin, Sparks, Nevada
Date: c. 2000
Length: 1¾"
Notes: A feeling of uneasiness often accompanies the viewer's first confrontation with a David Martin Scorpion.
Prices available on request.

Crappie
Dr. C. Baxter Kruger's Mediator Lure Co., Jackson, Mississippi
Date: c. 2001
Length: 7" overall
Notes: Made of wood, this beautiful Crappie features glass eyes, synthetic fiber fins and tail, and a textured foil covering beneath numerous coats of tinted and colored varnish.
Prices available on request.

Bluegill; Shad
Dr. C. Baxter Kruger's Mediator Lure Co., Jackson, Mississippi
Date: c. 2001
Length: 4½" overall
Notes: Utilizing the same unique construction as the previous Crappie, these two attractive lures feature very realistic paint work. The iridescent quality of Dr. Kruger's finish can be seen in the examples shown.
Prices available on request.

Ringed Bog Haunter Dragonfly
Peter Duguay, Mother Nature Lures, Cumberland Beach, Ontario
Date: c. 1999
Length: 3⅝"
Notes: Having begun his career as a lure maker by creating lures to fish with, Peter Duguay quickly graduated to making creative interpretations of insects which have become popular collectibles.
Prices available on request.

Thread Wasted Wasp
Peter Duguay, Mother Nature Lures, Cumberland Beach, Ontario
Date: c. 1999
Length: 3½"
Notes: This Wasp features Duguay's lathe-turned body, metal wings, and "wire" legs.
Prices available on request.

Hummingbird Moth
Peter Duguay, Mother Nature Lures, Cumberland Beach, Ontario
Date: c. 1999
Length: 3¼"
Notes: This brightly-painted moth features a front spinner and weedguard.
Prices available on request.

Bumblebee Moth
Peter Duguay, Mother Nature Lures, Cumberland Beach, Ontario
Date: c. 1999
Length: 3"
Notes: Similar to the previous lure, this moth features milky, opaque eyes.
Prices available on request.

Cranefly
Peter Duguay, Mother Nature Lures, Cumberland Beach, Ontario
Date: c. 1999
Length: 3¼"
Notes: This attractive two-hook lure is nicely painted and features protruding eyes and thin wings.
Prices available on request.

Marsh Treader
Peter Duguay, Mother Nature Lures, Cumberland Beach, Ontario
Date: c. 1999
Length: 3⅞"
Notes: This lure has the Duguay trademark features plus an implied sense of movement.
Prices available on request.

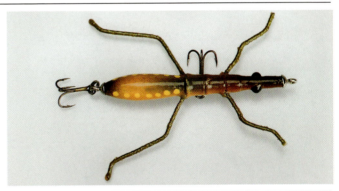

Bumblebee
Peter Duguay, Mother Nature Lures, Cumberland Beach, Ontario
Date: c. 1999
Length: 2"
Notes: Duguay's lures are produced in limited editions; the authors were lucky to snag this bee before the edition sold out.
Prices available on request.

Snout Beetle
Peter Duguay, Mother Nature Lures, Cumberland Beach, Ontario
Date: c. 1999
Length: 2½"
Notes: The "bug eyed" Snout Beetle features attractive paint and "wire" legs.
Prices available on request.

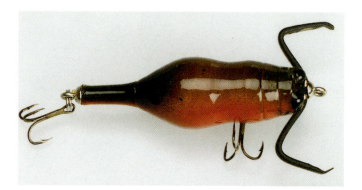

Water Scorpion

Peter Duguay, Mother Nature Lures, Cumberland Beach, Ontario
Date: c. 1999
Length: 3⅛"
Notes: The legs on this lure are shaped from metal and give the lure an aggressive stance.
Prices available on request.

Back Swimmer

Peter Duguay, Mother Nature Lures, Cumberland Beach, Ontario
Date: c. 1999
Length: 2½"
Notes: The Back Swimmer has flattened legs and attractive paint. A collection of Peter's lures makes a great display.
Prices available on request.

Luna Moth

Peter Duguay, Mother Nature Lures, Cumberland Beach, Ontario
Date: c. 2001
Notes: It is unusual to see a lure representing the large Luna Moth. This example features a single hook and large wooden wings.
Prices available on request.

Two-Spotted Ladybug

Peter Duguay, Mother Nature Lures, Cumberland Beach, Ontario
Date: c. 2002
Length: 2"
Notes: A frog lure similar to this Ladybug was made concurrently. Note the weedless hook design.
Prices available on request.

Rousseau Frog Decoy

Rich Rousseau, Mancelona, Michigan
Date: c. 1996
Length: 9"
Notes: Rich Rousseau's high-quality wildlife carvings are well-known in Michigan. This wonderful ice spearing frog decoy features glass eyes, moveable feet, and highly detailed paint.
Prices available on request.

Rousseau Crankbait
Rich Rousseau, Mancelona, Michigan
Date: c. 2001
Length: 2⅛"
Notes: Inspired by Heddon's Punkinseed, this attractive little lure features Rich's unusual scaled paint finish.
Prices available on request.

Rousseau Bluegill
Rich Rousseau, Mancelona, Michigan
Date: c. 2001
Length: 3½"
Notes: This interesting lure features glass eyes, carved scales, and a realistic sunfish paint job. The pectoral fins form the diving lip.
Prices available on request.

Rousseau Turtle
Rich Rousseau, Mancelona, Michigan
Date: c. 2001
Length: 3⅜"
Notes: Rousseau's stylized Turtle is designed to float realistically in the water.
Prices available on request.

"Spin Diver"
Gary Slama, Oregon
Date: c. 1993
Length: 2"
Notes: An excellent craftsman, Gary Slama creates lures ranging from oversized to miniature. His tiny lures are readily identified with the lures which inspired them, in this case, the Heddon Spin Diver.
Prices available on request.

"Swimming Minnow"
Gary Slama, Oregon
Date: c. 1993
Length: 2⅜"
Notes: This is Gary's miniaturized version of Heddon's #900 Swimming Minnow.
Prices available on request.

"Ice Decoy"
Gary Slama, Oregon
Date: c. 1993
Length: 2⅛"
Notes: This small ice spearing decoy is a copy of the Heddon "Batwing" decoy.
Prices available on request.

"Plug Oreno"
Gary Slama, Oregon
Date: c. 1993
Length: 1¼"
Notes: This Slama version of South Bend's Plug Oreno is amazingly true to scale.
Prices available on request.

"Whirl Oreno"
Gary Slama, Oregon
Date: c. 1993
Length: ⅝"
Notes: Gary Slama's miniature South Bend "Whirl Oreno."
Prices available on request.

"Multi Wobbler"
Gary Slama, Oregon
Date: c. 1993
Length: 2⅛"
Notes: Slama's Winchester "Multi-Wobbler" features moveable metal fins like the original.
Prices available on request.

"Kent Frog"
Gary Slama, Oregon
Date: c. 1993
Length: 1⅜"
Notes: At first glance, the Slama "Kent Frog" looks like it was made in the Pflueger factory like the original.
Prices available on request.

"Lady Bug"
Gary Slama, Oregon
Date: c. 1993
Length: 2½"
Notes: The Gary Slama version of the Moonlight Bait Company "Lady Bug."
Prices available on request.

"Gar Minnow"
Gary Slama, Oregon
Date: c. 1993
Length: 2¾", 3"
Notes: Shown are two Slama miniature copies of the Creek Chub Gar Minnow.
Prices available on request.

"Mouse"
Gary Slama, Oregon
Date: c. 1993
Length: 1⁷⁄₁₆"
Notes: Cleverly designed with paddling legs, this is Gary Slama's original version of a swimming mouse.
Prices available on request.

Sucker Minnow
Tony Smith, Macatawa Bait Co., Holland, Michigan
Date: c. 1983
Length: 5¼"
Notes: Tony Smith began carving lures and spearing decoys in 1979. Shown is Tony's first attempt at making a Sucker Minnow. Note the heavily textured paint finish.
Prices available on request.

Musky Brook Trout
Tony Smith, Macatawa Bait Co., Holland, Michigan
Date: c. 1997
Length: 6⁵⁄₈"
Notes: Tony's lures are all individually carved and painted by hand, and this example shows his frequently used decorative hook hanger design.
Prices available on request.

Dace Minnow
Tony Smith, Macatawa Bait Co., Holland, Michigan
Date: c. 1990
Length: 5"
Notes: This Dace Minnow features striking paint and unusual weedless side hooks.
Prices available on request.

Bluegill
Tony Smith, Macatawa Bait Co., Holland, Michigan
Date: c. 1998
Length: 3"
Notes: The special hook and attachment shown here is typical of unique designs of Tony Smith's.
Prices available on request.

Crappie
Tony Smith, Macatawa Bait Co., Holland, Michigan
Date: c. 1993
Length: 3¼"
Notes: This beautiful Crappie features glass eyes, dressed tail hook, elaborate hook attachment, and life-like carved gills.
Prices available on request.

Articulated Musky
Tony Smith, Macatawa Bait Co., Holland, Michigan
Date: c. 1996
Length: 7⅞"
Notes: This four-sectioned musky demonstrates Tony's creativity.
Prices available on request.

Walleye
Tony Smith, Macatawa Bait Co., Holland, Michigan
Date: c. 2001
Length: 4⅝"
Notes: Tony's lures often demonstrate a Native American influence in their paint patterns.
Prices available on request.

CONTEMPORARY LURES

Yellow Perch

Tony Smith, Macatawa Bait Co., Holland, Michigan

Date: c. 1993

Length: 4"

Notes: This lure features detailed carving on the mouth and gills, glass eyes, metal fins, and Tony's unique belly hook mounting system.

Prices available on request.

Catfish

Tony Smith, Macatawa Bait Co., Holland, Michigan

Date: c. 2001

Length: 4½"

Notes: Tony's catfish is a great example of innovative design blended with careful observation.

Prices available on request.

Musky Frog, top view

Tony Smith, Macatawa Bait Co., Holland, Michigan

Date: c. 1993

Length: 11¾" overall

Notes: Normally one view of a lure is sufficient to illustrate the important aspects of the design. This Musky Frog is a rare exception. Not only is this a very large lure, but it features Bing's weedless side hooks, Jamison Barbless leg hooks, leather feet, intricate paint and glass eyes. . . and that is just the top view.

Prices available on request.

Musky Frog, bottom view

Tony Smith, Macatawa Bait Co., Holland, Michigan

Date: c. 1993

Length: 11¾" overall

Notes: When viewed from the underside, the interesting features continue: multiple line tie, swept-back front legs and feet, and a carved mouth. . . this lure has commanding eye appeal.

Prices available on request.

Leather Footed Frog

Tony Smith, Macatawa Bait Co., Holland, Michigan

Date: c. 1995

Length: 2⅞" body

Notes: This sleek frog features glass eyes, leather feet, and an unusual weedguard.

Prices available on request.

Fly Size Frog
Tony Smith, Macatawa Bait Co., Holland, Michigan
Date: c. 2000
Length: 3⅝"
Notes: This little guy is the "fly size" version of the previous lure.
Prices available on request.

Fly Size Bluegill
Tony Smith, Macatawa Bait Co., Holland, Michigan
Date: c. 2001
Length: 1½"
Notes: This tiny Bluegill is one of the most popular Macatawa baits.
Prices available on request.

Fly Size Pike
Tony Smith, Macatawa Bait Co., Holland, Michigan
Date: c. 2001
Length: 3⅜"
Notes: Tony's Fly Size Pike is a very sleek and stylish little lure.
Prices available on request.

Fly Size Catfish
Tony Smith, Macatawa Bait Co., Holland, Michigan
Date: c. 2001
Length: 2½"
Notes: This little catfish looks great alongside the regular size catfish.
Prices available on request.

Fly Size Brook Trout
Tony Smith, Macatawa Bait Co., Holland, Michigan
Date: c. 2001
Length: 2½"
Notes: Tony's Fly Size lures may be purchased individually, but he also provides them in a 3-pack box. This little "Brookie" is nothing short of beautiful.
Prices available on request.

Fly Size Brown Trout
Tony Smith, Macatawa Bait Co., Holland, Michigan
Date: c. 2001
Length: 2½"
Notes: This brown trout is another Macatawa beauty.
Prices available on request.

Fly Size Rainbow Trout
Tony Smith, Macatawa Bait Co., Holland, Michigan
Date: c. 2001
Length: 2½"
Notes: Rounding out the Macatawa trout family is this attractive little rainbow.
Prices available on request.

Fly Size Walleye
Tony Smith, Macatawa Bait Co., Holland, Michigan
Date: c. 2001
Length: 2½"
Notes: Simple and attractive, this Walleye is a graceful design.
Prices available on request.

Fly Size Perch
Tony Smith, Macatawa Bait Co., Holland, Michigan
Date: c. 2001
Length: 2½"
Notes: This is Tony's fly size representation of a yellow perch.
Prices available on request.

Fly Size Dace Minnow
Tony Smith, Macatawa Bait Co., Holland, Michigan
Date: c. 2001
Length: 2½"
Notes: This is Tony's smallest Dace Minnow.
Prices available on request.

Beetle
Tony Smith, Macatawa Bait Co., Holland, Michigan
Date: c. 2001
Length: 2½"
Note: This great-looking beetle features wire legs, glass eyes, and beautiful paint.
Prices available on request.

Cricket
Tony Smith, Macatawa Bait Co., Holland, Michigan
Date: c. 1985
Length: 2"
Notes: Glass bead eyes, wire legs, double position linetie, and wings combine synergistically to give this lure enormous eye appeal.
Prices available on request.

Mayfly
Tony Smith, Macatawa Bait Co., Holland, Michigan
Date: c. 1991
Length: 2⅛" body
Notes: With similar features to the Cricket, this Mayfly is a very desirable collectible.
Prices available on request.

Musky Grasshopper
Tony Smith, Macatawa Bait Co., Holland, Michigan
Date: c. 1995
Length: 5"
Notes: Tony's favorite designs are his fanciful and imaginative creations like this musky size grasshopper.
Prices available on request.

Pentagon Minnow
Tony Smith, Macatawa Bait Co., Holland, Michigan
Date: c. 1999
Length: 6"
Notes: Featuring a more refined look than his fanciful lures, this five-sided lure features a fish tail, interesting hook cups, and beautiful paint.
Prices available on request.

Five-Sided Frog
Tony Smith, Macatawa Bait Co., Holland, Michigan
Date: c. 1997
Length: 7" overall
Notes: This stylish frog features kicking legs in combination with a five-sided body and glass eyes.
Prices available on request.

Flycasting Minnow
Tony Smith, Macatawa Bait Co., Holland, Michigan
Date: c. 1996
Length: 1½" body
Note: This tiny wiggling minnow features glass eyes and a fluted tail.
Prices available on request.

Sunfish
Richard Sundean, Brooklyn Park, Minnesota
Date: c. 2000
Length: 3⅛" overall
Notes: This little sunfish features glass eyes, carved gills, and beautiful paint. The clever tail is a buzz bait spinner.
Prices available on request.

Crappie
Richard Sundean, Brooklyn Park, Minnesota
Date: c. 2000
Length: 3⅞"
Notes: The Sundean Crappie features glass eyes, carved fins, and highly detailed paint.
Prices available on request.

Hinged Frog
Richard Sundean, Brooklyn Park, Minnesota
Date: c. 2000
Length: 3" overall
Notes: Both sets of legs are hinged through the body of this clever frog.
Prices available on request.

Walleye
Richard Sundean, Brooklyn Park, Minnesota
Date: c. 2000
Length: 5¾"
Notes: Clean and accurate, this Walleye features the expected Sundean details: glass eyes, carved fins and gills, and great paint.
Prices available on request.

Sucker
Richard Sundean, Brooklyn Park, Minnesota
Date: c. 2000
Length: 5¼"
Notes: This sleek sucker is a great example of stylized, minimal design.
Prices available on request.

Bug
Richard Sundean, Brooklyn Park, Minnesota
Date: c. 2000
Length: 2⅝"
Notes: Sundean's Bug features effective, economical, and tasteful design.
Prices available on request.

Bug
Richard Sundean, Brooklyn Park, Minnesota
Date: c. 2002
Length: 3⅜"
Notes: Featuring carved eyes and wings and fitted with a hand-made brass lip and hook rig, this bug also features a high-quality paint finish.
Prices available on request.

Musky Size Northern Frog
Richard Sundean, Brooklyn Park, Minnesota
Date: c. 2002
Length: 6½"
Notes: This beautifully finished Musky Frog features rotating front legs and hinged back legs attached with a handcrafted brass fitting.
Prices available on request.

Painted Turtle

Richard Sundean, Brooklyn Park, Minnesota
Date: c. 2002
Length: 3⅞"
This attractive turtle features a handmade brass lip which is reinforced with brass wire.
Prices available on request.

Five-Hook Minnow

Jack Swedberg, Webster, Wisconsin
Date: c. 1997
Length: 17¾"
Notes: Jack Swedberg has a passion for making oversized fishing lures for decoration and display. This lure is photographed next to a Heddon #150 to show its size.
Prices available on request.

Three-Hook Minnow

Jack Swedberg, Webster, Wisconsin
Date: c. 1999
Length: 11¾"
Notes: This is the three-hook version of the previous bait, modeled after the Heddon #100.
Prices available on request.

Surf Oreno

Jack Swedberg, Webster, Wisconsin
Date: c. 1999
Length: 13"
Notes: This is an oversized version of South Bend Bait Company's famous Surf-Oreno.
Prices available on request.

Spindiver

Jack Swedberg, Webster, Wisconsin
Date: c. 1997
Length: 14"
Notes: This Heddon Spindiver imitation features Jack Swedberg's signature and date beneath the diving lip. All Swedberg baits are signed and dated.
Prices available on request.

Tadpoly
Jack Swedberg, Webster, Wisconsin
Date: c. 1998
Length: 13"
Notes: This giant Tadpoly makes good use of Jack's crackleback paint.
Prices available on request.

Surf Pikie
Jack Swedberg, Webster, Wisconsin
Date: c. 1999
Length: 18"
Notes: Typical of Jack's accuracy, one might suspect that this lure is a standard Surf Pikie were it not for the listed size.
Prices available on request.

Truck Oreno
Jack Swedberg, Webster, Wisconsin
Date: c. 1999
Length: 14¾"
Notes: The standard South Bend Bait Company Truck Oreno is an imposing lure. This giant Swedberg version is even more imposing.
Prices available on request.

Vamp
Jack Swedberg, Webster, Wisconsin
Date: c. 1998
Length: 24"
Notes: There are Vamps, there are giant Vamps, then there is Jack's 24" monster Vamp!
Prices available on request.

8" Vamps
Jack Swedberg, Webster, Wisconsin
Date: c. 1998
Length: 8"
Notes: The desire to own and fish with the 8" size Vamp led Jack to become a lure maker. The eight colors shown represent a complete set of the Swedberg 8" Vamp.
Prices available on request.

Razorback

Leonard Thornton
Date: c. 1987
Length: 3¾"
Notes: The quintessential University of Arkansas fishing collectible.
Prices available on request.

Cork Floats

Steve White, Chesterfield, Missouri
Date: c. 1999
Notes: Although these are not fishing lures, one can't help but marvel at the design and craftsmanship in these handmade floats. Cork, walnut, and other hard and soft woods lend grace and subtlety to Steve's designs.
Prices available on request.

Fish Eat Fish Teeth Lure

Richard Whitehead, Colmesneil, Texas
Date: c. 1998
Length: 10½"
Notes: Perhaps one of Richard's most innovative ideas, this rubber-tailed fish with nails for teeth is eating a smaller fish.
Prices available on request.

Yellow Pike Teeth Lure

Richard Whitehead, Colmesneil, Texas
Date: c. 2001
Length: 6¾"
Notes: With five treble hooks, glass eyes, nail teeth, and attractive paint, this large lure has a lot of eye appeal and collectibility.
Prices available on request.

Elephant Nose

Richard Whitehead, Colmesneil, Texas
Date: c. 2001
Length: 5½"
Notes: Richard Whitehead's lures might best be categorized as contemporary folk art. Bright, distinct colors and imaginative designs contribute to the collectibility of Richard's lures.
Prices available on request.

Texas Swordfish
Richard Whitehead, Colmesneil, Texas
Date: c. 2001
Length: 6½"
Notes: This happy-looking fellow features fixed, opposing tail hooks, two belly trebles, and a long spinnered "sword."
Prices available on request.

Texas Convict Frog
Richard Whitehead, Colmesneil, Texas
Date: c. 2001
Length: 5"
Notes: This striped amphibian has rope front legs, glass eyes, and a hanging belly weight.
Prices available on request.

Minnows, old style
Charlie Wilson, The Minno Company, Lincoln, Nebraska
Date: c. 1998
Length: 5⅛", 3"
Notes: Charlie Wilson does not begin production on a new lure design until he is convinced that it will work in the water as a lure should. These beautiful minnows are early examples of Charlie's work.
Prices available on request.

Miller's Bay Minnow
Charlie Wilson, The Minno Company, Lincoln, Nebraska
Date: c. 2001
Length: 5¼"
Notes: Charlie makes all of his lures and components by hand with the exception of the hooks. Glass eyes, spinners, and beads are thus custom designed for each lure model.
Prices available on request.

Little Millers Minnow
Charlie Wilson, The Minno Company, Lincoln, Nebraska
Date: c. 2001
Length: 3¾"
Notes: The attractive paint and simple design suggest that this little minnow would be an effective fish catcher.
Prices available on request.

Moonshiner Minnow
Charlie Wilson, The Minno Company, Lincoln, Nebraska
Date: c. 2001
Length: 5"
Notes: A close examination of a Minno Company lure will always reveal smooth-working, custom-fitted components and immaculate paint.
Prices available on request.

Wilson Chub
Charlie Wilson, The Minno Company, Lincoln, Nebraska
Date: c. 2001
Length: 6¼"
Notes: With elaborate carved mouth and gills, this Chub features large handmade glass eyes and brass heart shaped diving lip.
Prices available on request.

Wharf Rat, Chipmunk finish
Charlie Wilson, The Minno Company, Lincoln, Nebraska
Date: c. 2001
Length: 4½"
Notes: This is a musky-size lure featuring a jointed head, hand-made ears, eyes, lip, and spinner legs.
Prices available on request.

Minnewashta Mouse
Charlie Wilson, The Minno Company, Lincoln, Nebraska
Date: c. 2001
Length: 2¾"
Notes: This little Mouse is the smaller relative of the wharf rat.
Prices available on request.

Dakota Frog
Charlie Wilson, The Minno Company, Lincoln, Nebraska
Date: c. 2001
Length: 5½"
Notes: This marvelous frog features trimmed deer hair hooks on the jointed legs.
Prices available on request.

Jointed Musky Sucker
Charlie Wilson, The Minno Company, Lincoln, Nebraska
Date: c. 2001
Length: 8"
Notes: This large lure features a jointed head, detailed gill carving, handmade glass eyes, and a nicely-fitted brass diving lip.
Prices available on request.

Musky Dragonfly
Charlie Wilson, The Minno Company, Lincoln, Nebraska
Date: c. 2001
Length: 3½"
Notes: Charlie's handmade wings provide the perfect accent for his delicate dragonfly.
Prices available on request.

North Bay Musky Minnow
Charlie Wilson, The Minno Company, Lincoln, Nebraska
Date: c. 2001
Length: 9¾" nose to tail
Notes: This magnificent Musky Minnow features two body joints hinged with intricate brass work, highly-detailed carving on gills, and mouth, and polished brass lip and tail.
Prices available on request.

Boji Twins
Charlie Wilson, The Minno Company, Lincoln, Nebraska
Date: c. 2001
Length: 5¾" overall
Notes: These Twins come packaged in a custom-fitted walnut box complete with a handmade screwdriver for loosening the screws on the interchangeable body parts.
Prices available on request.

Swimming Turtle
Charlie Wilson, The Minno Company, Lincoln, Nebraska
Date: 2002
Length: 3¾"
Notes: With a carved hollow shell, painted brass plate for the belly, moving legs and head, glass eyes, and brass diving lip, this lure has it all — original design, handmade hardware, and fishability. It just doesn't get any better.

CONTEMPORARY LURES

Show & Tell

One of the biggest thrills a fishing lure collector can experience comes from displaying their collection for others to look at and enjoy. It doesn't seem to matter if one is the owner or the viewer of the lures, the occasion nearly always makes for interesting conversation, respectful admiration, and a kindling of enthusiasm for the hobby.

Regardless of where it happens, be it an NFLCC fishing lure show, via e-mail or at the home of a fellow lure collector, "show and tell" helps to educate while furthering both interest and passion for the lure collecting hobby.

Since "show and tell" is such a vital part of what we do in lure collecting, it is with this chapter dedicated to the sharing of fishing lure information that we conclude this book.

Dudley and Deanie Murphy
Springfield, Missouri

Two contemporary spinners and a fly reel created by hand by Bob Baird. The lures feature sterling silver, 14K gold, and precious stones. The 2⅜" diameter reel features woolly mammoth side plates, mastodon ivory handle, Australian lightning ridge opal bearing and handle inlays, and a nickel silver frame. These exotic items represent a new level of expense and high quality in the hobby.
From the collection of Bob Baird.

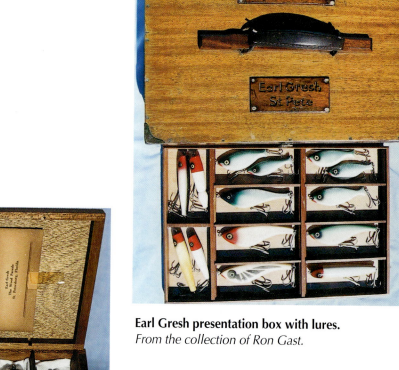

Earl Gresh presentation box with lures.
From the collection of Ron Gast.

A beautiful mahogany presentation box of lures
From the collection of Ron Gast.

364

A collection of Strikee lures made by the Natural Bait Co., Pasadena, California. *From the collection of John Anderson.*

A collection of Trenton Mad Mice. *From the collection of Matt Wickham.*

A display of Trenton lures. *From the collection of Matt Wickham.*

Ol' Skipper lures in boxes. *From the collection of Ron Hanley.*

An interesting collection of soft rubber Grube lures. *From the collection of Ron Hanley.*

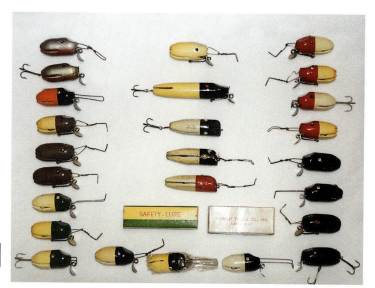

A great display of Safety-Lures.
From the collection of Ron Hanley.

A display of South Bend Fish Ferrets.
From the collection of James White.

Flyrod Fish Ferrets.
From the collection of George Chrisman.

Flyrod Fish Ferrets.
From the collection of George Chrisman.

Clint Brown's Select-A-Bait lure kit.
From the collection of Dudley Murphy.

Plucky 4-pack.
From the collection of Dudley Murphy.

Marathon Spin-O-Bug Kit.
From the collection of Dudley Murphy.

A nice display of #740 Punkinseeds.
From the collection of Riley Smith.

#730 Punkinseeds.
From the collection of Riley Smith.

An attractive display of #9630 plastic Punkinseeds.
From the collection of Riley Smith.

A display of various Punkinseeds.
From the collection of Riley Smith.

A salesman's sample ring of #380 Tiny Punkinseeds.
From the collection of Riley Smith.

A salesman's sample ring of Heddon Tiny Torpedos.
From the collection of Riley Smith.

A salesman's sample ring of Heddon Cousins.
From the collection of Riley Smith.

A salesman's sample ring of Heddon Chuggers and Tiny Torpedos.
From the collection of Riley Smith.

Development stages of Bug R Bird.
From the collection of Ron Hanley.

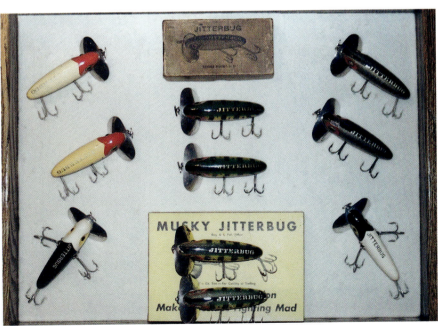

Musky Jitterbugs and boxes.
From the collection of Ron Hanley.

Arbogast salesman's sample kit.
From the collection of Ron Hanley.

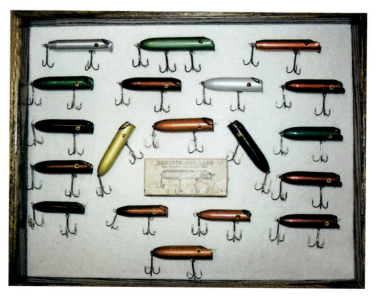

Attractive display of Bright-Eye-Lures.
From the collection of Ron Hanley.

A small collection of Glitterfish.
From the collection of Rick Edmisten.

A collection of Hawk lures.
From the collection of Charles and Annette Sanders.

370

A Glo-Bug display card with lure.
From the collection of Dudley Murphy.

Realistic flyrod lures by William F. Blades.
From the collection of Dudley Murphy.

William F. Blades flies.
From the collection of Bill Calhoun.

A small collection of interesting, inexpensive modern flies.
From the collection of Dudley Murphy.

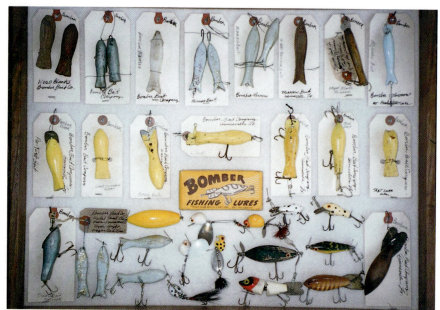

An assortment of prototypes and factory test baits from the Bomber Bait Co.
From the collection of Debbie & Rufus Harris.

A selection of Bomber Bait Co. experimental lures.
From the collection of Debbie & Rufus Harris.

Experimental and prototypical lures from the Bomber Bait Co.
From the collection of Debbie & Rufus Harris.

Full-color set of Bomber Looboyle Specials.
From the collection of Debbie & Rufus Harris.

Full color set of Bomber Knot Heads (large and small). Note the two prototypes above the box.
From the collection of Debbie & Rufus Harris.

A collection of CCBCO lures in Blue Flash finish.
From the collection of Bob from Long Island.

South Bend Fish Obite collection.
From the collection of Bob from Long Island.

Mystic Minnow in the box with interchangeable heads and bodies.
From the collection of Dudley Murphy.

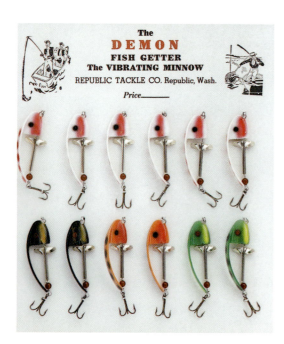

Demon display card, Republic Tackle Co., Republic, Washington.
From the collection of Dudley Murphy.

"Paw Paw Frog Pond."
From the collection of David Stalnaker.

Prototype lures from J.B. Woods' tackle box. No. 1 is a special color in Dipsy Doodle. Top center lure is 2¼".
From the collection of David Stalnaker.

A nice collection of CCBCO #2700 Baby Pikies.
From the collection of Ron Hanley.

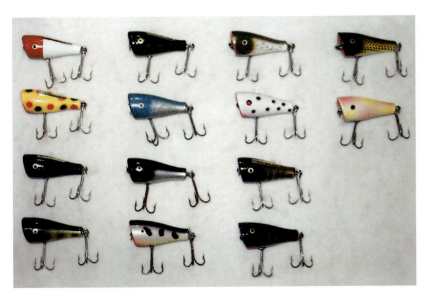

A collection of CCBCO 5900 paint eye Baby Plunkers.
From the collection of Ron Hanley.

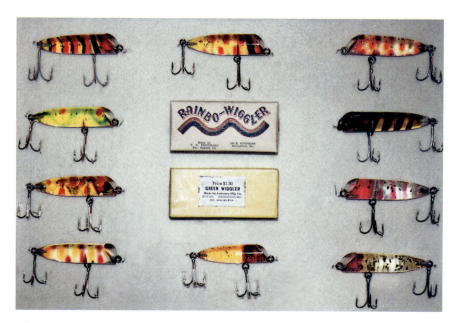

A beautiful display of Rainbo-Wigglers, Springfield, Missouri.
From the collection of Ron Hanley.

Staley-Johnson Twin Fins and Honeys.
From the collection of Rich Dickman.

"Booze bottles."
From the collection of Rick Dickman.

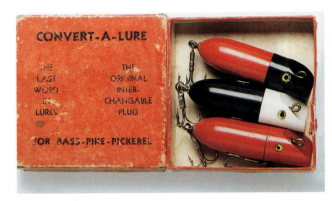

Convert-a-lure kit.
From the collection of Dudley Murphy.

A color collection of Bon-Net lures.
From the collection of Michael Muth.

A color collection of Arbogast Jitterbugs in a special notched display, allowing the observer to view the lures as if they are floating in the water.
From the collection of Bill Mitzel.

Seigle's night fishing minnows and night fishing floats. Hinton, Oklahoma, 1934.

Display card of Irish Shad by Mubago Bait Co., Lexington, Kentucky, c. 1952 – 1954.

Shakespeare lures by Inglis, Canada.
From the collection of Rick Edmisten.

A collection of boxed P & K lures.
From the collection of Dennis McNulty.

A collection of Bill DeWitt Pyra-Shell lures.

"Tackle Your Business," book-bound salesman's sample lure kit by Marathon, 1957.

"Time to Retire," book-bound salesman's sample lure kit by Marathon, 1951.

A spinning kit by Horrocks-Ibbotson.

Buck Perry's Spoonplug 5-pack.
From the collection of Dudley Murphy.

Weller spinning lure kit.
From the collection of Dudley Murphy.

Al's Goldfish spinning kit.
From the collection of Dudley Murphy.

A spinning kit by B & H, Harrison, New York.
From the collection of Dudley Murphy.

Tony's Tackle box by Tony Accetta.
From the collection of Dudley Murphy.

An Airex spinning kit.
From the collection of Dudley Murphy.

A variety of colorful and interesting spinning lures.
From the collection of Dudley Murphy.

Beacon Deluxe lure kit.
From the collection of Dudley Murphy.

An interesting MagicSnell lure with interchangeable tails.
From the collection of Dudley Murphy.

A pair of Abu spinner kits.
From the collection of Dudley Murphy.

A factory assortment box of Garcia spinning lures.
From the collection of Dudley Murphy.

Wonderful collection of Wood Mfg. Co. #1200 Series Doodlers. All 19 original colors are shown.

From the collection of Ray Rodgers.

A great collection of Wood Mfg. Co. lures. All 19 original colors of the #400 Series Dipsy Doodle are on the left side and the corresponding 19 colors of the #500 Series Dipsy Doodle are on the right.

From the collection of Ray Rodgers.

Paul Bunyan Electrolures.
From the collection of Rich Sundean.

A color collection of Paul Bunyan Transparent Dodgers.
From the collection of Rich Sundean.

2002 Winchester Christmas "Two-pack" fishing tackle classics.
From the collection of Rick Edmisten.

Fly Rod critters three-pack by Ron Hoseney.
From the collection of Dudley Murphy.

2001 Winchester "four pack" Fishing Tackle classics.
From the collection of Rick Edmisten.

Fly Rod trout six-pack by Ron Hoseney.
From the collection of Dudley Murphy.

Eger Bait Manufacturing Co.
Baby Dillinger 0 Series ...170
Bull Nose Frog ...169
Eger Darter 1500 Series ...169
Junior Dillinger 200 Series ...169
Sea Dillinger 400 Series ...170
Sea Sargeant ...170

E.H. LeBlanc
Water Ranger ...203

E.H. Peckinpaugh
The Baitcasting Feather Minnow ...225

Electralure
Electralure ...170

Electrolure Co.
Electrolure ...170

Electronic Units Co.
Jumping Jo ...171

E.L. Jacobs
Jacobs Polly-Frog ...192

Elman "Bud" Stewart
Crawdad ...252
Crippled Minnow ...251
Crippled Mouse ...251
Crippled Wiggler ...251
One-eyed Minnow ...251

E.R. Barber
Reel Shad ...139

Erwin Weller Co.
Flipper ...272

Etchen Tackle Co.
Helga-Devil ...172

Evans Walton Company
Weed Queen ...173

E.V. Selby and Co.
Flathead ...239

Ewell Parker Co.
The Ewelure ...173

Fair Play Industries
Bubble Minnie ...174
Bubble Sally ...174

Falls Bait Co.
Big Inch ...295
"Falls Minnow" ...295
Fish-N-Fool ...295
Inch Minnow ...295

F.E. Chester Manufacturing Co.

"Artie" Mack's Magic Minnow ...159
Dazzler ...159

Felmlee Enterprises
"Fingerling Bull Head" ...296
"Fingerling Minnow" ...296
"Fingerling Shiner" ...296
"Spinnered Eel" ...296
"Yellow Perch" ...296

Fetchi-Lure Company
Pop-Eye ...174

F.H. Horvath, Little Workshop
The Twiggler Bait ...190

Finn-Kala
Finn-Kala ...297

Fishathon Bait Manufacturing Co.
Dizzy Crawdad ...175
Dizzy Diver ...174
Dizzy Floater ...175

Fisher-Motors
Twirlo ...297

F. Jordan Mfg.
Jordan's Dirigible Minnow ...197

Florida Fishing Tackle Co.
Dalton Special ...175

Fly Boy Lures, Inc.
Fly Boy ...175

F.M.F. Lures
Twinkle Bug ...174

Foster Enterprises
Rocket Racer ...175

France
Asspoon ...297
Calico Cat ...297
CP Swing ...298
Lessor ...298
Pecos Jointed Top Minnow ...299
Pecos Swiveled Devon ...299
Regeut ...298
"Stabil" ...298
Vivif ...298

Frank Steel, Inc.
Steel's Wigglefrog ...250

Fred Arbogast
Arbo-Gaster ...127
Arby "Hanger" ...128
Dekalb Lure ...131
Dorado ...128

Fly Rod Hawaiian ...130
Fred's Frog ...128
Hawaiian #4 ...130
Hula Dancer ...127
Hula Popper ...126
Hula Popper (flyrod) ...127
Hula Popper (spinning) ...126
Hula Popper (ultra lite) ...127
Hum-Bug ...131
Hustler ...128
Jitterbug (flyrod size) ...126
Jitterbug Group ...125
Jitterbug (plastic) ...125
Jitterbug (spinning) ...126
Jitterbug (weedless) ...126
Jitterbug (wood) ...124
Jitterbug (wood, peanut size) ...124
Jitterbug (wood, single hook) ...124
Jointed Jitterbug ...125
Mopar Dart ...130
Mud Bug ...131
Musky Jitterbug (wood) ...125
#1 Hawaiian Wiggler (runs deep) ...129
#1 Hawaiian Wiggler (runs medium) ...129
#2 Hawaiian Wiggler (runs shallow) ...129
Phred's Phydeaux ...129
Snooker ...129
Spinning Tin Liz ...131
Sputterbug ...127
Sputter Fuss ...130
Tin Liz, flyrod size ...131
Tipsy ...128
Twin Liz ...130

Fred Young
Big-O ...281, 282
Big-O Rattler ...282
Little Fred ...282
Mr. Fred ...281
Small Big-O ...282
Topwater Bait ...282

F.S. Burroughs and Co., Inc.
Aqua-Bat ...157
The Croaker ...157
The Tad-Pole ...157

Fury Manufacturing Co.
Fury ...176

F.W. Cook Company, Inc.
Cook's 500 ...163
Cook's Goldblume ...163

Gale Allen
Potbelly ...120

Gardner Specialty Company
Twin Dancer ...176

INDEX BY COMPANY

INDEX BY COMPANY

INDEX BY COMPANY

INDEX BY COMPANY

INDEX BY COMPANY

INDEX BY COMPANY

INDEX BY COMPANY

INDEX BY COMPANY

INDEX BY COMPANY

INDEX BY COMPANY

INDEX BY COMPANY

INDEX BY COMPANY

INDEX BY COMPANY

INDEX BY COMPANY

INDEX BY COMPANY

INDEX BY COMPANY

Index By Lure

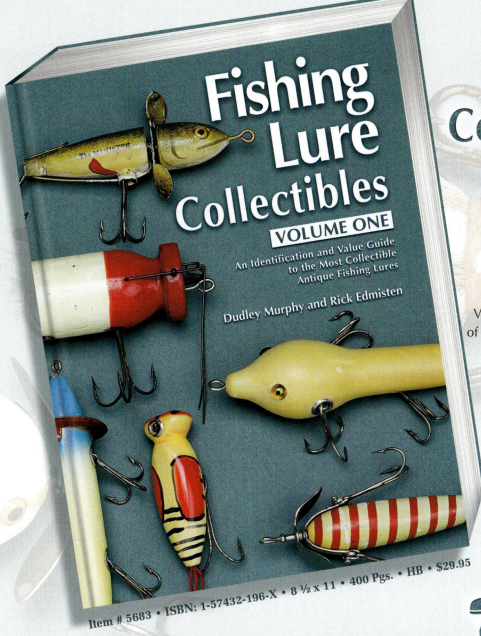

COLLECTOR BOOKS

Informing Today's Collector

For over two decades we have been keeping collectors informed on trends and values in all fields of antiques and collectibles.

FISHING LURES, GUNS & KNIVES

5616	Big Book of **Pocket Knives**, Stewart & Ritchie	.19.95
5355	**Cattaraugus** Cutlery Co., Stewart & Ritchie	.19.95
5906	Collector's Encyclopedia of **Creek Chub Lures** & Collectibles, 2nd Ed., Smith	.29.95
5929	Commercial **Fish Decoys**, Baron	.29.95
5683	**Fishing Lure** Collectibles, Vol. I, 2nd Ed., Murphy/Edmisten	.29.95
6141	**Fishing Lure** Collectibles, Vol. II, Murphy	.29.95
5258	**Fishing Lure** Collectibles Bible, Streater/Murphy/Edmisten	.24.95
5912	The **Heddon** Legacy – A Century of Classic Lures, Roberts/Pavey	.29.95
6028	**Modern Fishing Lure** Collectibles, Lewis	.24.95
6131	**Modern Fishing Lure** Collectibles Vol. II, Lewis	.24.95
6132	**Modern Guns**, 14th Ed., Quertermous	.14.95
5603	19th Century **Fishing Lures**, Carter	.29.95
5166	Std. Gde. to **Razors**, 2nd Ed., Ritchie/Stewart	.9.95
6031	Standard **Knife** Collector's Guide, 4th Ed., Ritchie/Stewart	.14.95

INDIAN ARTIFACTS, TOOLS & PRIMITIVES

1868	**Antique Tools**, Our American Heritage, McNerney	.9.95
1426	**Arrowheads & Projectile Points**, Hothem	.7.95
6021	**Arrowheads** of the Central Great Plains, Fox	.19.95
5362	Collector's Guide to **Keen Kutter Cutlery & Tools**, Heuring	.19.95
4943	Field Gde. to **Flint Arrowheads & Knives** of the N. Amer. Indian, Tully	.9.95
1668	**Flint Blades & Projectile Points**, Tully	.24.95
2279	**Indian Artifacts** of the Midwest, Book I, Hothem	.14.95
3885	**Indian Artifacts** of the Midwest, Book II, Hothem	.16.95
4870	**Indian Artifacts** of the Midwest, Book III, Hothem	.18.95
5685	**Indian Artifacts** of the Midwest, Book IV, Hothem	.19.95
5826	**Indian Axes** & Stone Related Artifacts, 2nd Ed., Hothem	.19.95
2164	**Primitives**, Our American Heritage, McNerney	.9.95
1759	**Primitives**, Our American Heritage, Series II, McNerney	.14.95

TOYS & CHARACTER COLLECTIBLES

2333	Antique & Collectible **Marbles**, 3rd Ed., Grist	.9.95
5900	Collector's Guide to **Battery Toys**, 2nd Ed., Hultzman	.24.95
6123	**Breyer Animal** Collector's Guide, 3rd Ed., Browell	.19.95
5150	**Cartoon Toys** & Collectibles, Longest	.19.95
4559	Collectible **Action Figures**, 2nd Ed., Manos	.17.95
5149	Collector's Guide to **Bubble Bath** Containers, Moore/Pizzo	.19.95
5038	Collector's Guide to **Diecast Toys** & Scale Models, 2nd Ed., Johnson	.19.95
5169	Collector's Guide to **T.V. Toys** & Memorabilia, 1960s & 1970s, 2nd Ed., Davis/Morgan	.24.95
4566	Collector's Guide to **Tootsietoys**, 2nd Ed., Richter	.19.95
4945	**G-Men & FBI Toys** & Collectibles, Whitworth	.18.95

5593	**Grist's Big Book of Marbles**, 2nd Ed.	.24.95
3970	Grist's Machine-Made & Contemporary **Marbles**, 2nd Ed.	.9.95
6128	**Hot Wheels**, the Ultimate Redline Guide, Clark/Wicker	.24.95
4950	**Lone Ranger** Collector's Reference & Value Guide, Felbinger	18.95
5267	**Matchbox Toys**, 1947–1998, 3rd Ed., Johnson	.19.95
5830	**McDonald's** Collectibles, 2nd Ed., Henriques/DuVall	.24.95
5673	**Modern Candy Containers** & Novelties, Miller	.19.95
1540	**Modern Toys** 1930 – 1980, Baker	.19.95
5365	**Peanuts Collectibles**, Id. & Value Gde., Podley-Bang	.24.95
5274	**Rock-n-Roll** Treasures, Hilton/Moore	.19.95
5619	**Roy Rogers and Dale Evans** Toys & Memorabilia, Coyle	.24.95
5920	Schroeder's Collectible **Toys**, Antique to Modern Price Guide, 2002 8th Ed.	.17.95
6040	**Star Wars** Super Collector's Wish Book, Carlton	.29.95
5908	**Toy Car** Collector's Guide, Johnson	.19.95

FURNITURE

3716	American **Oak** Furniture, Book II, McNerney	.12.95
6012	**Antique Furniture**-A Basic Primer on Furniture	.12.95
1118	Antique **Oak** Furniture, Hill	.7.95
2132	Collector's Encyclopedia of **American** Furniture, Vol. I, The Darkwoods, Swedberg	.24.95
3720	Collector's Encyclopedia of **American** Furniture, Vol. III, 18th & 19th Century Furniture, Swedberg	.24.95
5359	Early **American Furniture**, A Practical Guide for Collectors, Obbard	.12.95
3906	**Heywood-Wakefield** Modern Furniture, Id. & 2001 Value Guide, Rouland	.18.95
1885	**Victorian** Furniture, Our American Heritage, McNerney	.9.95
3829	**Victorian Furniture**, Our Amer. Heritage, Book II, McNerney	.9.95

PAPER COLLECTIBLES & BOOKS

4633	**Big Little Books**, A Collector's Reference & Value Guide, Jacobs	.18.95
5902	**Boys' & Girls' Book Series**, Jones	.19.95
4852	Collectible **Compact Disc** Price Guide, 2nd Ed., Cooper	.17.95
4710	Collector's Guide to **Children's Books**, 1850 – 1950, Jones	.18.95
5153	Collector's Guide to **Children's Books**, Vol. II, Jones	.19.95
5596	Collector's Guide to **Children's Books**, 1950 – 1975, Vol. III, Jones	19.95
1441	Collector's Guide to **Post Cards**, Wood	.9.95
5031	Collector's Guide to **Early 20th Century American Prints**, Ivankovich	.19.95
4864	Collector's Guide to **Wallace Nutting** Pictures, Ivankovich	.18.95
5926	**Duck Stamps**, Chappell	.9.95
2081	Guide to Collecting **Cookbooks**, Allen	.14.95
2080	Price Guide to **Cookbooks** & Recipe Leaflets, Dickinson	.9.95
3973	**Sheet Music** Reference & Price Gde., 2nd Ed., Guiheen/Pafik	.19.95
6041	**Vintage Postcards** for the Holidays, Reed	.24.95
4733	Whitman **Juvenile Books**, Brown	.17.95

COLLECTOR BOOKS
Informing Today's Collector

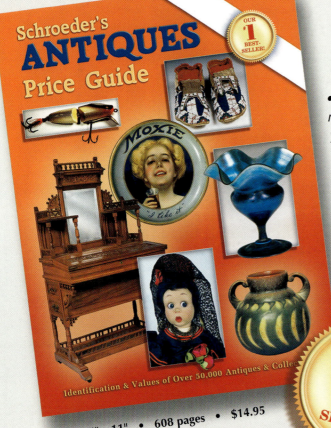